WARRANTS FOR LANDS

IN

SOUTH CAROLINA

Volume I: 1672–1679
Volume II: 1680–1692
Volume III: 1692–1711

EDITED BY

A. S. SALLEY, JR.

WARRANTS FOR LANDS

IN

SOUTH CAROLINA

Volume I: 1672–1679
Volume II: 1680–1692
Volume III: 1692–1711

EDITED BY

A. S. SALLEY, JR.

CLEARFIELD

Warrants for Lands in South Carolina 1672–1679
Originally published
Columbia, South Carolina, 1910

Warrants for Lands in South Carolina 1680–1692
Originally published
Columbia, South Carolina, 1911

Warrants for Lands in South Carolina 1692–1711
Originally published
Columbia, South Carolina, 1915

Reprinted, three volumes in one, for
Clearfield Company, Inc. by
Genealogical Publishing Co., Inc.
Baltimore, Maryland
1998

International Standard Book Number: 0-8063-4818-6

Made in the United States of America

Warrants for Lands

IN

South Carolina

1672-1679

EDITED BY

A. S. SALLEY, JR.
Secretary of the Historical Commission of South Carolina

Printed for
The Historical Commission of South Carolina
By The State Co., Columbia, S. C.
1910

Carolina./

By the grand Councill

You are forthwth. to admeasure and lay out or cause to be layd out upon the land lying between Ashley River and Wandoe River twelve thousand acres of land for a Collony in a square as much as Navigable Rivers will ℘mitt, bounding the same wth. limitts running directly from East to West and from North to South begining upon Ashley River towards the South at a place there knowne by the name of the Oyster Poynt, And a Plott thereof fairly drawne you are to returne to us with all convenient speed whereof you are not to fayle; Given under our hands this xxxth. day of Aprill 1672./

John Yeamans
Maurice Mathews Tho: Gray
Will: Owen: John Godfrey

To John Culpeper
Surveyo^{r} Generall
or his lawfull Dep^{ty}.

Carolina./

By the Governo^{r} by and with the advice and consent of the Councill.

You are forthwth to cause to be admeasured and layd out for S^{r}. Peter Colleton Barr^{t}: one of the Lords Prop^{rs}. of this Province, M^{r}. Thomas Colleton M^{r}. James Colleton and Capt: John Godfrey one hundred and sixty acres of land for their present planting nere Charles Towne being now in the possession of the s^{d} Capt: Godfrey not p^{r}judicing or removing the lines of any other persons lands lying next the same And a Certificate fully specifying the scituacon and bounds thereof, you are to returne to us with all convenient speed and for your soe doeing this shall be your sufficient warr^{t}: Given under my hand this xxist day of May: 1672./

John Yeamans

To John Culpeper
Surveyo^{r} Generall./

Carolina./

By the Governour by and with the advice and consent of the Councill

You are forthwth to cause to be admeasured and layd out for S^{r}. Peter Colleton Barr^{t}: One of the Lords Prop^{rs}. of this Province Mr Thomas Colleton, Mr James Colleton, and Capt: John Godfrey two hundred acres of land being the proporcon allowed to them by the Lords Prop^rs^. concessions for two serv^ts^. namely Thomas Smith and John Chaplen arriveing in Aprill 1672. in such place as you shall be directed by the said Capt: John Godfrey their Agent soe as the same be not within the compass of any lands heretofore layd out or marked to be layd out for any other person or Towne nor prejudiciall to any such lines or bounds and if the same happen upon any navigable River or any River capable of being made navigable, you are to allow only the one fifth part of the depth thereof by the water side And a Certificate fully specifying the scituacon and bounds thereof you are to returne to us wth all convenient speed and for your soe doeing this shall be your sufficient warr^t^. Given under my hand at Charles Towne this xxi^th^. day of May 1672./

John Yeamans

To John Culpeper
Surveyo^r^ Generall./

Carolina./ By the Governo^r^ by and with the advice and consent of the Councill

You are forthw^th^ to cause to be admeasured and layd out for S^r^. Peter Colleton Barr^t^: one of the Lords Prop^rs^. of this Province, M^r^. Thomas Colleton M^r^. James Colleton and Capt: John Godfrey three thousand acres of land pursuant to the said S^r^. Peter Colletons Instructions ꝑduced and shewed to us, in such place as you shall be directed by the sd Capt: John Godfrey soe as the same be not w^th^in the compass of any lands heretofore layd out or marked to be layd out for any other person or Towne nor prejudiciall to any such lines or bounds, and if the same happen upon any navigable River or any River capable of being made navigable you are to lay out only one fifth ꝑ^te^. of the depth thereof by the water side and a Certificate fully specifying the scituacon and bounds thereof you are to returne to us with all convenient speed and for your soe doeing this shall be your sufficient Warr^t^. Given under my hand at Charles Towne this xxi^th^ day of May: 1672./

To John Culpeper John Yeamans.
Surveyo^r^ Generall./

Carolina./ By the Governo^r^ by and with the advice and consent of the Councill

You are forthwith to admeasure and lay out for Sr Peter Colleton Barr^t^. one of the Lords prop^rs^. of this province, Mr Thomas Colleton M^{r}. James Colleton and Capt: John Godfrey that small Track or ꝑcell of land nere Charles Towne bounding upon the land herewith to be layd out to the s^{d} S^{r}. Peter Colleton &c. and the westward of the lands layd out for Capt: Thomas Gray and Mr John ffoster not p^{r}judicing or removing the bounding lines of any lands lying next the same And a Certificate fully specifying the scituacon bounds and quantity thereof you are to returne to us with all convenient speed and for your soe doeing this shall be your sufficient warr^{t}. Given under my hand this xxith day of May: 1672./

John Yeamans

To John Culpeper
Surveyo^{r}. Generall./

Carolina./

By the Governo^{r} by and with the
advice and consent of the Councill

You are forthwth to cause to be admeasured and layd out for Mr Stephen Bull One hundred and seaventy acres of land being the proporcon allowed to him for two serv^{ts}. namely Robert Lockier and Simon Hughes arriveing in August: 1671 by the Lords prop^{rs}. concessions in such place as you shall be directed by him soe as the same be not within the compass of any lands heretofore layd out or marked to be layd out for any other person or Towne nor p^{r}judiciall to any such lines or bounds, and if the same happen upon any navigable River or any River capable of being made navigable you, are to allow only one fifth part of the depth thereof by the water side, And a Certificate fully specifying the scituacon and bounds thereof you are to returne to us with all convenient speed and for your soe doeing this shall be your sufficient warr^{t}. Given under my hand at Charles Towne this xxith. day of May 1672./

John Yeamans

To John Culpeper
Surveyo^{r}. Generall./

Carolina./

By the Governo^{r} by and with the
advice and consent of the Councill

You are forthwth—to cause to be admeasured and layd out for M^{r}. Stephen Bull fower hundred acres of land being the proporcon allowed to him by the lords prop^{rs} concessions for himselfe and two serv^{ts}. namely Dudly Woodyer, and John Larmott arriveing in the first ffleet deducting soe much therefrom as his Towne lott and Tenn acre lott amounts to (if any he hath) in such place as you shall be directed by him soe as the same be not within the compass of any lands heretofore layd out or marked to be layd out for any other person or Towne nor p^{r}judiciall to any such lines or bounds and if the same happen upon any navigable River or any River capable of being made navigable you are to allow only one fifth part of the depth thereof by the waterside, And a Certificate fully specifying the scituacon and bounds thereof you are to returne to us wth. all convenient speed and for your soe doeing this shall be your sufficient warr^{t}. Given under my hand at Charles Towne this xxith. day of May: 1672./

John Yeamans

To John Culpeper
Surveyo^{r}. Generall./

Carolina./

By the Governo^{r} by and with the advice and consent of the Councill

You are forthwth. to cause to be admeasured and layd out for M^{r}. Stephen Bull One hundred acres of land being the proporcon allowed to him by the Lords prop^{rs}. concessions for one Servt. namely Alexander Lilly arriveing in Aprill 1671. in such place as you shall be directed by him soe as the same be not within the compass of any lands heretofore layd out or marked to be layd out for any other person or Towne nor prejudiciall to any such lines or bounds and if the same happen upon any navigable River or any River capable of being made navigable you are to allow only the fifth part of the depth thereof by the waterside and a Certificate fully specifying the scituacon and bounds thereof you are to returne to us with all convenient speed and for your soe doeing this shall be your sufficient warr^{t}. Given under my hand at Charles Towne this xxith. day of May: 1672./

John Yeamans

To John Culpeper
Surveyo^{r}. Generall

Carolina./

By the Governour by and with the advice and consent of the Councill—

You are forthw^th^ to cause to be admeasured and layd out for Capt: John Godfrey five hundred acres of land being the proporcon allowed to him by the lords propriet^rs^. concessions (for his disbursm^ts^. on the discovery of this Province by Capt: Hilton) in such place as you shall be directed by him soe as the same be not within the compass of any lands heretofore layd out or marked to be layd out for any other person or Towne, nor prejudiciall to any such lines or bounds, and if the same happen upon any navigable River or any River Capable of being made navigable you are to lay out only One fifth part of the depth thereof by the water side, And a Certificate fully specifying the scituacon and bounds thereof you are to returne to us with all convenient speed and for yor soe doeing this shall be your sufficient warr^t^. Given under my hand at Charles Towne this xxi^th^ day of May 1672./

John Yeamans

To John Culpeper
Surveyo^r^ Generall./

Carolina./

By the Governo^r^ by and with the advice and consent of the Councill

You are forthw^th^ to cause to be admeasured and layd out for David Abercromby one hundred acres of land (deducting his tenn acre lott) being the proporcon allowed to him by the lords prop^rs^ concessions arriveing in August 1671./ in such place as you shall be directed by him or his Attorney so as the same be not within the compass of any lands heretofore layd out or marked to be layd out for any other person nor prejudiciall to any such lines or bounds and if the same happen upon any navigable River or any River capable of being made navigable you are to allow only one fifth part of the depth thereof by the water side and a Certificate fully specifying the scituacon and bounds thereof you are to returne to us with all convenient speed and for your soe doeing this shall be your sufficient warr^t^. Given under my hand at Charles Towne this xxi^th^ day of May: 1672.

John Yeamans

To John Culpeper
Surveyo^r^. Generall/

Carolina./

By the Governo[r] by and with the advice and consent of the Councill }

You are forthw[th] to cause to be admeasured & layd out for Cap[t]: George Thompson five hundred acres of land being the proporcon allowed to him by the lords prop[rs]. concessions (for his disbursements on the discovery of this Province by Cap[t]: Hilton) in such place as you shall be directed by him or his Attorney soe as the same be not w[th]in the compass of any lands heretofore layd out or marked to be layd out for any other person or Towne nor p[r]judiciall to any such lines or bounds and if the same happen upon any navigable River or any River capable of being made navigable you are to allow only the one fifth part of the depth thereof by the water side; And a Certificate fully specifying the scituacon and bounds thereof you are to returne to us with all convenient speed and for your soe doeing this shall be yor sufficient warr[t]. Given under my hand at Charles Towne this xxi[th]. day of May: 1672./

John Yeàmans

To John Culpeper
Surveyo[r] Generall/

Carolina./

By the Governo[r] by and with the advice and consent of the Councill }

You are forthw[th]. to cause to be admeasured and layd out for William Gray thirty acres of land for his present planting nere Charles Towne in such place as you shall be directed by him soe as the same be not within the compass of any lands heretofore layd out or marked to be layd out for any other person nor p[r]judiciall to any such lines or bounds And a Certificate fully specifying the scituacon and bounds thereof you are to returne to us with all convenient speed, and for your soe doing this shall be your sufficient warr[t]. Given under my hand at Charles Towne this xxi[th]. day of May: 1672./

John Yeamans

To John Culpeper
Surveyo[r]. Generall/

Carolina./

By the Governo^{r} by and with the advice & consent of the Councill

You are forthwth. to cause to be admeasured and layd out for M^{r}. Thomas Smith and Mr James Smith two hundred acres of land being the proporcon allowed to them by the lords prop^{rs}. concessions for two Serv^{ts}. namely Henry Lumpton and Thomas Vayle arriveing in August 1671 in such place as you shall be directed by them or either of their Attorney or Attorneys soe as the same be not wthin the compass of any lands heretofore layd out or marked to be layd out for any other person or Towne, nor p^{r}judiciall to any such lines or bounds, and if the same happen upon any navigable River or any River capable of being made navigable you are to allow only one fifth Ꝑ^{te}. of the depth thereof by the water side And a Certificate fully specifying the scituacon and bounds thereof you are to returne to us with all convenient speed and for your soe doeing this shall be your sufficient warr^{t}. Given under my hand at Charles Towne this xxist day of May: 1672./

John Yeamans.

To John Culpeper
Surveyo^{r} Generall./

Carolina./

By the Governo^{r} by and with the advice and consent of the Councill

You are forthwth to cause to be admeasured and layd out for Henry Jones one hundred acres of land being the proporcon allowed to him by the lords prop^{rs} concessions (arriveing a Servt. in the first ffleet) in such place as yo^{u} shall be directed by him soe as the same be not within the compass of any lands heretofore layd out or marked to be layd out for any other person or Towne nor prejudiciall to any such lines or bounds and if the same happen upon any navigable River or any River capable of being made navigable you are to allow only the fifth part of the depth thereof by the water side And a Certificate fully specifying the scituacon and bounds thereof you are to returne to us with all convenient speed and for yor soe doeing this shall be your sufficient warr^{t}. Given under my hand at Charles Towne this xxith day of May: 1672./

John Yeamans

To John Culpeper
Surveyo^{r} Generall./

Carolina./

By the Governo^{r} by and with the advice and consent of the Councill }

You are forthwth to cause to be admeasured and layd out for Richard Poore tenn acres of land for his present planting nere Charles Towne in such place as you shall be directed by him soe as the same be not wthin the compass of any lands heretofore layd out or marked to be layd out for any other ℘erson nor p^{r}judiciall to any such lines or bounds; And a Certificate fully specifying the scituacon and bounds thereof you are to returne to us with all convenient speed and for your soe doeing this shall be your sufficient warr^{t}. Given under my hand at Charles Towne aforesaid this xxith. day of May: 1672./

John Yeamans.

To John Culpeper
Surveyo^{r}. Generall./

Carolina./

By the Governo^{r} by and wth the advice & consent of the Councill }

You are forthwth to cause to be admeasured and layd out for Thomas Holten seaventy acres of land being the proporcon due to him for and on the behalfe of Judith his Wife arriveing in August 1671 by the Lords Prop^{rs}. concessions, in such place as you shall be directed by him soe as the same be not within the compass of any lands heretofore layd out or marked to be layd out for any other ℘son or Towne nor prejudiciall to any such lines or bounds, and if the same happen upon any navigable River or any River capable of being made navigable, you are to allow only the fifth part of the depth thereof by the water side, and a Certificate fully specifying the scituacon & bounds thereeof you are to returne to us with all convenient speed, & for your soe doing this shall be your sufficient warr^{t}. Given under my hand at Charles Towne this viijth day of June= 1672./

John Yeamans

To John Culpeper
Surveyo^{r} Generall./

Carolina./

By the Governo^{r} by and wth the advice and consent of the Councill }

You are forthwth to admeasure for Thomas Hart one Towne lott in James Towne and Tenn acres of land nere the said Towne for a planting lott, observing the forme and methode wch you have been formerly directed in concerning the said Towne and not prejudicing the lines of any lands lying next the said lotts, and a Certificate fully specifying the scituacon and bounds thereof you are to returne to us with all convenient speed and for yor soe doeing this shall be your sufficient warr^{t}. Given under my hand at Charles Towne this viijth. day of June 1672.

John Yeamans

To John Culpeper
Surveyo^{r} Generall./

Carolina/

By the Governo^{r} by and wth the— advice and consent of the Councill }

You are forthwth to cause to be admeasured and layd out for Phillip Comerton one hundred acres of land being the proporcon allowed to him by the lords prop^{rs} concessions arriveing in February $167\frac{0}{1}$: deducting therefrom his Towne & Tenn acre lott if any he hath in such place as you shall be directed by him soe as the same be not within the compass of any lands heretofore layd out or marked to be layd out for any other person or Towne, nor; p^{r}judiciall to any such lines or bounds, and if the same happen upon any navigable River or any River capable of being made navigable you are to allow only the fifth part of the depth thereof by the water side And a Certificate fully specifying the scituacon and bounds thereof you are to returne to us with all convenient speed and for yor soe doeing this shall be yor. sufficient warr^{t}. Given under my hand at Charles Towne this fifth day of June 1672.

John Yeamans

To John Culpeper
Surveyo^{r} Generall./

Carolina./

By the Governo^{r} by and wth the advice & consent of the Councill }

You are forthwth to admeasure and lay out for Thomas Williams One Towne lott in James Towne and tenn acres of land nere the said Towne for a planting lott observing the forme and method which you have been formerly directed in concerning the said Towne and not p^{r}judicing the lines of any lands lying next the said lotts; And a Certificate fully specifying the scituacon and bounds thereof you are to returne to us with all convenient speed and for yor. soe doeing this shall be yor sufficient warr^{t}. Given under my hand at Charles Towne this viijth day of June: 1672./

John Yeamans

To John Culpeper
Surveyo^{r} Generall./

Carolina/

By the Governour by and wth the
Advice and consent of the Councill

You are forthwth to admeasure and lay out for Elinor Burnett Widdow tenn acres of land nere James Towne for a planting lott observing the forme and methode which you have been formerly directed in and not p^{r}judicing the lines of any lands lying next the same, and a Certificate fully specifying the scituacon and bounds thereof you are to returne to us wth all convenient speed and for yor soe doeing this shall be yor sufficient warr^{t}. Given under my hand at Charles Towne this viijth day of June: 1672./

John Yeamans

To John Culpeper
Surveyo^{r} Generall/

Carolina./

By the Governour by and with the
advice and consent of the Councill

You are forthwth to cause to be admeasured and layd out for Barnaby Bull One hundred and fifty acres of land (deducting his Towne lott and tenn acre lott if any he hath) being the proporcon allowed to him by the Lords prop^{rs} concessions arriveing in the first ffleet in such place as you shall be directed by him soe as the same be not within the compass of any lands heretofore layd out or marked to be layd out for any other ℘son or Towne nor p^{r}judiciall to any such lines or bounds, and if the same happen upon any navigable River or any River capable of being made navigable yo^{u} are to allow only the fifth part of the depth thereof by the water side And a Certificate fully specifying the scituacon & bounds thereof you are to returne to us wth all convenient speed and for yor soe doeing this shall be yor. sufficient warr^{t}. Given under my hand at Charles Towne this viijth. day of June: 1672./

John Yeamans

To John Culpeper
Surveyo^{r} Generall./

Carolina./

By the Governour by and with the advice and consent of the Councill

You are forthwth to cause to be admeasured and layd out for John Carr One hundred acres of land being the proporcon allowed to him by the Lords prop^{rs}. concessions arriveing in the first ffleet in such place as you shall be directed by him soe as the same be not within the compass of any lands heretofore layd out or marked to be layd out for any other ℘son or Towne nor p^{r}judiciall to any such lines or bounds and if the same happen upon any navigable River or any River capable of being made navigable you are to allow only the fifth part of the depth thereof by the water side And a Certificate fully specifying the scituacon & bounds thereof yo^{u} are to returne to us wth all convenient speed and for yor. soe doeing this shall be yor sufficient warr^{t}. Given under my hand at Charles Towne this viijth. day of June: 1672./

John Yeamans

To John Culpeper
Surveyo^{r} Generall./

Carolina./

By the Governo^{r} by and with the advice and consent of the Councill

You are forthwth to cause to be admeasured and layd out for Samuell Boswood two hundred and forty acres of land being the proporcon allowed to him by the lords prop^{rs}. concessions for Mary his Wife, Elizabeth & Margarett his Daughters arriveing in June 1671. in such place as you shall be directed by him soe as the same be not within the compass of any lands heretofore layd out or marked to be layd out for any other ℘son or Towne, nor p^{r}judiciall to any such lines or bounds and if the same happen upon any navigable River or any River capable of being made navigable you are to allow only the fifth part of the depth thereof by the water side And a Certificate fully specifying the scituacon and bounds thereof you are to returne to us wth all convenient speed, & for yor soe doeing this shall be yor sufficient warr^{t}. Given under my hand at Charles Towne this viijth day of June 1672./

John Yeamans.

To John Culpeper
Surveyo^{r} Generall

Carolina./

By the Governo^{r} by and with the advice and consent of the Councill }

You are forthwth to cause to be admeasured and layd out for Henry Jones One hundred acres of land being the proporcon allowed to him by the Lords prop^{rs}. concessions (arriveing a serv^{t} in in the first ffleet) in such place as you shall be directed by him soe as the same be not wthin the compass of any lands heretofore layd out or marked to be layd out for any other ℘son or Towne nor p^{r}judiciall to any such lines or bounds and if the same happen upon any navigable River or any River capable of being made navigable you are to allow only the fifth part of the depth thereof by the water side, and a Certificate fully specifying the scituacon & bounds thereof you are to returne to us with all convenient speed; and for yor soe doeing this shall be yor sufficient warr^{t}. Given under my hand at Charles Towne this xxist day of May; 1672./

John Yeamans

To John Culpeper.
Surveyo^{r} Generall./

Carolina./

By the Governour by and with the advice and consent of the Councill }

You are forthwth to cause to be admeasured and layd out for Nicholas Bushell One hundred acres of land being the proporcon allowed to him by the lords prop^{rs} concessions arriveing in August 1671./ in such place as you shall be directed by him or his Attorney soe as the same be not wthin the compass of any lands heretofore layd out or marked to be layd out for any other ℘son or Towne nor p^{r}judiciall to any such lines or bounds and if the same happen upon any navigable River or any River capable of being made navigable you are to allow only the fifth ℘^{te}. of the depth thereof by the water side; and a Certificate fully specifying the scituacon and bounds thereof you are to returne to us with all convenient speed and for yor soe doeing this shall be yor sufficient warr^{t}. Given under my hand at Charles Towne this viijth day of June 1672./

John Yeamans

To John Culpeper
Surveyo^{r} Generall./

Carolina./

By the Governo^{r} by and wth the advice and consent of the Councill

You are forthwth to cause to be admeasured & layd out for Christopher Edwards Twenty acres of land for his present planting nere Charles Towne in such place as you shall be directed by him soe as the same be not within the Compass of any lands heretofore layd out or marked to be layd out for any other person nor p^{r}judiciall to any such lines or bounds, And a Certificate fully specifying the scituacon and bounds thereof you are to returne to us with all convenient speed and for yor soe doeing this shall be yor sufficient warr^{t}. Given under my hand at Charles Towne this xviijth. day of June 1672./

John Yeamans

To John Culpeper
Surveyo^{r} Generall./

Carolina./

By the Governo^{r} by and wth the— advice and consent of the Councill

You are forthwth to cause to be admeasured and layd out for Mr Thomas Clutterbooke of Barbadoes six hundred and seaventy acres of land being the proporcon allowed to him by the Lords prop^{rs} concessions (that is to say) five hundred acres for his disbursm^{ts} on the discovery of this province by Capt: Hilton and one hundred and seaventy acres for two Serv^{ts}. namely Robert Thomas & Mary Thomas arriveing in ffebruary 167$\frac{0}{1}$. in such place as you shall be directed by him or his Attorney soe as the same be not within the compass of any lands heretofore layd out or marked to be layd out for any other person or Towne nor prejudiciall to any such lines or bounds; and if the same happen upon any navigable River or any River capable of being made navigable you are to allow only the fifth part of the depth thereof by the water side; And a Certificate fully specifying the scituacon & bounds thereof you are to returne to us with all convenient speed; and for your soe doeing this shall be yor sufficient warr^{t}. Given under my hand at Charles Towne this viijth day of June: 1672./

John Yeamans

To John Culpeper
Surveyo^{r} Generall./

Carolina./

By the Governo^r^ by and wth the advice and consent of the Councill }

You are forthw^th^ to cause to be admeasured and layd out for Mr Christopher Portman thirty acres of land nere Charles Towne for his present planting bounding the same to the southward of the land there allready layd out for Mr John Culpeper and Mr John Robinson & not prejudicing the lines of any lands lying next the same, And a Certificate fully specifying the scituacon & bounds thereof you are to returne to us with all convenient speed and for your soe doeing this shall be yor sufficient warr^t^. Given under my hand at Charles Towne this twenty nineth day of June 1672./

John Yeamans

To John Culpeper
Surveyo^r^ Generall./

Carolina./

By the Governour by and with the advice and consent of the Councill }

You are forthw^th^ to cause to be admeasured and layd out for Sr Peter Colleton, one of the Lords prop^rs^ of this province, M^r^. Thomas Colleton, Mr James Colleton & Capt: John Godfrey fifty acres of land by them purchased of the Heires of Mr Paul Smith deceased and now in the possession of the said John Godfrey as appeares bounding the same Westward of the land layd out to Mr William Owen nere this Towne and not prejudicing the lines of any lands lying next the same And a Certificate fully specifying the scituacon and bounds thereof, you are to returne to us with all convenient speed and for your soe doeing this shall be your sufficient warr^t^. Given under my hand at Charles Towne this xxix^th^ day of June 1672./

John Yeamans

To John Culpeper
Surveyo^r^ Generall./

Carolina./

By the Governour by and with the advice and Consent of the Councill. }

You are forthwith to cause to be admeasured and layd out for Mr Thomas Smith and Mr James Smith fifty acres of land nere this Towne for their present planting bounding the same Northward of the land to be layd out for Sr Peter Colleton One of the lords prop^{rs}. of this province Mr Thomas Colleton, Mr James Colleton and Capt. John Godfrey formerly belonging to Mr Paul Smith deceased not prejudicing the lines of any lands lying next the same; and a Certificate fully specifying the scituacon and bounds thereof you are to returne to us with all convenient speed and for yor soe doeing this shall be yor sufficient warr^{t}. Given under my hand at Charles Towne this xxixth. day of June 1672./

John Yeamans

To John Culpeper
Surveyo^{r} Generall./

Carolina./

By the Governour by and with the advice and consent of the Councill }

You are forthwith to cause to be admeasured and layd out for Henry Wood Two hundred acres of land (deducting his tenn acre lott)being the full quantity allowed to him by the lords proprietors Concessions for himselfe and Alice his Wife arriveing in the first ffleet bounding the same between the land late belonging to Mr William Scrivener and Mr William Owen towards the West and a ꝑcell of ground comonly knowne by the name of the watering place towards the East, & not p^{r}judicing or removeing the lines of any lands lying next the same And if the same happen upon any navigable River or any River capable of being made navigable you are to allow only the fifth part of the depth thereof by the waterside And a certificate fully specifying the scituacon and bounds thereof you are to returne to us with all convenient speed and for yor soe doeing this shall be yor sufficient warr^{t}. Given under my hand at Charles Towne this xxixth day of June 1672./

John Yeamans

To John Culpeper
Surveyo^{r} Generall./

Carolina./

By the Governo^{r} by and with the advice & consent of the Councill— }

You are forthwth to cause to be admeasured and layd out for Henry Hughes forty acres of land for his present planting nere Charles Towne in such place as you shall be directed by him soe as the same be not within the compass of any lands heretofore layd out or marked to be layd out for any other person nor prejudiciall to any such lines or bounds, And a certificate fully specifying the scituacon and bounds thereof you are to returne to us wth all convenient speed and for your soe doeing this shall be yor sufficient warr^{t}. Given under my hand at Charles Towne this xxixth day of June 1672./

John Yeamans

To John Culpeper
Surveyo^{r} Generall./

Carolina./

By the Governo^{r} by and with the advice and consent of the Councill

You are forthwith to cause to be admeasured and layd out for Susanna Kinder Tenn acres of land for her present planting bounding the same upon the North part of the lands layd out as a Tenn acre lott for Mr William Owen and Mr William Scrivener in his life time nere Charles Towne not p^{r}judicing the lines of any lands lying next the same, And a Certificate fully specifying the scituacon and bounds thereof you are to returne to us wth all convenient speed, and for your soe doeing this shall be yor sufficient warr^{t}. Given under my hand at Charles Towne aforesaid this 29th day of June 1672/

John Yeamans

To John Culpeper
Surveyo^{r} Generall./

Carolina./

By the Governo^{r} by and with the advice and consent of the Councill

You are forthwith to cause to be admeasured and layd out for John Terrey One Towne lott in James Towne observing the forme & methode which you have been formerly directed in concerning the said Towne and not p^{r}judicing the lines of any lands lying next the said lott; and a Certificate fully specifying the scituacon and bounds thereof you are to returne to us with all convenient speed and for your soe doeing this shall be yor sufficient warr^{t}. Given under my hand at Charles Towne this ninth day of July 1672./

John Yeamans

To John Culpeper
Surveyo^{r} Generall./

Carolina./

By the Governo^{r} by and with the advice and consent of the Councill

You are forthwth to cause to be admeasured and layd out for John Lawrison thirty acres of land nere James Towne for a planting lott, observing the forme & method which yo^{u} have been formerly directed in, & not p^{r}judicing the lines of any lands lying next the same; And a Certificate fully specifying the scituacon and bounds thereof you are to returne to us with all convenient speed, and for yor. soe doeing this shall be yor sufficient warr^{t}. Given under my hand at Charles Towne this ninth day of July 1672./

John Yeamans

To John Culpeper
Surveyo^{r} Generall./

Carolina./

By the Governo^{r} by and with the advice and consent of the Councill

You are forthwth. to cause to be admeasured and layd out for Edmund Fogertee one Towne lott in James Towne observing the forme and methode which you have been formerly directed in concerning the said Towne, and not p^{r}judicing the lines of any lands lying next the said lott And a Certificate fully specifying the scituacon and bounds thereof you are to returne to us with all convenient speed; and for your soe doeing this shall be yor= sufficient warr^{t}. Given under my hand at Charles Towne this ninth day of July: 1672./

John Yeamans

Carolina./

By the Governo^{r} by and with the advice and consent of the Councill

You are forthwith to cause to be admeasured and layd out for Samuell Boswood seaventy acres of land (deducting his tenn acre lott if any he hath) being the full proporcon due to him by the lords prop^{rs}. concessions for One servant namely Ann Workeup arriveing in August 1671./ in such place as you shall be directed by him soe as the same be not within the compass of any lands heretofore layd out or marked to be layd out for any other person or Towne, nor p^{r}judiciall to any such lines or bounds; and if the same happen upon any navigable River or any River capable of being made navigable you are to allow only the fifth part of the depth thereof by the waterside; And a Certificate fully specifying the scituacon and bounds thereof you are to returne to us with all convenient speed and for yor soe doeing this shall be your sufficient warr^t^. Given under my hand at Charles Towne this ninth day of July 1672./

John Yeamans

To John Culpeper
Surveyo^r^ Generall./

Carolina./

By the Governo^r^ by and with the advice and consent of the Councill }

You are forthw^th^ to cause to be admeasured and layd out for John Boone one hundred acres of land being the proporcon allowed to him, by the lords prop^rs^. concessions, (arriveing in the first ffleet) in such place as you shall be directed by him soe as the same be not within the compass of of any lands heretofore layd out or marked to be layd out for any other person or Towne nor p^r^judiciall to any such lines or bounds and if the same happen upon any navigable River or any River capable of being made navigable you are to allow only the fifth part of the depth thereof by the water side, And a Certificate fully specifying the scituacon & bounds thereof you are to returne to us with all convenient speed And for your soe doing this shall be yor sufficient warr^t^. Given under my hand at Charles Towne this ninth day of July: 1672./

John Yeamans.

To John Culpeper
Surveyo^r^ Generall./

Carolina./

By the Governo^r^ by and with the advice and consent of the Councill }

You are forthw^th^ to cause to be admeasured and layd out for Mr Richard Conant One Towne lott in James Towne and Twenty acres of land nere the said Towne for his present planting (now in the possession of the said Richard Conant) observing the forme and methode which you have been formerly directed in concerning the said Towne and not p^r^judicing the lines of any lands lying next the s^d^ lotts; And a Certificate fully specifying the scituacon and bounds thereof you are to returne to us with all convenient speed; and for your soe doeing this shall be yo[r] sufficient warr[t]. Given under my hand at Charles Towne this ninth day of July 1672/

John Yeamans.

To John Culpeper
Surveyo[r] Generall/

Carolina./

By the Governo[r] by and with the advice and consent of the Councill }

You are forthw[th]. to cause to be admeasured and layd out for M[r] Robert Richardson One Towne lott in James Towne and Twenty acres of land nere the said Towne for a planting lott observing the forme and methode which you have been directed in concerning the said Towne and not prejudicing the lines of any lands lying next the said lotts; And a Certificate fully specifying the situacon and bounds thereof you are to returne to us with all convenient speed and for your soe doeing this shall be your sufficient warr[t]. Given under my hand at Charles Towne this nineth day of July 1672./

John Yeamans

To John Culpeper
Surveyo[r] Generall./

Carolina./

By the Governo[r] by and with the advice & consent of the Councill. }

You are forthw[th] to cause to be admeasured and layd out for William Bevin one hundred acres of land (being the proporcon allowed to him by the Lords Proprietors concessions arriveing a Serv[t]. in the first ffleet) in such place as yo[u]. shall shall be directed by him soe as the same be not w[th]in the compass of any lands heretofore layd out or marked to be layd out for any other person or Towne nor p[r]judiciall to any such lines or bounds and if the same happen upon any navigable River or any River capable of being made navigable yo[u]. are to allow only the fifth part of the depth thereof by the water side; and a Certificate fully specifying the scituacon and bounds thereof you are to returne to us with all convenient speed and for yo[r]. soe doeing this shall be yo[r] sufficient warr[t]. Given under my hand at Charles Towne this xxvij[th] day of July 1672

John Yeamans

To John Culpeper
Surveyo[r] Generall./

Carolina./

By the Governo[r] by and with the advice and consent of the Councill.

You are forthwith to admeasure and lay out for a Towne on the Oyster Poynt all that poynt of land there formerly allotted for the same adding thereto one hundred & fifty acres of land or soe much thereof, as you shall find to be proporconable for the said one hundred and fifty acres in the breadth of land formerly marked to be layd out for M[r] Henry Hughes, M[r] John Coming and Affera his now wife, and James Robinson estimated to seaven hundred acres, and contained between the lands then allotted to be layd out for M[r] Richard Cole to the North and a marked Tree formerly designed to direct the bounding line of the said Towne to the South And a Certificate fully specifying the scituacon bounds and quantity thereof you are to returne to us with all convenient speed And for yo[r] soe doing this shall be yo[r] sufficient warr[t]. Given under my hand at Charles Towne this Seaven and twentieth day of July 1672./

John Yeamans

To John Culpeper
Surveyo[r] Generall./

Carolina./

By the Governo[r]. by and with the advice and consent of the Councill

You are forthwith to cause to be admeasured and lay out for M[r] Henry Hughes two hundred & twenty five acres of land (being the proporcon allowed to him by the lords Prop[rs] Concessions for himselfe & the half share of one Serv[t] namely John Neale arriveing in the first ffleet) or soe much thereof as you shall find to be proporconable for the same on the Southward part of that breadth of land estimated to five hundred and fifty acres of land and conteyned between the lands now to be layd out for a Towne on the Oyster poynt to the South and the lands marked to be layd out for M[r] Richard Cole to the North, And a Certificate fully specifying the scituacon quantity and bounds thereof you are to returne to us wth all convenient speed And for yo[r] soe doing this shall be yo[r] sufficient warr[t]. Given under my hand at Charles Towne this xxvij[th]. day of July 1672./

John Yeamans

To John Culpeper
Surveyo[r] Generall./

Carolina./

By the Governo^r^ by and with the advice and consent of the Councill }

You are forthw^th^ to cause to be admeasured and layd out for Mr John Coming Three hundred and twenty five acres of land being the proporcon allowed to him by the Lords Prop^rs^. Concessions for himselfe Affera his Wife and the halfe share of one Servt. namely John Neale arriveing in the first ffleet, or soe much thereof as you shall find to be contained between the lines of the lands allotted to be layd out to Mr Henry Hughes to the South and Mr Richard Cole to the North without prejudicing either of the said lines And a Certificate specifying the scituacon bounds and quantity thereof you are to returne to us with all convenient speed And for yor soe doeing this shall be yor sufficient warr^t^. Given under my hand at Charles Towne this xxvij^th^ day of July 1672./

John Yeamans

To John Culpeper
Surveyo^r^ Generall./

Carolina./

By the Governo^r^ by and with the advice and consent of the Councill }

You are forthw^th^ to cause to be admeasured and layd out for Richard Cole foure hundred and fifty acres of land (being the full proporcon due to him by the lords prop^rs^. concessions for himselfe and two Serv^ts^. namely Dennis Mahoone and Richard Crossland arriveing in the first ffleet) or soe much thereof as is or shall be found to be conteyned between the lines of the lands allotted to be layd out M^r^. John Coming and Affera his Wife to the South and Mr Joseph Dalton to the North without prejudicing or removeing either of the said allotted lines (deducting soe much therefrom as his Towne lott and Tenn acre lott amounts to if any he hath) And a Certificate fully specifying the scituacon bounds and quantity thereof yo^u^ are to returne to us wth all convenient speed and for yor soe doeing this shall be yor sufficient warr^t^. Given under my hand at Charles Towne this xxvij^th^ day of July 1672./

John Yeamans

To John Culpeper
Surveyo^r^ Generall./

Carolina./

By the Governo^r by and with the advice and consent of the Councill—

You are forthw^th to cause to be admeasured and layd out for Mr Joseph Dalton Eleaven hundred and fifty acres of land (being the proporcon allowed to him by the lords prop^rs. concessions for Seaven Serv^ts.. namely George Prideaux Tho: Young William Chambers, John Dawson William Rhodes William Burges and Jane Lawson, arriveing in the first ffleet) or soe much thereof as is or shall be found to be conteined between the lines of the lands allotted to be layd out to Richard Cole to the South and George Beadon and Hugh Carterett to the North, without prejudicing or removeing either of the said allotted lines (deducting soe much therefrom as his Towne lott and Tenn acre lott amounts to if any he hath) And a Certificate fully specifying the scituacon bounds and quantity thereof you are to returne to us wth all convenient speed and for yor soe doeing this shall be yor sufficient warr^t. Given under my hand at Charles Towne this xxvij^th day of July 1672./

John Yeamans

To John Culpeper
Surveyo^r Generall

Carolina./

By the Governo^r by & wth the advice & consent of the Councill

You are forthw^th to cause to be admeasured & layd out for George Beadon and Hugh Carterett three hundred acres of land (being the proporcon allowed to them by the Lords prop^rs. concessions for themselves arriveing in the first ffleet) or soe much thereof as is or shall be found to be conteyned to be between the lines of the lands allotted to be layd out to Mr Joseph Dalton to the South and Mr Thomas Thompson to the North without p^rjudicing or removeing either of the said allotted lines (deducting soe much therefrom as his Towne lott and Tenn acre lott amounts to if any he hath) And a Certificate fully specifying the scituacon bounds & quantity thereof you are to returne to us with all convenient speed and for yor soe doeing this shall be yor sufficient warr^t. Given under my hand at Charles Towne this xxvij^th day of July 1672./

John Yeamans

To John Culpeper
Surveyo^r Generall./

Carolina./

By the Governo^{r} by and with the advice and consent of the Councill }

You are forthwth to cause to be admeasured and layd out for Mr Thomas Thompson three hundred acres of land (being the proporcon allowed to him by the Lords prop^{rs}. concessions for him selfe and Sarah his Wife arriveing in the first ffleet) or soe much thereof as is or shall be found to be conteyned between the lines of the lands allotted to be layd out to George Beadon & Hugh Carterett to the South and Henry Simonds to the North without p^{r}judicing or removeing either of the said allotted lines (deducting soe much therefrom as his Towne lott & Tenn acre lott amounts to if any he hath) And a Certificate fully specifying the scituation bounds and quantity thereof you are to returne to us with all convenient speed and for yor soe doeing this shall be yor sufficient warr^{t}. Given under my hand at Charles Towne this xxvijth day of July. 1672./

John Yeamans

To John Culpeper
Surveyo^{r} Generall./

Carolina./

By the Governo^{r} by and wth the advice & consent of the Councill }

You are forthwth to cause to be admeasured and layd out for Mr Henry Simonds One hundred and fifty acres of land being the proporcon allowed to him by the Lords Prop^{rs} concessions for himselfe arriveing in the first ffleet or soe much thereof as is or shall be found to be conteyned between the lines of the lands allotted to be layd out to Mr Thomas Thompson to the South and Mr Joseph Pendarvis to the North without p^{r}judicing or removeing either of the said allotted lines (deducting soe much therefrom as his Towne lott and Tenn acre lott amounts to if any he hath) And a Certificate fully specifying the scituacon bounds and quantity thereof you are to returne to us with all convenient speed and for your soe doeing this shall be your sufficient warr^{t}. Given under my hand at Charles Towne this xxvijth day of July 1672./

John Yeamans

To John Culpeper
Surveyo^{r} Generall./

Carolina./

By the Governor^{r} by and with the
advice and consent of the Councill

You are forthwth to cause to be admeasured & layd out for Joseph Pendarvis two hundred and fifty acres of land (being the proporcon allowed to him by the lords prop^{rs} concessions for Elizabeth his Wife and Priscilla her Daughter arriveing in the first ffleet) or soe much thereof as is or shall be found to be conteined between the lines of the lands allotted to be layd out to Mr Henry Simonds to the South and William Kennis to the North wthout p^{r}judicing or removeing either of the said allotted lines (deducting soe much therefrom as his Towne lott and Tenn acre lott amounts to if any he hath) And a Certificate fully specifying the scituacon bounds & quantity thereof you are to returne to us wth all convenient speed and for yor. soe doeing this shall be yor sufficient warr^{t}. Given under my hand at Charles Towne this xxvijth day of July 1672.

John Yeamans

To John Culpeper
Surveyo^{r} Generall./

Carolina./

By the Governo^{r} by and with the
advice and consent of the Councill

You are forthwth to cause to be admeasured & layd out for William Kennis foure hundred acres of land being the full proporcon allowed to him by the lords prop^{rs}. Concessions for himselfe Joanna his Wife and William his Sonn arriveing in the first ffleet or soe much thereof as is or shall be found to be conteyned between the lines of the lands allotted to be layd out to Joseph Pendarvis to the South and John Williamson to the North without p^{r}judicing or removeing either of the said allotted lines (deducting soe much therefrom as his Towne lott and Tenn acre lott amounts to if any he hath) And a Certificate fully specifying the scituacon, bounds and quantity thereof you are to returne to us with all convenient speed and for yor. soe doeing this shall be yor sufficient warr^{t}. Given under my hand at Charles Towne this xxvijth day of July 1672./

John Yeamans

To John Culpeper
Surveyo^{r} Generall./

Carolina./

By the Governo^{r} by and with the
advice & consent of the Councill

You are forthwth to cause to be admeasured and layd out for John Williamson foure hundred and fifty acres of land being the proporcon allowed to him by the Lords prop^{rs} concessions for himselfe and two Serv^{ts}. namely Edmund Pursell & John Kinsell arriveing in the first ffleet; or soe much thereof as is or shall be found to be conteyned between the lines of the lands allotted to be layd out to William Kennis to the South and Mr Samuell West to the North without p^{r}judicing or removeing either of the said allotted lines (deducting soe much therefrom as his Towne lott and Tenn acre lott amounts to if any he hath) And a Certificate fully specifying the scituacon bounds & quantitie thereof you are to returne to us with all convenient speed and for your soe doeing this shall be yor sufficient warr^{t}. Given under my hand at Charles Towne this xxvijth day of July 1672./

John Yeamans

To John Culpeper
Surveyo^{r} Generall./

Carolina./

By the Governo^{r} by and with the
advice and censent of the Councill

You are forthwth to cause to be admeasured and layd out for M^{r}. Samuell West foure hundred and fifty acres of land (being the proporcon allowed to him by the Lords Prop^{rs} Concessions for himselfe and two Serv^{ts}. namely William West and Andrew Searle arriveing in the first ffleet) or soe much thereof as is or shall be found to be conteyned between the lines of the lands allotted to be layd out to John Williamson to the South and Mr Ralph Marshall to the North without prejudicing or removeing either of the said Allotted lines (deducting soe much therefrom as his Towne lott and tenn acre lott amounts to if any he hath. And a Certificate fully specifying the scituacon bounds and quantity thereof you are to returne to us with all convenient speed and for yor soe doeing this shall be yor sufficient warr^{t}. Given under my hand at Charles Towne this xxvijth day of July 1672./

John Yeamans

To John Culpeper
Surveyo^{r} Generall./

Carolina./

By the Governo^{r} by and with the
advice and consent of the Councill

You are forthwith to cause to be admeasured and layd out for Major Thomas Gray seaven hundred acres of land being the quantity allowed for seaven servants namely William Gray, Richard Poore, Dermott Scrawhall William Backwell Evan Howell Rich^{d}. Bargener and Sam: Boswood arriveing in ffebruary and June 1671. in some place not yett layd out or marked to be layd out for any other person and if the same happen upon any River or navigable place you are to allow only the fifth part of the depth thereof by the water side And a Certificate specifying the scituacon and bounds thereof you are to returne to us with all convenient speed And for your soe doeing this shall be yor sufficient warr^{t}. Given under my hand at Charles Towne this xxiiijth day of August 1672.

John Yeamans

To John Culpeper
Surveyo^{r} Generall./

Carolina./

By the Governo^{r} by and wth the
advice and consent of the Councill

You are forthwth to cause to be admeasured and layd out for Capt^{t}: Thomas Jenner one hundred and fifty acres of land (deducting soe much therefrom as his Town lott amounts to) being the full proportion due to him for and on the behalfe of John More Marriner deceased according to an Order of the late Governo^{r} & Councill dated the xxiiijth ffebruary 167$\frac{0}{1}$ bounding the same upon Stonoe Creeke to the North and the Marsh on Ashley River to the East observing as nere as conveniently you may to allow only the fifth part of the depth thereof by the waterside. And a Certificate fully specifying the scituacon & bounds thereof you are to returne to us with all convenient speed and for your soe doeing this shall be your sufficient warr^{t}. Given under my hand at Charles Towne this xxiiijth day of August 1672

John Yeamans

To John Culpeper
Surveyo^{r} Generall./

Carolina/

By the Governour by and with the
advice and consent of the Councill

You are forthwith to cause to be admeasured and layd out for Teige Canty fower and twenty acres of land bounding the same to the

Southward of the lands there layd out for George Canty James Donaghoe & Phillip Comerton without prejudicing or removing the lines of any lands lying next the same, observing as nere as conveniently you may to allow only the fifth ℘^{t}. of the depth thereof by the water side And a Certificate fully specifying the scituacon and bounds thereof you are to returne to us wth all convenient speed And for your soe doeing this shall be your sufficient warr^{t}. Given under my hand at Charles Towne this xxiiijth day of August 1672.

John Yeamans

To John Culpeper
Surveyo^{r} Generall./

Carolina/

By the Governour by and with the
advice and consent of the Councill

You are forthwth to cause to be admeasured and layed out for Capt: Robert Gibbs ninety acres of land bounding the same southward on Stonoe Creeke and Westward on Capt: Jenners land there without prejudicing or removeing the lines of any lands lying next the same observing as nere as conveniently you may to allow only the fifth part of the depth thereof by the water side And a Certificate fully specifying the scituacon and bounds thereof you are to returne to us with all convenient speed and for your soe doeing this shall be your sufficient warr^{t}. Given under my hand at Charles Towne this xxiiijth day of August 1672/

John Yeamans

To John Culpeper
Surveyo^{r} Generall./

Carolina./

By the Governo^{r} by and with the
advice and consent of the Councill

You are forthwth to lay out sixty acres of land on the Westward of ninety acres of land herewith to be layd out for Capt: Robt. Gibbs soe as the same may be added to the said ninety acres for the said Capt: Gibbs in case the said Capt: Gibbs transport six persons more to settle the same before the expiracon of foure Monthes next ensuing according to an Order of the Grand Councill on y^{t} behalfe and a Certificate whereof you are to returne to us wth all convenient speed

And this shall be yor sufficient warr^{t}. Given under my hand at Charles Towne this vjth day of August 1672./

John Yeamans

To John Culpeper
Surveyo^{r} Generall./

Carolina/

By the Governo^{r} by and with the
advice & consent of the Councill

You are forthwth to admeasure and lay out for Mr Robert Browne tenn acres of land nere this Towne bounding to the Eastward of the land late belonging to Mr Henry Hughes And a Certificate specifying the scituacon and bounds thereof you are to returne to us with all convenient speed and for your soe doeing this shall be your sufficient Warrant Given under my hand at Charles Towne this xxiiijth day of August 1672./

John Yeamans

To John Culpeper
Surveyo^{r} Generall./

Carolina./

By the Governo^{r} by and with the
advice and consent of the Councill

You are forthwith to cause to be admeasured and layd out for Richard Poore one hundred acres of land being the full proporcon allowed to him by the Lords Prop^{rs}. Concessions arriveing in February 167$\frac{0}{1}$ in such place as you shall be directed by him soe as the same be not within the compass of any lands heretofore layd out or marked to be layd out for any other person or Towne nor prejudiciall to any such lines or bounds and if the same happen upon any navigable River or any River capable of being made navigable you are to allow only the fifth part of the depth thereof by the water side; (deducting soe much therefrom as his Towne lott and tenn acre lott amounts to if any he hath) And a Certificate fully specifying the scituacon and bounds thereof you are to returne to us with all convenient speed and for your soe doeing this shall be yor sufficient warr^{t}. Given under my hand at Charles Towne this xxxth. day of August 1672./

John Yeamans

To John Culpeper
Surveyo^{r} Generall./

Carolina./

By the Governo[r] by and with the advice and consent of the Councill

You are forthw[th] to cause to be admeasured and layd out for M[r] John Pinkard two hundred acres of land being the full proporcon allowed to him by the lords prop[rs]. concessions for Mary his Wife and one Serv[t] namely James Purvys arriveing in August 1672 in such place as you shall be directed by him soe as the same be not within the compass of any lands not yett layd out or marked to be layd out for any other person or Towne nor prejudiciall to any such lines or bounds and if the same happen upon any navigable River or any River capable of being made navigable you are to allow only the fifth part of the depth thereof by the water side And a Certificate fully specifying the scituacon and bounds thereof you are to returne to us with all convenient speed and for your soe doeing this shall be your sufficient warr[t]. Given under my hand at Charles Towne this seaventh day of September 1672./

John Yeamans

To John Culpeper
Surveyo[r] Generall./

Carolina./

By the Governo[r] by and with the advice and consent of the Councill

You are forthw[th] to cause to be admeasured and layd out for Thomas Holton Twenty acres of land for his present planting in such place as you shall be directed by him soe as the same be not within the compass of any lands not yett layd out or marked to be layd out for any other person or Towne nor prejudiciall to any such lines or bounds and if the same happen upon any navigable River or any River capable of being made navigable you are to allow only the fifth part of the depth thereof by the waterside And a Certificate fully specifying the scituacon and bounds thereof you are to returne to us with all convenient speed and for your soe doeing this shall be your sufficient warr[t]. Given under my hand at Charles Towne this vij[th]. day of September 1672 John Yeamans

To John Culpeper
Surveyo[r]. Generall./

Carolina./

By the Governo^{r} by and with the advice and consent of the Councill }

You are forthwith to cause to be admeasured and layd out for Christopher Edwards One hundred and seaventy acres of land being the proporcon allowed to him by the Lords Propriet^{rs} concessions for Margarett his Wife and Anne his Daughter arriveing in ffebruary $167\frac{0}{1}$ in such place as you shall be directed by him soe as the same be not within the compass of any lands heretofore layd out or marked to be layd out by any other person or Towne nor prejudiciall to any such lines or bounds and if the same happen upon any navigable River or any River capable of being made navigable you are to allow only the fifth part of the depth thereof by the water side And a Certificate fully specifying the scituacon and bounds thereof you are to returne to us with all convenient speed and for your soe doeing this shall be your sufficient warr^{t}. Given under my hand at Charles Towne this vijth day of September 1672./

John Yeamans

To John Culpeper
Surveyo^{r} Generall./

Carolina./

By the Governo^{r} by and with the advice and consent of the Councill }

You are forthwth to cause to be admeasured and layd out for John Sullivan one hundred and fifty acres of land (being the proporcon allowed to him by the lords prop^{rs} concessions for himselfe arriveing in the first ffleet) in such place as you shall be directed by him soe as the same be not within the compass of any lands heretofore layd out or marked to be layd out for any other person or Towne nor p^{r}judiciall to any such lines or bounds and if the same happen upon any navigable River or any River capable of being made navigable you are to allow only the fifth part of the depth thereof by the waterside And a Certificate fully specifying the scituacon and bounds thereof you are to returne to us with all convenient speed and for your soe doeing this shall be yor sufficient warr^{t}. Given under my hand at Charles Towne this xxxth day of August 1672./

John Yeamans

To John Culpeper
Surveyo^{r} Generall./

Carolina./

By the Governo[r] by and with the advice & consent of the Councill }

You are forthw[th] to cause to be admeasured and layd out for Thomas Ingrum One hundred and fifty acres of land being the full proporcon allowed to him by the lords prop[rs] concessions arriveing in the first ffleet in such place as you shall be directed by him soe as the same be not within the compasse of any lands heretofore layd out or marked to be layd out for any other ꝑson or Towne nor p[r]judiciall to any such lines or bounds and if the same happen upon any navigable River or any River capable of being made navigable you are to allow only the fifth part of the depth thereof by the waterside (deducting soe much therefrom as his Towne lott and tenn acre lott amounts to if any he hath) And a Certificate fully specifying the scituacon & bounds thereof you are to returne to us with all convenient speed and for your soe doeing this shall be your sufficient warr[t]. Given under my hand at Charles Towne this xxx[th]. day of August 1672/ John Yeamans

To John Culpeper
Surveyo[r] Generall./

Carolina./

By the Governo[r] by and wth the advice and consent of the Councill }

You are forthw[th] to cause to be admeasured and layd out for Dennis Mahoon one hundred acres of land (being the proporcon allowed to him by the Lords prop[rs] Concessions arriveing a Serv[t] in the first ffleet) in such place as you shall be directed by him soe as the same be not within the compass of any lands heretofore layd out or marked to be layd out for any other person or Towne nor prejudiciall to any such lines or bounds and if the same happen upon any navigable River or any River capable of being made navigable you are to allow only the fifth part of the depth thereof by the water side, And a Certificate fully specifying the scituacon and bounds thereof you are to returne to us with all convenient speed and for your soe doeing this shall be your sufficient Warr[t]. Given under my hand at Charles Towne this xxx[th] day of August 1672/

John Yeamans

To John Culpeper
Surveyo[r] Generall./

Carolina./

By the Governo^r^ by and with the advice and consent of the Councill

You are forthw^th^ to cause to be admeasured and layd out for Nathaniell Dartnell one hundred acres of land being the full proporcon allowed to him by the Lords propriet^rs^ concessions arriveing a Servt. in the first ffleet in such place as you shall be directed by him soe as the same be not within the compass of any lands heretofore layd out or marked to be layd out for any other person or Towne nor p^r^judiciall to any such lines or bounds and if the same happen upon any navigable River or any River capable of being made navigable you are to allow only the fifth part of the depth thereof by the water side and a Certificate fully specifying the scituacon and bounds thereof you are to returne to us with all convenient speed and for your soe doeing this shall be your sufficient warr^t^. Given under my hand at Charles Towne this xxx^th^. day of August 1672./ John Yeamans

To John Culpeper
Surveyo^r^ Generall./

Carolina./

By the Governo^r^ by and with the advice and consent of the Councill

You are forthwith to cause to be admeasured and layd out for Mr Thomas Hurt three hundred and seaventy acres of land being the full proporcon allowed to him by the Lords Propriet^rs^. concessions for himselfe and two Serv^ts^. namely Joseph Pendarvis George Higgs and Elizabeth Stonhall arriveing in August 1671. (deducting soe much therefrom as his Towne lott and tenn acre lott amounts to if any he hath) in such place as you shall be directed by him soe as the same be not within the compass of any lands heretofore layd out or marked to be layd out for any other person or Towne nor prejudiciall to any such lines or bounds and if the same happen upon any navigable River or any River capable of being made navigable you are to allow only the fifth part of the depth thereof by the water side And a Certificate fully specifying the scituacon and bounds thereof you are to returne to us with all convenient speed and for your soe doeing this shall be your sufficient Warr^t^. Given under my hand at Charles Towne this vij^th^. day of September 1672./

John Yeamans

To John Culpeper
Surveyo^r^ Generall./

Carolina./

By the Governo^r^ by and with the
advice and consent of the Councill

You are forthwith to cause to be admeasured and layd out for Hugh Sherdon One hundred acres of land (deducting therefrom his Towne lott and tenn acre lott if any he hath) being the full proporcon allowed to him by the Lords prop^rs^ concessions arriveing a Servt. in the first ffleet in such place as you shall be directed by him soe as the same be not within the compass of any lands heretofore layd out or marked to be layd out for any other person or Towne nor prejudiciall to any such lines or bounds and if the same happen upon any navigable River or any River capable of being made navigable you are to allow only the fifth part of the depth thereof by the water side and a Certificate fully specifying the scituacon and bounds thereof you are to returne to us with all convenient speed and for your soe doeing this shall be your sufficient warr^t^. Given under my hand at Charles Towne this vij^th^ day of September 1672/

John Yeamans

To John Culpeper
Surveyo^r^ Generall./

Carolina./

By the Governo^r^ by and with the
advice and consent of the Councill

You are forthw^th^ to cause to be admeasured and layd out for Mr Henry Simonds seaventy acres of land being the proporcon allowed to him for and on the behalfe of ffrancis his Wife arriveing in August 1671 by the lords propriet^rs^ concessions in such place as you shall be directed by him soe as the same be not within the compass of any lands heretofore layd out or marked to be layd out for any other person or Towne nor prejudiciall to any such lines or bounds and if the same happen upon any navigable River or any River capable of being made navigable you are to allow only the fifth part of the depth thereof by the waterside and a Certificate fully specifying the scituacon and bounds thereof you are to returne to us with all convenient speed and for your soe doeing this shall be your sufficient warr^t^. Given under my hand at Charles Towne this seaventh day of September 1672./

John Yeamans

To John Culpeper
Surveyo^r^ Generall./

Carolina./

By the Governo^r by and with the advice and consent of the Councill

You are forthwith to cause to be admeasured and layd out for Anthony Churne One hundred and fifty acres of land or soe much thereof as is or shall be found to be conteyned between the lines of the lands allotted to be layd out to Richard Deyos towards the South and John Hawkes towards the North without prejudicing or removeing either of the said allotted lines (deducting soe much therefrom as his Towne lott and two acre lott amounts to) being the full proporcon allowed to him by the Lords proprietors concessions for himselfe arriveing in the first ffleet; And a Certificate fully specifying the scituacon bounds and quantity thereof you are to returne to us with all convenient speed and for your soe doeing this shall be your sufficient warr^t. Given under my hand at Charles Towne this vij^th day of September 1672

John Yeamans

To John Culpeper
Surveyo^r Generall

Carolina./

By the Governo^r by and with the advice and consent of the Councill

You are forthwith to cause to be admeasured and layd out for Anthony Churne One hundred acres of land for Elizabeth his Wife being the full quantity allowed to her (arriveing a Servt in the first ffleet) by the lords Propriet^rs concessions.: in such place as you shall be directed by him soe as the same be not within the compass of any lands heretofore layd out or marked to be layd out for any other person or Towne nor prejudiciall to any such lines or bounds and if the same happen upon any navigable River or any River capable of being made navigable you are to allow only the fifth part of the depth thereof by the water side and a Certificate fully specifying the scituacon and bounds thereof you are to returne to us with all convenient speed and for your soe doeing this shall be your sufficient warr^t. Given under my hand at Charles Towne this vij^th. day of Septemb^r. 1672/

John Yeamans

To John Culpeper
Surveyo^r Generall./

Carolina./

By the Governor[r] by and with the advice and consent of the Councill }

You are forthw[th] to cause to be admeasured and layd out for Capt: fflor: ô Sullivan One thousand Nine hundred acres of land (deducting soe much therefrom as his Towne lott and tenn acre lott amounts to) being the proporcon allowed to him by the lords Propriet[rs] concessions for him selfe and twelve Serv[ts]. namely Elizabeth Dimock Rich: Alexander Stephen Wheelwright, John Dale John Mare George White, W[m] Bevin Bryan ffitzpatrick Daniell Sullivan John Scott Aaron Allouron and Teige Shugeron arriveing in the first ffleet in such place as you shall be directed by him soe as the same be not within the compass of any lands heretofore layd out or marked to be layd out for any other person or Towne nor p[r]judiciall to any such lines or bounds and if the same happen upon any navigable River or any River capable of being made navigable you are to allow only the fifth part of the depth thereof by the water side And a Certificate fully specifying the scituacon and bounds thereof you are to returne to us with all convenient speed and for your soe doeing this shall be your sufficient warr[t]. Given under my hand at Charles Towne this vij[th] day of September 1672/

John Yeamans

To John Culpeper
Surveyo[r] Generall./

Carolina/

By the Governo[r] by and with the advice and consent of the Councill }

You are forthw[th]. to cause to be admeasured and layd out for Capt: fflor: ô Sullivan one hundred acres of land being the proporcon allowed to him by the Lords propriet[rs] Concessions for one serv[t]. namely John Frezer Jun[r]= arriveing in August 1671. in such place as you shall be directed by him soe as the same be not within the compass of any lands heretofore layd out or marked to be layd out for any other person or Towne nor p[r]judiciall to to any such lines or bounds and if the same happen upon any navigable River or any River capable of being made navigable you are to allow only the fifth part of the depth thereof by the water side and a Certificate fully specifying the scituacon and bounds thereof you are to returne to us with all convenient speed and for your soe doeing this shall be your sufficient warr[t]. Given under my hand at Charles Towne this vij[th] day of September 1672 John Yeamans

To John Culpeper
Surveyo[r] Generall./

Carolina./

By the Governo[r] by and with the advice and consent of the Councill

You are forthw[th] to cause to be admeasured and layd out for Capt: fflor: ô Sullivan Sixty acres of land for his present planting nere Charles Towne bounding the same to the Eastward of the lands allready layd out for Mrs Priscilla Bourke and not prejudiciall to the lines of any lands lying next the same and a Certificate fully specifying the scituacon and bounds thereof you are to returne to us with all convenient speed and for your soe doeing this shall be your sufficient Warr[t]. Given under my hand at Charles Towne aforesaid this nineth day of September 1672/

John Yeamans

To John Culpeper
Surveyo[r] Generall./

Carolina./

By the Governo[r] by and with the advice and consent of the Councill

You are forthw[th] to cause to be admeasured and layd out for Oliver Spencer Twenty acres of land for his present planting in such place as you shall be directed by him soe as the same be not within the compass of any lines heretofore layd out or marked to be layd out for any other person or Towne nor prejudiciall to any such lines or bounds And a Certificate fully specifying the scituacon and bounds thereof you are to returne to us with all convenient speed and for your soe doeing this shall be your sufficient warr[t]. Given under my hand at Charles Towne this xi[th]. day of September 1672./

John Yeamans

To John Culpeper
Surveyo[r] Generall./

Carolina./

By the Governo[r] by and with the advice & consent of the Councill

You are forthw[th] to cause to be admeasured and layd out for John Attkins One Towne lott in James Towne observing the forme and method which you have been directed in concerning the s[d] Towne and not prejudicing the lines of any lands lying next the said lott And a Certificate fully specifying the scituacon and bounds thereof you are to returne to us with all convenient speed and for your soe doeing this shall be your sufficient warr[t]. Given under my hand at Charles Towne this seaven & twentieth day of September 1672/

John Yeamans

To John Culpeper
Surveyo[r] Generall./

Carolina./

By the Governo[r]: by and with the advice & consent of the Councill—

You are forthwith to cause to be admeasured and layd out for John Attkins two hundred acres of land being the full proporcon allowed to him by the Lords Proprietors concessions for him selfe and Rachell his Wife arriveing in July 1672 (deducting soe much therefrom as his Towne lott amounts to) in such place as you shall be directed by him soe as the same be not within the compass of any lands not yett layd out or marked to be layd out for any other person or Towne nor prejudiciall to any such lines or bounds and if the same happen upon any navigable River or any River capable of being made navigable you are to allow only the fifth part of the depth thereof by the water side and a Certificate fully specifying the scituacon and bounds thereof you are to returne to us with all convenient speed and for your soe doeing this shall be yo[r] sufficient Warr[t]. Given under my hand at Charles Towne this xxvij[th] day of September 1672/

John Yeamans

To John Culpeper
Surveyo[r] Generall./

Carolina./

By the Governo[r] by and with the advice and consent of the Councill

You are forthw[th] to cause to be admeasured and layd out for John Wells one Towne lott in James Towne observing the forme & method which you have been formerly directed in concerning the s[d] Towne and not prejudicing the lines of any lands lying next the said lott and a Certificate fully specifying the scituacon and bounds thereof you are to returne to us with all convenient speed and for your soe doeing this shall be your sufficient Warr^{t}. Given under my hand at Charles Towne this xxvijth. day of September 1672.

John Yeamans

To John Culpeper
Surveyo^{r} Generall/

Carolina./

By the Governo^{r} by and with the advice and consent of the Councill

You are forthwth. to cause to be admeasured and layd out for John Wells One hundred acres of land being the full proporcon allowed to him by the lords Proprietors concessions for himselfe arriveing in August 1672 (deducting soe much therefrom as his Towne lott amounts to) in such place as you shall be directed by him soe as the same be not wthin the compass of any lands not yett layd out nor marked to be layd out for any other person or Towne nor prejudiciall to any such lines or bounds and if the same happen upon any navigable River or any River capable of being made navigable you are to allow only the fifth part of the depth thereof by the water side and a Certificate fully specifying the scituacon and bounds thereof you are to returne to us with all convenient speed and for your soe doeing this shall be your sufficient Warr^{t}. Given under my hand at Charles Towne this xxvijth. day of September 1672.

John Yeamans

To John Culpeper
Surveyo^{r} Generall./

Carolina./

By the Governo^{r} by and with the advice and consent of the Councill

You are forthwth to cause to be admeasured and layd out for Mr Henry Pretty one hundred acres of land being the full proporcon allowed to him by the lords proprietors concessions for himselfe arriveing in Aprill 1672: (deducting soe much therefrom as his Towne lott amounts to) in such place as you shall be directed by him soe as the same be not within the compass of any lands not yett layd out or marked to be layd out for any other person or Towne nor prejudiciall to any such lines or bounds and if the same happen upon any navigable River or any River capable of being made navigable you are to allow only the fifth part of the depth thereof by the water side And a Certificate fully specifying the scituacon and bounds thereof you are to returne to us with all convenient speed and for yor soe doeing this shall be your sufficient warr^{t}. Given under my hand at Charles Towne this xxvijth. day of September 1672.

John Yeamans

To John Culpeper
Surveyo^{r} Generall./

Carolina./

By the Governo^{r} by and with the
advice and consent of the Councill

You are forthwth to cause to be admeasured and layd out for Mr William Morrill acres of land bounding the same to the Eastward of the lands allready layd out to Anthony Churne and John Hawkes and to the Westward of Wando River without p^{r}judicing or removeing the lines of any lands lying next the same And a Certificate fully specifying the scituacon and bounds thereof you are to returne to us with all convenient speed and for your soe doeing this shall be your sufficient Warr^{t}. Given under my hand at Charles Towne this xxviijth day of September 1672

John Yeamans

To John Culpeper
Surveyo^{r} Generall./

Carolina./

By the Governo^{r} by and with the
advice and consent of the Councill

You are forthwith to cause to be admeasured and layd out for Mr Christopher Berrow three hundred acres of land being the full proporcon allowed to him by the Lords Propriet^{rs} concessions for himselfe and Elizabeth his Wife; in such place as you shall be directed him soe as the same be not within the compass of any lands heretofore layd out or marked to be layd out for any other person or Towne nor prejudiciall to any such lines or bounds and if the same happen upon any navigable River or any River capable of being made navigable you are to allow only the fifth part of the depth thereof by the water side And a Certificate fully specifying the scituacon and bounds thereof you are to returne to us with all convenient speed and for your soe doeing this shall be your sufficient warr^{t}. Given under my hand at Charles Towne this xxxth day of September 1672

John Yeamans

To John Culpeper
Surveyo^{r} Generall./

Carolina/

By the Governo[r] by and with the advice & consent of the Councill

You are forthwith to cause to be admeasured and layd out for M[r] Thomas Norvill five hundred acres of land being the full proporcon allowed to him by the lords proprietors concessions for his disbursements on the discovery of this Province by Cap[t]: Hilton in such place as you shall be directed by him soe as the same be not within the compass of any lands heretofore layd out or marked to be layd out for any other person or Towne nor prejudiciall to any such lines or bounds and if the same happen upon any navigable River or any River capable of being made navigable you are to allow only the fifth part of the depth thereof by the waterside And a Certificate fully specifying the scituacon and bounds thereof you are to returne to us with all convenient speed and for your soe doeing this shall be your sufficient Warr[t]. Given under my hand at Charles Towne this xxx[th] day of September 1672./

John Yeamans

To John Culpeper
Surveyo[r] Generall./

Carolina./

By the Governour by and with the advice and consent of the Councill

You are forthw[th]. to cause to be admeasured and layd out for M[r]. Bartholomew Reese five hundred acres of land being the full proporcon allowed to him by the Lords Propriet[rs] concessions (for his disbursments on the discovery of this province by Cap[t]: Hilton) in such place as you shall be directed by him soe as the same be not w[th]in the compass of any lands heretofore layd out or marked to be layd out for any other person or Towne, nor prejudiciall to any such lines or bounds and if the same happen upon any navigable River or any River capable of being made navigable you are to allow only the fifth part of the depth thereof by the waterside and A Certificate fully specifying the scituacon and bounds thereof you are to returne to us with all convenient speed and for your soe doeing this shall be yo[r]. sufficient Warr[t]. Given under my hand at Charles Towne this xxx[th]. day of September 1672./

John Yeamans

To John Culpeper
Surveyo[r] Generall./

Carolina./

By the Governour by and with the advice and consent of the Councill

You are forthwth to cause to be admeasured and layd out for Mr Ralph Marshall tenn acres of land for his present planting in such place as you shall be directed by him soe as the same be not wthin the compass of any lands heretofore layd out or marked to be layd out for any other person, or prejudiciall to any such lines or bounds And a Certificate fully specifying the scituacon and bounds thereof you are to returne to us with all convenient speed and for yor soe doeing this shall be your sufficient Warr^{t}. Given under my hand at Charles Towne this xxxth. day of September 1672/

John Yeamans

To John Culpeper
Surveyo^{r} Generall./

Carolina./

By the Governour by and with the advice and consent of the Councill

You are forthwith to cause to be admeasured and layd out for Mr Peter Herne foure hundred acres of land as part of a greater quantity of land due to him by the Lords proprietors concessions in the Collony of James Towne in such place there as you shall be directed by him soe as the same be not within the compass of any lands heretofore layd out or marked to be layd out for any other person or Towne nor p^{r}judiciall to any such lines or bounds and if the same happen upon any navigable River or any River capable of being made navigable you are to allow only the fifth part of the depth thereof by the waterside and a Certificate fully specifying the scituacon and bounds thereof you are to returne to us with all convenient speed and for your soe doeing this shall be your sufficient warr^{t}. Given under my hand at Charles Towne this xvjth. day of Octob^{r} 1672./

John Yeamans

To John Culpeper
Surveyo^{r} Generall./

Carolina./

By the Governo^{r} by and with the advice and consent of the Councill

You are forthwth to cause to be admeasured and layd out for Mr Richard Chapman one hundred and thirty acres of land bounding the same to the Eastward of the lands allotted to be laid out for Mr Henry Woodward and not prejudicing the lines of any lands lying next the same And a Certificate fully specifying the scituacon and bounds thereof you are to returne to us with all convenient speed and for your soe doeing this shall be your sufficient warr^t. Given under my hand at Charles Towne this xvj^th. day of October 1672./

John Yeamans

To John Culpeper
Surveyo^r Generall./

Carolina./

By the Governo^r: by and with the advice and consent of the Councill }

You are forthw^th to cause to be admeasured and layd out for Mrs Priscilla Burke forty acres of land for her present planting bounding the same to the Westward of the land allotted to be layd out for Capt: fflorence ô Sullivan and not p^rjudicing the lines of any lands lying next the same And a Certificate fully specifying the scituacon and bounds thereof you are to returne to us with all convenient speed and for your soe doeing this shall be your sufficient warr^t. Given under my hand at Charles Towne this xvj^th. day of October 1672./

John Yeamans

To John Culpeper
Surveyo^r Generall./

Carolina

By the Governo^r: by and with the advice and Consent of ye Councill }

You are forthwith to cause to be admeasured and laid out for M^r: Henry: Woodward one hundred and fifty acres of land being the full proporcon allowed to him by the Lords prop^rs. concessions for himselfe arriveing in the first ffleet bounding the same to the Northward of the lands allready layd out for Mr James Jones and not prejudicing the lines of any lands lying next the same, and you are to allow only the fifth part of the depth thereof by the waterside And a certificate fully specifying the scituacon and bounds thereof you are to returne to us with all convenient speed and for yor soe doeing this shall bee your sufficient Warr^t. Given under my hand at Charles Towne this xviij^th. day of October 1672./

John Yeamans

To John Culpeper
Surveyo^r Generall/

Carolina./ By the Governo^r^ by and with the advice and consent of the Councill }

You are forthw^th^ to cause to be admeasured and layd out for Mr John Coming three hundred and seaventy five acres of land being the proporcon allowed to him by the Lords prop^rs^. concessions for himselfe Affera his wife and the halfe share of one servant namely John Neale arriveing in the first ffleet or soe much thereof as you shall find to be proporconable for the same on the Westward part of that breadth of land estimated to seaven hundred and fifty acres and contained between the lines of the land layd out for Mr Richard Cole to the North and the land allotted to be laid out for a Towne on the Oyster poynt to the South the same breadth being devided with three proporcons or parts vizt. the said three hundred seaventy five acres, two hundred twenty five and one hundred and fifty acres; and a Certificate fully specifying the scituacon & bounds and quantity thereof you are to returne to us with all convenient speed and for your soe doeing this shall be yor sufficient warr^t^. Given under my hand at Charles Towne this xviij^th^. day of October 1672./

John Yeamans

To John Culpeper
Surveyo^r^ Generall./

Carolina./ By the Governo^r^: by and with the advice & consent of the major part of the Councill }

You are forthw^th^. to cause to be admeasured and laid out for Mr John Coming eight hundred and tenn acres of land, five hundred & seaventy acres whereof being the proporcon allowed to him by the lords prop^rs^: concessions for five men Serv^ts^. and one woman Servt. arriveing in August 1671/ namely Samuell Lucas, George Gantlett, John Chambers, Phillip Orrill, Michaell Lovering, and Rachell ffranck, and two hundred and forty acres of land deficient of a fformer warr^t^: (deducting soe much therefrom as his Towne lott and tenn acre lott amounts to if any he hath) in such place as you shall be directed by him or his Attorney soe as the same be not w^th^in the compass of any lands heretofore laid out or marked to be laid out for any other person or Towne nor p^r^judiciall to any such lines or bounds, allowing only the fifth part of the depth thereof by the water side; and a Certificate fully specifying the scituacon & bounds thereof yo^u^. are to returne to us with all convenient speed And for your soe doeing this shall be your sufficient warr^t^. Given under my hand at Charles Towne this xxiij^d^ day of November 1672

John Yeamans

To John Culpeper
Surveyo^r^ Generall./

Carolina/

By the Governo^r^ by and with the advice & consent of the major part of the Councill

You are forthw^th^ to cause to be admeasured and laid out for Originall Jackson One hundred acres of land being the full proporcon allowed to him by the Lords prop^rs^: concessions for Millicent his Wife arriveing in the first ffleet, in such place as yo^u^ shall be directed by him soe as the same be not within the compass of any lands heretofore laid out or marked to be laid out for any other person or Towne nor p^r^judiciall to any such lines or bounds and if the same happen upon any navigable River or any River capable of being made navigable, you are to allow only the fifth part of the depth thereof by the water side, and a Certificate fully specifying the scituacon and bounds thereof you are to returne to us wth all convenient speed and for your soe doeing this shall be yor sufficient warr^t^. Given under my hand at Charles Towne this xxiij^th^ day of November 1672

John Yeamans

To John Culpeper
Surveyo^r^ Generall./

Carolina./

By the Governo^r^ by and w^th^: the advice and consent of the major part of the Councill

You are forthw^th^. to cause to be admeasured and laid out for Thomas Fluellin One hundred acres of land in the Collony of James Towne being the full proporcon allowed to him by the lords prop^rs^: concessions for himselfe arriveing in December 1671 (deducting soe much therefrom as his Towne lott and tenn acre lott amounts to if any he hath) in such place in the said Collony as you shall be directed by him soe as the same be not w^th^in the compass of any lands heretofore laid out or marked to be laid out for any other person nor p^r^judiciall to any such lines or bounds, allowing only the fifth part of the depth thereof by the water side; And a Certificate fully specifying the scituacon and bounds thereof you are to returne to us with all convenient speed and for yor soe doeing this shall be yor sufficient warr^{t}. Given under my hand at Charles Towne this xxiij^{d} day of November 1672./ John Yeamans

To John Culpeper
Surveyo^{r} Generall./

Carolina./

By the Governo^{r} by and wth the advice and consent of the major part of the Councill

You are forthwth to cause to be admeasured and laid out for Mary Brotherhood seaventy acres of land being the full proporcon allowed to her by the Lords Prop^{rs}: concessions for her selfe arriveing in August 1671 in such place as you shall be directed by her soe as the same be not within the compass of any lands heretofore laid out or marked to be laid out for any other person or Towne nor prejudiciall to any such lines or bounds and if the same happen upon any navigable River or any River capable of being made navigable you are to allow only the fifth part of the depth thereof by the water side; And a Certificate fully specifying the scituacon and bounds thereof you are to returne to us with all convenient speed and for your soe doeing this shall be your sufficient warrant Given under my hand at Charles Towne this xxiijth. day of November 1672.

John Yeamans

To John Culpeper
Surveyo^{r} Generall./

Carolina./

By the Governo^{r} by and with the advice and consent of the major part of the Councill

You are forthwth to cause to be admeasured and laid out for Thomas Williams one hundred acres of land in the Collony of James Towne being part of a greater quantity of land due to him by the Lords Prop^{rs}: concessions in such place in the said Collony as you shall be directed by him soe as the same be not within the compass of any lands heretofore laid out or marked to be laid out for any other person nor p^{r}judiciall to any such lines or bounds allowing only the fifth part of the depth thereof by the water side, And a Certificate fully specifying the scituacon and bounds thereof you are to returne to us wth. all convenient speed and for yor soe doeing this shall be yor sufficient warr^{t}. Given under my hand at Charles Towne this xxiijth day of November 1672.

John Yeamans

To John Culpeper
Surveyo^{r}: Generall./

Carolina./

By the Governo^{r}: by and with the advice and consent of the major part of the Councill }

You are forthwth to cause to be admeasured and laid out for Robert Goffe two hundred acres of land being the full proporcon allowed to him by the Lords Prop^{rs}: concessions for himselfe and one Servt. namely John Robry arriveing in July 1672 in such place as you shall be directed by him soe soe as the same be not within the compass of any lands heretofore laid out or marked to be laid out for any other person or Towne nor p^{r}judiciall to any such lines or bounds and if the same happen upon any navigable River or any River capable of being made navigable you are to allow only the fifth part of the depth thereof by the water side; And a Certificate fully specifying the scituacon and bounds thereof you are to returne to us with all convenient speed and for yor soe doeing this shall be yor sufficient warr^{t}. Given under my hand at Charles Towne this xxiijth day of November 1672 John Yeamans

To John Culpeper
Surveyo^{r}: Generall./

Carolina./

By the Governo^{r} by and with the advice & consent of the major part of the Councill }

You are forthwth to cause to be admeasured and laid out for George Beadon Administrator of Mr Paul Smith deceased seaven hundred acres of land being the full proporcon allowed by the Lords prop^{rs}: concessions for the s^{d} Mr Paul Smith, M^{r}. John Boon, William Cockfield, Andrew Burne & Elizabeth Smith Serv^{ts}: arriveing in the first ffleet in such place as yo^{u} shall be directed by the s^{d} George Beadon soe as the same be not wthin the compass of any lands heretofore laid out or marked to be laid out for any other person or Towne nor p^{r}judiciall to any such lines or bounds (deducting soe much therefrom as the Tenn acre lott and Towne lott of the s^{d} Mr Paul Smith amounts to) and if the same happen upon any navigable River or any River capable of being made navigable you are to allow only the fifth part of the depth thereof by the water side and a Certificate fully specifying the scituacon and bounds thereof you are to returne to us with all convenient speed and for yor soe doeing this shall be your sufficient warr^{t}. Given under my hand at Charles Towne this xxiijth day of November 1672/

John Yeamans

To John Culpeper
Surveyo^{r} Generall./

Carolina./

By the Governo^r^ by and wth the advice and consent of the major part of the Councill

You are forthw^th^ to cause to be admeasured and laid out for Thomas Turpin one hundred acres of land being the full proporcon allowed to him by the Lords prop^rs^: concessions for himselfe arriveing in Aprill 1671 (deducting soe much therefrom as his Towne lott and tenn acre lott amounts to if any he hath) in such place as you shall be directed by him soe as the same be not within the compass of any lands heretofore laid out or marked to be laid out for any other person or Towne nor prejudiciall to any such lines or bounds and if the same happen upon any navigable River or any River capable of being made navigable you are to allow only the fifth part of the depth thereof by the water side And a Certificate fully specifying the scituacon and bounds thereof you are to returne to us with all convenient speed and for yor soe doeing this shall be your sufficient warr^t^. Given under my hand at Charles Towne this xxiij^th^. day of November 1672/

To John Culpeper
Surveyo^r^ Generall./

John Yeamans

Carolina./

By the Governo^r^ by and with the advice & consent of the major part of the Councill

You are forthw^th^ to cause to be admeasured and laid out for Mr Thomas Buttler fower hundred acres of land being the full proporcon allowed to him by the Lords Prop^rs^: concessions for himselfe and three Servants namely Otho Christopher John Cattell, and Thomas Mackanellor arriveing in August 1672 in such place as you shall be directed by him soe as the same be not within the compass of any lands heretofore laid out or marked to be laid out for any other person or Towne nor p^r^judiciall to any such lines or bounds, and if the same happen upon any navigable River or any River capable of being made navigable you are to allow only the fifth part of the depth thereof by the water side And a Certificate fully specifying the scituacon and bounds thereof you are to returne to us with all convenient speed And for your soe doeing this shall be your sufficient warr^t^. Given under my hand at Charles Towne this xxiij^th^ day of November 1672/

John Yeamans

To John Culpeper
Surveyo^r^ Generall./

Carolina./

By the Governo^{r} by and with the advice
& consent of the major part of the Councill

You are forthwth to cause to be admeasured and laid out for John Faulconer Extor: to Edward Roberts deceased one hundred acres of land being the full proporcon allowed to him by the Lords Prop^{rs}: concessions arriveing in February 167$\frac{0}{1}$ (deducting soe much therefrom as the Towne lott and ten acre lott of the said Edward Roberts amounts to if any he hath) in such place as you shall be directed by the said John ffaulconer soe as the same be not wthin the compass of any lands heretofore laid out or marked to be laid out for any other person or Towne nor p^{r}judiciall to any such lines or bounds and if the same happen upon any navigable River or any River capable of being made navigable you are to allow only the fifth part of the depth thereof by the waterside, And a Certificate fully specifying the scituacon and bounds thereof you are to returne to us with all convenient speed and for your soe doeing this shall be your sufficient warr^{t} Given under my hand at Charles Towne this xxiijth day of November 1672./ John Yeamans

To John Culpeper
Surveyo^{r} Generall./

Carolina./

By the Governo^{r} by and with the advice &
consent of the major part of the Councill

You are forthwth to cause to be admeasured and laid out for John Faulconer one hundred acres of land (deducting soe much therefrom as his Towne lott and tenn acre lott amounts to if any he hath) being the full proporcon allowed to him by the Lords Prop^{rs}: concessions for himselfe arriveing in September 1670 bounding the same to the Northward of the lands herewith to be laid out to him as Extor: to Edward Roberts deceased observing as nere as conveniently you may to allow only the fifth part of the depth thereof by the water side and not to p^{r}judice the lines of any lands lying next the same And a Certificate fully specifying the scituacon and bounds thereof you are to returne to us wth all convenient speed and for your soe doeing this shall be your sufficient warr^{t}. Given under my hand at Charles Towne this xxiijth. day of November 1672

John Yeamans

To John Culpeper
Surveyo^{r} Generall./

Carolina./

By the Governo^{r}: by and wth the advice and consent of the major part of the Councill

You are forthwth to cause to be admeasured and laid out for Capt^{t}: Robert Donne Seaventy acres of land being the full proporcon allowed to him by the Lords Prop^{rs} concessions for Elizabeth his Wife arriveing in August 1671./ in such place as you shall be directed by him soe as the same be not within the compass of any lands heretofore laid out or marked to be laid out for any other person or Towne nor p^{r}judiciall to any such lines or bounds and if the same happen upon any navigable River or any River capable of being made navigable you are to allow only the fifth part of the depth thereof by the water side, and a Certificate fully specifying the scituacon and bounds thereof you are to returne to us with all convenient speed and for your soe doeing this shall be your sufficient Warr^{t}. Given under my hand at Charles Towne this xxiijth. day of November 1672./

John Yeamans

To John Culpeper
Surveyo^{r} Generall./

Carolina./

By the Governo^{r} by and with the advice and consent of the major part of the Councill

You are forthwth to cause to be admeasured and laid out for John Pinke One hundred acres of land (deducting soe much therefrom as his Towne lott and tenn acre lott amounts to if any he hath) being the full proporcon allowed to him by the Lords prop^{rs} concessions for one Servant namely George Saker arriveing in ffebruary 167$\frac{0}{1}$ in such place as you shall be directed by him soe as the same be not within the compass of any lands heretofore laid out or marked to be laid out for any other person or Towne nor p^{r}ejudiciall to any such lines or bounds and if the same happen upon any navigable River or any River capable of being made navigable you are to allow only the fifth part of the depth thereof by the water side And a Certificate fully specifying the scituacon and bounds thereof you are to returne to us with all convenient speed and for your soe doeing this shall be your sufficient warr^{t}. Given under my hand at Charles Towne this xxiijth day of November 1672/

John Yeamans

Carolina/

By the Governo^{r} by and with the advice and consent of the major part of the Councill }

You are forthwth to cause to be admeasured and laid out for Capt: fflorence ô Sullivan Extor: of Michael Moron deceased fower hundred acres of land being the full proporcon allowed to the said Michaell Moron for himselfe, his Wife and One child arriveing in the first fleet by the Lords Prop^{rs}: concessions (deducting therefrom his Towne lott and Tenn acre lott if any he hath) in such place as you shall be directed by the said Capt: ô Sullivan soe as the same be not wthin the compass of any lands heretofore laid out or marked to be laid out for any other person or Towne nor p^{r}judiciall to any such lines or bounds and if the same happen upon any navigable River or any River capable of being made navigable you are to allow only the fifth part of the depth thereof by the water side And a Certificate fully specifying the Scituacon and bounds thereof you are to returne to us with all convenient speed and for your soe doeing this shall be your Sufficient Warr^{t}. Given under my hand at Charles Towne this xxiijth day of November 1672

To John Culpeper Surveyo^{r} Generall./ John Yeamans

Carolina/

By the Governour by and with the advice and consent of the major part of the Councill }

You are forthwth to cause to be admeasured and laid out for Capt: Nathanieel Sayle and Mr James Sayle Extors: of Col: William Sayle deceased thirteen hundred acres of land being the proporcon allowed by the lords prop^{rs} concessions for the said Coll: William Sayle Capt: Nathanieel Sayle M^{rs}: Mary Gand & Charles Rilley, George Roberts, John Senr a Negroe Elizabeth a Negro and John Junr a Negroe arriveing in the first ffleet and Thomas Parker and William a Negroe arriveing in September 1670 in the Collony of James Towne in such place there as yo^{u} shall be directed by them or their Attorneys soe as the same be not wthin the compass of any lands heretofore laid out or marked to be laid out for any other person and not p^{r}judicing the lines of any lands lying next the same and allowing the fifth part of the depth thereof by the water side And a Certificate fully specifying the scituacon and bounds thereof you are to returne to us with all convenient speed and for your soe doeing this

shall be yor sufficient warr^{t}. Given under my hand at Charles Towne this xxiijth day of November 1672./
To John Culpeper
Surveyo^{r} Generall./

Carolina./

By the Governo^{r} by and with the advice and consent of the major part of the Councill

You are forthwth to cause to be admeasured and laid out for Mr John Maverick one hundred acres of land being the full proporcon allowed to him by the Lords prop^{rs}: concessions for himselfe arriveing in February 1670 (deducting soe much therefrom as his Towne lott and tenn acre lott amounts to if any he hath) in such place as you shall be directed by him soe as the same be not wthin the compass of any lands heretofore laid out or marked to be laid out for any other person or Towne nor p^{r}judiciall to any such lines or bounds and if the same happen upon any navigable River or any River capable of being made navigable you are to allow only the fifth part of the depth thereof by the water side; And a Certificate fully specifying the scituacon and bounds thereof you are to returne to us with all convenient speed and for yor soe doeing this shall be your sufficient warr^{t}. Given under my hand at Charles Towne this xxiijth day of November 1672 John Yeamans
To John Culpeper
Surveyo^{r} Generall./

Carolina/

By the Governo^{r} by and with the advice and consent of the major part of the Councill

You are forthwth to cause to be admeasured and laid out for John Culpeper three hundred and seaventy acres of land being the full proporcon allowed to him by the Lords prop^{rs}: concessions for himselfe and Crow a Negro arriveing in ffebruary 167$\frac{0}{1}$ and Judith his Wife and one servant namely Alice Thomas, arriveing in December 1671./ (deducting soe much there from as his Towne lott and tenn acre lott amounts to if any he hath) in such place as you shall be directed by him soe as the same be not within the compass of any lands heretofore laid out or marked to be laid out for any other person or Towne nor prejudiciall to any such lines or bounds and if the same happen upon any navigable River or any River capable of being made navigable you are to allow only the fifth part of the depth thereof by the waterside And a Certificate fully specifying the scituacon and bounds thereof you are to returne to us with all convenient speed and for your soe doeing this shall be your sufficient warr^{t}. Given under my hand at Charles Towne this ij^{d} day of December 1672/

To John Culpeper
Surveyo^{r} Generall./

John Yeamans

Carolina./

By the Governo^{r} by and wth. the advice and consent of the major part of the Councill

You are forthwth to cause to be admeasured and laid out for M^{rs}: Jane Robinson one hundred and Seaventy acres of land being the full proporcon allowed to her by the Lords prop^{rs}: concessions for herselfe and Grace a Negro arriveing in ffebruary 167$\frac{0}{1}$ (deducting soe much there from as her Towne lott and tenn acre lott amounts to if any she hath) in such place as you shall be directed by Capt: John Robinson and Mr John Culpeper her Attorneys soe as the same be not within the compass of any lands heretofore laid out or marked to be laid out for any other person or Towne nor p^{r}judiciall to any such lines or bounds and if the same happen upon any navigable River or any River capable of being made navigable you are to allow only the fifth part of the depth thereof by the waterside And a Certificate fully specifying the scituacon and bounds thereof you are to returne to us with all convenient speed and for your soe doeing this shall be yor sufficient warr^{t}. Given under my hand at Charles Towne this ij^{d} day of December 1672/

John Yeamans

To John Culpeper
Surveyo^{r}: Generall./

Carolina./

By the Governo^{r}: by and with the advice and consent of the major part of the Councill

You are forthwth: to cause to be admeasured and laid out for Capt: John Robinson two hundred acres of land being the full proporcon allowed to him by the Lords Prop^{rs}: concessions for himselfe and One Negro namely Yackae arriveing in ffebruary 167$\frac{0}{1}$ (deducting soe much there from as his Towne lott and tenn acre lott amounts to if any he hath) in such place as you shall be directed by him soe as the same be not within the compass of any lands heretofore laid out or marked to be laid out for any other person or Towne nor prejudiciall to any such lines or bounds and if the same happen upon any navigable River or any River capable of being made navigable you are to allow only the fifth part of the depth thereof by the water side And a Certificate fully specifying the scituacon and bounds thereof you are to returne to us with all convenient speed and for your soe doeing this shall be yor sufficient warr^{t}. Given under my hand at Charles Towne this ij^{d} day of December 1672./

John Yeamans

To John Culpeper
Surveyo^{r}. Generall./

Carolina./

By the Governo^{r} by and with the advice and consent of the major part of the Councill }

You are forthwth. to cause to be admeasured and laid out for Richard Cole Eight hundred acres of land being the full proporcon allowed to him by the Lords prop^{rs}: concessions for Eight Serv^{ts}. namely John Barnes John Stryde, John Cooke, Edward Willson, Edward Deale, John Rivers, Anthony ffleming, Ambrose Adams arriveing in August 1671. in such place as you shall be directed by him soe as the same be not wth.in the compass of any lands heretofore laid out or marked to be laid out for any other person or Towne nor prejudiciall to any such lines or bounds and if the same happen upon any navigable River or any River capable of being made navigable you are to allow only the fifth part of the depth thereof by the water side And a Certificate fully specifying the scituacon and bounds thereof you are to returne to us with all convenient speed and for your soe doeing this shall be your sufficient warr^{t}. Given under my hand at Charles Towne this vijth. day of December 1672./

John Yeamans

To John Culpeper
Surveyo^{r} Generall./

Carolina./

By the Governo^{r}: by and with the advice & consent of the major part of the Councill }

You are forthwth to cause to be admeasured and laid out for Richard Deyos three hundred acres of land being the full proporcon allowed to him by the Lords prop^{rs}: concessions for himselfe and one Servt. namely Christopher Edwards arriveing in the first ffleet, or soe much thereof as is or shall be found to be conteyned between the lines of the lands allotted to be laid out to Thomas Norris to the South and Anthony Churne to the North (deducting soe much therefrom as his Towne lott and two acre lott amounts to) And a Certificate fully specifying the scituacon bounds and quantity thereof you are to returne to us with all convenient speed And for your soe doeing this shall be yor sufficient warr^{t}. Given under my hand at Charles Towne this vijth. day of December 1672./

John Yeamans

To John Culpeper
Surveyo^{r} Generall./

Carolina./

By the Governo^{r}: by and with the advice and consent of the major part of the Councill

You are forthwth to cause to be admeasured and laid out for Mr William Owen thirteen hundred and twenty acres of land being the full proporcon allowed to him by the Lords prop^{rs}: concessions for himselfe, John Barley and Christopher Swaine Mr William Scrivener Robert Hunt, John Williams, and Benjamin Gilbert, arriveing in the first ffleet, John Reese and Elizabeth Braine, arriveing in ffebruary $167\frac{0}{1}$. and Thomas Clarke arriveing in Aprill 1671./ (deducting soe much therefrom as his Towne lott and tenn acre lott amounts to) in such place as you shall be directed by him soe as the same be not within the compass of any lands heretofore laid out or marked to be laid out for any other person or Towne nor prejudiciall to any such lines or bounds and if the same happen upon any navigable River or any River capable of being made navigable you are to allow only the fifth part of the Depth thereof by the water side And a Certificate fully specifying the scituacon and bounds thereof you are to returne us with all convenient speed and for your soe doeing this shall be your sufficient warr^{t}. Given under my hand at Charles Towne this viith day of December 1672

John Yeamans

To John Culpeper
Surveyo^{r} Generall./

Carolina./

By the Governo^{r}: by and with the advice and consent of the major part of the Councill

You are forthwith to cause to be admeasured and laid out for Mr John ffoster that vacant land that lyes nere James Towne between the lands of Mr Peter Herne, and Mr James Jones, and not p^rjudicing the lines of any lands lying next the same And a Certificate fully specifying the scituacon bounds and quantity thereof you are to returne to us with all convenient speed and for your soe doeing this shall be your sufficient warr^t. Given under my hand at Charles Towne this xij^th day of December 1672./

John Yeamans

To John Culpeper
Surveyo^r Generall./

Carolina./

By the Governo^r: by and with the advice and consent of the major part of the Councill }

You are forthw^th. to cause to be admeasured and laid out for John Wattkins One hundred acres of land being the full proporcon allowed to him by the Lords prop^rs: concessions for himselfe arriveing a serv^t: in ffebruary 1670 in such place as you shall be directed by him soe as the same be not within the compass of any lands heretofore laid out or marked to be laid out for any other person or Towne nor p^rejudiciall to any such lines or bounds and if the same happen upon any navigable River or any River capable of being made navigable you are to allow only the fifth part of the depth thereof by the water side And a Certificate fully specifying the scituacon and bounds thereof you are to returne to us wth. all convenient speed And for your soe doeing this shall be yor sufficient warr^t. Given under my hand at Charles Towne this xviij^th. day of January 1672/

John Yeamans

To John Culpeper
Surveyo^r: Generall./

Carolina./

By the Governo^r: by and wth the advice and consent of the major part of the Councill }

You are forthw^th. to cause to be admeasured and laid out for M^r: Amos Jeffors foure hundred acres of land being part of a greater quantity of land due to him by the Lords prop^rs: concessions in such place as yo^u shall be directed by him soe as the same be not within the compass of any lands heretofore laid out or marked to be laid out for any other person or Towne nor p^rjudiciall to any such lines or bounds and if the same happen upon any navigable River or any River capable of being made navigable you are to allow only the fifth part of the depth thereof by the waterside And a Certificate fully specifying the scituacon and bounds thereof you are to returne to us with all convenient speed and for your soe doeing this shall be your sufficient warr[t]. Given under my hand at Charles Towne this xxiiij[th]. day of December 1672

To John Culpeper Surveyo[r]: Generall./ John Yeamans

Carolina./

By the Governo[r]: by and wth. the advice and consent of the major part of the Councill—

You are forthw[th]. to cause to be admeasured and laid out for Christopher Edwards Eighty acres of land being part of a greater quantity of land due to him by the lords prop[rs]: concessions in such place as you shall be directed by him soe as the same be not within the compass of any lands heretofore laid out or marked to be laid out for any other person or Towne nor p[r]judiciall to any such lines or bounds and if the same happen upon any navigable River or any River capable of being made navigable you are to allow only the fifth part of the depth thereof by the water side and a Certificate fully specifying the scituacon and bounds thereof you are to returne to us with all convenient speed and for your soe doeing this shall be your sufficient warr[t]. Given under my hand at Charles Towne this xviij[th] day of January 1672.

To John Culpeper Surveyo[r] Generall./ John Yeamans

Carolina./

By the Governo[r] by and with the advice and consent of the major part of the Councill

You are forthw[th] to cause to be admeasured and laid out for Thomas Archcraft One hundred acres of land being the full proporcon allowed to him by the Lords proprietors concessions for himselfe arriveing a serv[t] in ffebruary 1670 in such place as yo[u] shall be directed by him soe as the same be not within the compass of any lands heretofore laid out or marked to be laid out for any other person or Towne nor p[r]judiciall to any such lines or bounds and if the same happen upon any navigable River or any River capable of being made navigable you are to allow only the fifth part of the depth thereof by the water side And a Certificate fully specifying the scituacon and bounds thereof you are to returne to us with all convenient speed and for your soe doeing this shall be yo[r] sufficient warr[t]. Given under my hand at Charles Towne this xviij[th] day of January 1672

To John Culpeper
Surveyo[r] Generall./

John Yeamans

Carolina./

You[u]. are forthw[th]. to cause to be admeasured and laid out for Evan Jones tenn acres of land for his present planting in the Collony of Charles Towne in such place in the s[d] Collony as you shall be directed by him soe as the same be not w[th]in the compass of any lands heretofore laid out or marked to be laid out for any other person nor prejudiciall to any such lines or bounds And a Certificate fully specifying the scituacon and bounds thereof you are to returne to us w[th]. all convenient speed and for your soe doeing this shall be your sufficient warrant Given under our hands at Charles Towne this first day of March 167$\frac{2}{3}$/

To John Culpeper
Surveyo[r] Generall./

John Yeamans
Joseph West
John Godfrey
Maurice Mathews

Carolina

You are forthwith to cause to be admeasured and laid out for John Bassent one Towne lott in James Towne and tenn acres of land for his p[r]sent planting in such place neere the sd Towne as you shall be directed by him soe as the same be not within the compasse of any lands heretofore laid out or marked to be laid out for any other person, nor p[r]judiciall to any such lines or bounds, & a Certificate fully specifieing the scittuacon, and bounds thereof you are to returne to us with all convenient speed & for yo[r] soe doeing this shall be yo[r]. sufficient warr[t]: Given und[r]: our hands at Charles Towne this xviij[th]: day of Aprill 1673./

Mau: Mathews
Will: Owen/

John: Yeamans
Joseph: West
John: Godfrey

Carolina

You are forthwith to cause to be admeasured and laid out for John: Berton one hundred acres of land being the proportion allowed to him by the Lords proprieto[rs]: Concessions arriveing in ffebruary 1670. in such place as he shall direct you, soe as the same be not within the compasse of any lands heretofore laid out or marked to be laid out for any other person, and if the same happen upon any navigable river or any river capable of being made navigable, You are to allow onely the fifth part of the depth thereof by the waterside, And a Certificate fully specifieing the scittuacon and bounds thereof you are to returne to us with all convenient speed, And for yor: soe doeing this shall be yor: sufficient warr^{t}: Given und^{r}. our hands at Charles Towne this iij^{d}: day of May 1673/

John: Yeamans
To M^{r}: John Culpeper Joseph: West
Surveyo^{r}: Gen^{ll}: Will: Owen John: Godfrey

Carolina
You are forthwith to cause to be admeasured and laid out for M^{rs}: Dorcas: Smith two hundred and seaventy acres of land (being the proportion allowed to her by the Lords proprieto^{rs}: Concessions for herself, and two slaves namely Andrew & Jone Negroes, in such place as you shall be directed by her, soe as the same be not within the compasse of any lands heretofore laid out or marked to be laid out for any other person or use, and if the same happen upon any Navigable river or any river capable of being made navigable you are to allow onely the fifth part of the depth thereof by the waterside, And a Certificate fully specifieing the scittuacon and bounds thereof you are to returne to us with all convenient speed and for yor: soe doeing this shall be yor: suff^{t}: warr^{t}: Given und^{r}: our hands at Charles Towne this xxvjth: day of Aprill 1673/

To John: Culpeper John Yeamans
Surveyo^{r}: Gen^{ll}:/ Maurice Mathews Jos: West
Willm Owen John: Godfrey

Carolina
You are forthwith to cause to be admeasured and laid out for John: May one hundred acres of land being the proportion allowed by the Lords prop^{rs}: Concessions to him arriveing a serv^{t}: in the month of Aprill 1670, in such place as he shall direct you, soe as the same be not within the compasse of any lands heretofore laid out, or marked to be laid out for any other person or Towne, and if the same happen upon any navigable river or any river capable of being made navigable you are to allow onely the fifth part of the depth thereof by the waterside, And a Certificate fully specifieing the scittuacon and bounds thereof you are to returne to us with all convenient speed

and for yor soe doeing this shall be yor: sufft: wart: Given und^r: our hands at Charles Towne this iij^d: day of May 1673./

To M^r: John: Culpeper Surveyo^r: Gen^ll:/ — Will: Owen, John: Yeamans, Joseph: West, John: Godfrey

Carolina

You are forthwith to cause to be admeasured and laid out for Capt. Nathaneel: Sayle and M^r: James Sayle Extors of Coll W^m: Sayle deceased one thousand and fifty acres of land being the proporcon allowed by the Lords proprieto^rs: Concessions for the sd Coll William Sayle, Nathan: Sayle, Charles Rilly, George: Roberts, John Senr: a Negroe Eliz: a Negroe, and John Junr a Negroe arriveing in the first fleet, and William a Negroe arriveing in september 1670.) neare James Towne, in such place there as you shall be directed by them or their Attorneys, soe as the same be not within the Compasse of any lands heretofore laid out for any other person or use, and not p^rjudiceing the lines of any lands lyeing next ye same, alloweing onely the fifth part of ye depth thereof by the waterside: And a Certificate fully specifieing the scittuacon and bounds thereof you are to returne to us with all convenient speed And for yor: soe doeing this shall be yor: sufficient war^t: Given und^r: our hands at Charles Towne this xxij^d: day of March 1672./

To John Culpeper Surveyo^r. Gen^ll:/ — Maurice Mathews, John Yeamans, Joseph: West, Tho: Gray./

Carolina

You are forthwith to cause to be admeasured and laid out for M^r: William: Thomas two hundred and seaventy acres of land being the proporcon allowed to him by the Lords proprieto^rs. Concessions for 3 serv^ts: namely W^m: Cason, and Richard and Salisbury two Negroes arriveing in May 1673 in such place as you shall be directed by him, soe as the same be not within the compasse of any lands heretofore laid out or marked to be laid out for any other person, and if the same happen upon any navigable river, or any river capable of being made navigable you are to allow onely the fifth part of the depth thereof by the waterside, and a Certificate fully specifieing the scittuacon and bounds thereof you are to returne to us with all convenient speed, And for yor: soe doeing this shall be yor: sufft:

wart: Given undr: our hands at Charles Towne this xth: day of May 1673./

To Mr: John: Culpeper Surveyor: Genll:/ John: Yeamans Will: Owen John: Godfrey Maur: Mathews

Carolina

You are forthwith to cause to be admeasured and laid out for Mr: William Thomas three hundred and forty acres of land being the proporcon allowed to him by the Lords proprs: Concessions for himself and three servants namely Willm Jones, Ann Jones & one child arriveing in May 1673 in such place as you shall bė directed by him, soe as the same be not within the compasse of any lands heretofore laid out, or marked to be laid out, for any other person, And if the same happen upon any Navigable river, or any river capable of being made Navigable you are to allow onely the fifth part of the depth thereof by the waterside, and a Certificate fully specifieing the scittuacon and bounds thereof, you are to returne to us with all convenient speed, And for yor: soe doeing this shall be yor: sufft: wart: Given undr: our hands at Charles Towne this xth: day of May 1673./

To Mr: John: Culpeper Surveyor: Genll: John: Yeamans Will: Owen John: Godfrey Maur: Mathews

Carolina

You are forthwith to cause to be admeasured and laid out for Mr: William Thomas two hundred acres of land being the proportion allowed to him by the Lords proprs: Concessions for two servts: namely William: Jackson—and Tho: Hunt ——— arriveing in May 1673 in such place as you shall be directed by him, soe as the same be not within the compasse of any lands heretofore laid out or marked to be laid out, for any other person, and if the same happen upon any navigable river or any river capable of being made navigable you are to allow onely the fifth part of the depth thereof by the waterside and a Certificate fully specifying the scittuacon and bounds thereof you are to returne to us with all convenient speed, And for yor: soe doeing this shall be yor: sufft: wart: Givėn undr: our hands at Charles Towne this xth: day of May 1673./

To Mr: John: Culpeper Surveyor: Genll:/ John: Yeamans Will: Owen John: Godfrey Maur: Mathews

Carolina

You are forthwith to cause to be admeasured and laid out for Coll Joseph West four hundred and seaventy acres of land, two hundred acres whereof being ye residue of the proportion allowed to him by the Lords prop[rs]: Concessions for himself and two serv[ts]: namely Abraham: Smith, and Millicent How arriveing in the first fleet, and 270: acres for M[rs]: Joanna West, James Bryan, & Elizabeth Baker arriveing in Aug[t]: 1671 in such place as you shall be directed by him soe as the same be not within the compasse of any lands heretofore laid out or marked to be laid out for any other person or Towne, and if the same happen upon any Navigable river, or any river capable of being made navigable you are to allow onely the fifth part of the depth thereof by the waterside, And a Certificate fully specifieing the scittuacon and bounds thereof you are to returne to us with all convenient speed, And for yo[r]: soe doeing this shall be yo[r]: sufficient war[t]: Given und[r]: our hands at Charles Towne this x[th]: day of May 1673./

To M[r]: John: Culpeper
Surveyo[r]: Gen[ll]:/

John: Yeamans
Will: Owen John: Godfrey
Maur: Mathews

Carolina

You are forthwith to admeasure and lay out for John Gardner a certaine parcell of land to ye north side of Ashley River and to the Eastward of John: Sullivans land, and the westward of Bryan ffitzpatricks land soe as the same doe not exceed one hundred acres alloweing the breadth to be the fifth part of the depth thereof, And a Certificate fully specifieing the scittuacon, bounds and quantity thereof you are to returne to us with all convenient speed, And for yo[r]: soe doeing this shall be yo[r]: suff[t]: war[t]: Given und[r]: our hands at Charles Towne this x[th]: day of May 1673/

To M[r]: John: Culpeper
Surveyo[r]: Gen[ll]:/

John: Yeamans
Will: Owen. Joseph: West
John: Godfrey

Carolina

You are forthwith to cause to be admeasured and laid out for John: Boon seaventy acres of land being the proporcon allowed to him by the Lords proprieto[rs]: Concessions for one serv[t]. by name Benjamin: Wood arriveing in December 1671 in such place as you shall be directed by him, soe as the same be not within the compasse of any lands heretofore laid out or marked to be laid out for any other person or Towne, and if the same happen upon any Navigable river you are to allow onely the fifth part of the depth thereof by the water side, and a Certificate fully specifieing the scittuacon and bounds thereof you are to returne to us with all convenient speed, and for yor: soe doeing this shall be yor: suff^{t}: war^{t}: Given und^{r}: our hands at Charles Towne this ij^{d}: day of June 1673./

To M^{r}: John Culpeper
Surveyo^{r}: Gen^{ll}:/

John: Yeamans
Will: Owen Joseph: West
John: Godfrey

Carolina./

By the Governo^{r} by and with the advice and consent of the major part of the Councill

You are forthwth. to cause to be admeasured and laid out for Mr Edward Mathews One hundred acres of land being the full proporcon allowed to him by the Ld^{s}. prop^{rs}: Concessions for one Servt. namely Thomas Steere arriveing in August 1671 in such place as you shall be directed by him soe as the same be not within the compass of any lands heretofore laid out or marked to be laid out for any other person or Towne nor p^{r}judiciall to any such lines or bounds, and if the same happen upon any navigable River or any River capable of being made navigable you are to allow only the fifth part of the depth thereof by the water side; And a Certificate fully specifying the scituacon and bounds thereof you are to returne to us with all convenient speed and for your soe doeing this shall be your sufficient Warr^{t}. Given under my hand at Charles Towne this xviijth: day of January 1672/

To John Culpeper
Surveyo^{r} Generall./

John Yeamans

Carolina/

You are forthwth. to cause to be admeasured and laid out for Mr Thomas Lane seaven hundred and forty acres of land being the full proporcon allowed to him by the Lords prop^{rs} concessions for himselfe, Mathew Harris and Robert Leeds arriveing in July 1672. and Trisimus Morrison, John Hooper, David Derling, Hester Lane and Judith Lane arriveing in May 1673./ in such place as you shall be directed by him soe as the same be not within the compass of any lands heretofore laid out or marked to be laid out for any other person or Towne nor prejudiciall to any such lines or bounds and

if the same happen upon any navigable River or any River capable of being made navigable you are to allow only the fifth part of the depth thereof by the water side and a Certificate fully specifying the scituacon and bounds thereof you are to returne to us with all convenient speed and for your soe doeing this shall be your sufficient warr^{t}. Given under our hands at Charles Towne this 18— day of January 1673
To John Culpeper
Surveyo^{r} Generall./

Carolina
You are forthwith to admeasure and lay out for Evan: Jones four score acres of land being ye residue of the land allowed to him by the Lords proprieto^{rs}: concessions arriveing in ffebr 167$\frac{0}{1}$ in such place as he shall direct you, soe as ye same be not within the compasse of any lands heretofore laid out, or marked to be laid out for any other person or Towne, and if the same upon any navigable river you are to allow onely the fifth part of the depth thereof by the waterside. And a Certificate fully specifieing the scittuation and bounds thereof, you are to returne to us with all convenient speed: And for yor: soe doeing this shall be yor: sufficient warr^{t}: Given und^{r}: our hands at Charles Towne this xxviijth: day of August 1673/

To Capt^{t}: Stephen: Bull
Surveyo^{r}:[1]/

John: Yeamans
Joseph: West
Mau: Mathews
William: Owen

Carolina./
You are forthwth. to cause to be admeasured and laid out for William Cockfield One hundred acres of land being the full proporcon allowed to him by the Lords Proprietors concessions (arriveing a Servt in the first ffleet) in such place as you shall be directed by him soe as the same be not within the compass of any lands heretofore laid out or marked to be laid out for any other person or Towne nor prejudiciall to any such lines or bounds and if the same happen

[1] "Foras much as John Culpeper Surveyo^{r} Generall hath run away from this Settlem^{t}: soe that divers persons are exceedingly injured haveing none to lay out their lands; It is therefore ordered and resolved that Mr Stephen Bull Mr John Yeamans and Stephen Wheelewright be commissionated surveyors during pleasure, and that they doe attend the grand Councill next sitting."—Journal of the Grand Councill, July 12, 1673.

upon any navigable River or any River capable of being made navigable you are to allow only the fifth part of the depth thereof by the water side; And a Certificate fully specifying the scituacon and bounds thereof you are to returne to us with all convenient speed and for your soe doeing this shall be your sufficient Warr^{t}. Given under our hands at Charles Towne this fowerth day of October 1673./

To Capt: Stephen: Bull
Surveyo^{r}

John Yeamans
Joseph West
Will: Owen
Maurice Mathews

Carolina./

You are forthwth. to cause to be admeasured and laid out for Mathew English seaventy acres of land being the full proporcon allowed to him by the lords prop^{rs} concessions arriveing in ffebruary 1670 in such place as you shall be directed by him soe as the same be not within the compass of any lands heretofore laid out or marked to be laid out for any other person or Towne nor prejudiciall to any such lines or bounds and if the same happen upon any navigable River or any River capable of being made navigable you are to allow only the fifth part of the depth thereof by the water side And a Certificate fully specifying the scituacon and bounds thereof you are to returne to us wth all convenient speed and for your soe doeing this shall be your sufficient warrant; Given under our hands at Charles Towne this fourth day of October 1673./

To Capt Stephen Bull
Surveyo^{r}./

John Yeamans
Joseph West
Will: Owen
Maurice Mathews

Carolina./

You are forthwth to cause to be admeasured and laid out for Mr Thomas Smith seaventy acres of land being the proporcon allowed to him by the Lords prop^{rs} concessions for one Servt by name Elinor Stranton arriveing in ffebruary 1672 in such place as you shall be directed by him soe as the same be not within the compass of any lands heretofore laid out or marked to be laid out for any other person or Towne nor prejudiciall to any such lines or bounds and if the same happen upon any navigable River or any River capable of being made navigable you are to allow only the fifth part of the depth thereof by the water side and a Certificate fully specifying the Scituacon and bounds thereof you are to returne to us wth all convenient speed and for yor. soe doeing this shall be yor. sufficient warr^t^. Given under our hands at Charles Towne this xxiiij^th^ day of November 1673./ John Yeamans

To Stephen Wheelwright
Surveyo^r^./

You are forthwith to cause to be admeasured and laid out for M^r^: William: Morrill four hundred and seaventy acres of land being the proportion allowed to him by the Lords prop^rs^: Concessions for himself & John: Morrill his sonne arriveing in December 1671, & three servants namely Nathaneel: Wigmore, Richard: Wells, & Susan; arriveing in August 1672 in such place as you shall be directed by him; soe as ye same be not within any lands heretofore laid out or marked to be laid out for any other person or use, and if the same happen upon any Navigable river or any river capable of being made navigable; you are to allow onely the fifth part of the depth thereof by ye waterside And a Certificate fully specifieing the scittuacon and bounds thereof you are to returne to us with all convenient speed and for your soe doeing this shall be yor: sufficient warr^t^: Given und^r^: our hands at Charles Towne this xvij^th^: day of January 167¾/

To Capt: Stephen: Bull
Surveyo^r^:/

Will: Owen John: Yeamans
Joseph: West
John: Godfrey

Carolina

you are forthwith to cause to be admeasured and laid out for Thomas: Archcroft two hundred and eighty acres of land being allowed to him by the Lords proprieto^rs^: Concessions for himself his wife & two Children, arriveing in ffebruary 1670, in such place as you shall be directed by him, being not injurious to any lands heretofore laid out or marked to be laid out, for any other use, & if ye same happen upon any Navigable river, or any river capable of being made navigable, you are to allow onely the fifth part of ye depth thereof by ye waterside, And a Certif. fully specifieing ye scittuacon & bounds thereof you are to returne to us with all convenient speed, And for yor soe doeing this shall be yor sufficient warr^t^: Given und^r^: our hands at Charles Towne this vij^th^: day of March 167¾ .

John: Yeamans
Joseph: West
John: Godfrey
Maur: Mathews.

Carolina
you are forthwith to cause to be admeasured & laid out for Mr: John Yeamans one Towne Lott in James Towne, not yet taken up observeing the forme & method which have been formerly directed concerning the sd Towne and not injurious to any lands lyeing next the same, And a Certificate fully specifieing the Scittuacon & bounds thereof you are to returne to us, with all convenient speed, and for yor soe doeing this shall be yor: sufficient wart: Given undr: our hands at Charles Towne this xxvijth: day of March 1674.

To Capt: Stephen: Bull Surveyor

Mau: Mathews. John: Yeamans Joseph: West John: Godfrey

Carolina
you are forthwith to cause to be admeasured & laid out for Mr. John: ffallock eight hundred and eighty acres of land allowed to him, by ye Lords proprs: Concessions for himself, his wife, four Children, & four servts. namely John: Horton Richard: Morgan, James: Green, Eusebius: Beale arriveing in March 1674 in such place as you shall be directed by him, being not injurious to any lands heretofore laid out for any other person or use, & if the same happen upon any Navigable river or any river capable of being made navigable, you are to allow onely the fifth part of ye depth thereof by ye water side, And a Certificate fully specifieing the scittuation & bounds thereof, you are to returne to us with all convenient speed And for yor soe doeing this shall be yor. sufficient wart: Given undr: our hands at Charles Towne this xxvijth: day of March 1674.

To Mr: John: Yeamans Surveyor:

Mau: Mathews. John: Yeamans Joseph: West John: Godfrey

Carolina
you are forthwith to admeasure & lay out for mr: Thomas: Hurt three hundred and seaventy acres of land allowed to him by ye Lords proprs: Concessions for himself and two servts: namely Joseph pendarvis, George Higgs and Elizabeth Stonehall arriveing in Augt: 1671 in such place as you shall be directed by him, soe as the same be not injurious to any lands heretofore laid out or marked to be laid out for any other use and if the same happen upon any Navigable river or any river capable of being made navigable you are onely to allow the fifth part of the depth thereof by ye waterside;

And a Certificate fully specifieing the quantity & bounds thereof you are to returne to us with all convenient speed, & for yor: soe doeing this shall be yor: sufficient war^{t}: Given und^{r}: our hands at Charles Towne this vijth: day of March 167$\frac{3}{4}$/

To Capt: Stephen: Bull Surveyo^{r}: — Mau: Mathews. John: Yeamans, Joseph: West, John: Godfrey

Carolina

you are forthwith to cause to be admeasured & laid out for m^{r}: Thomas: Hurt one hundred & twenty eight acres of land being ye residue of ye land allowed to Mary his wife by ye Lords prop^{rs}: Concessions arriveing in the first ffleet, in such place as you shall be directed by him being not injurious to any lands heretofore laid out or marked to be laid out for any other use, and if the same happen upon any Navigable river or any river capable of being made Navigable, you to allow onely ye fifth part of ye depth thereof by ye water side: And a Certificate fully specifieing the Scittuacon & bounds thereof you are to returne to us with all convenient speed, and for yor: soe doeing this shall be yor: suff^{t}: war^{t}: Given und^{r}: our hands this vijth: day of March 167$\frac{3}{4}$

To Capt: Stephen: Bull Surveyo^{r}: — Mau: Mathews. John Yeamans, Joseph: West, John: Godfrey

Carolina

You are forthwith to admeasure and lay out for Christopher: Swaine one hundred acres of land allowed to him by the Lords proprieto^{rs}. Concessions for himselfe arriveing a serv^{t}. in the first fleet in such place as you shall be directed by him being not injurious to any lands heretofore laid out for any other person or use, and if the same happen upon any navigable river, or any river capable of being made navigable, you are to allow onely the fifth part of ye depth thereof by ye waterside, And a Certificate fully specifieing the scittuacon and bounds thereof you are to returne to us with all convenient speed & for yor soe doeing this shall be yor suff^{t}: war^{t}: Given und^{r}: our hands at Charles Towne this xxvijth day of March 1674/

To Capt: Stephen: Bull Surveyo^{r}:/ — Mau: Mathews. John: Yeamans, Joseph: West, John: Godfrey

Carolina./

You are forthwth to cause to be admeasured and laid out for Capt: Stephen Bull fower hundred acres of land allowed to him by the Ld^{s}. prop^{rs}: concessions for himselfe and two Serv^{ts}. namely Dudley Woodier and John Larmott arriveing in the first ffleet, deducting soe much therefro as his Towne lott and tenn acre lott amounts to (if any he hath) in such place as you shall be directed by him, soe as the same be not within the compass of any lands heretofore laid out for any other use, and if the same happen upon any navigable River or any River capable of being made navigable yo^{u} are to allow only the fifth part of the depth thereof by the water side, and a Certificate fully specifying the scituacon & bounds thereof you are to returne to us wth all convenient speed and for yor soe doeing this shall be your sufficient warr^{t}., Given under our hands at Charles Towne this xviijth day of Aprill 1674./

To John Yeamans Surveyor/ — John Yeamans, Mau: Mathews, Joseph West

Carolina/

Yo^{u} are forthwth to cause to be admeasured and laid out for Capt: Stephen Bull One hundred & Seaventy acres of land allowed to him for two Serv^{ts}. namely Robert Locker and Simon Hughes arriveing in August 1671 by the Ld^{s}. prop^{rs}: concessions, in such place as yo^{u} shall be directed by him soe as the same be not within the compass of any lands heretofore laid out or marked to be laid out for any other use, and if the same happen upon any navigable River or any River capable of being made navigable yo^{u}. are to allow only the fifth part of the depth thereof by the water side and a Certificate fully specifying the scituacon and bounds thereof you are to returne to us with all convenient speed and for yor soe doeing this shall be your sufficient warr^{t}. Given under our hands at Charles Towne this xviijth day of Aprill 1674./

To John Yeamans Surveyo^{r}./ — John Yeamans, Mau: Mathews. Joseph West

Carolina/

You are forthwth to cause to be admeasured & laid out for Capt: Stephen Bull One Hundred acres of land allowed to him by the Ld^{s}: prop^{rs}: concessions for one Servt. namely Alexander Lilly arriveing in Aprill 1671 in such place as you shall be directed by him soe as the same be not within the compass of any lands heretofore laid out or marked to be laid out for any other use and if the same happen upon any navigable River or any River capable of being made navigable you are to allow only the fifth part of the depth thereof by the water side, And a Certificate fully specifying the scituacon & bounds thereof you are to returne to us with all convenient speed and for your soe doeing this shall be your sufficient warr^{t}. Given under our hands at Charles Towne this xviijth. day of Aprill 1674./

To John Yeamans Surveyor./

John Yeamans
Joseph West
Mau: Mathews

Carolina./

You are forthwth to cause to be admeasured and laid out for Capt^{t}: George Thompson five hundred acres of land for his disburs-m^{ts}. by Capt^{t}: Hilton in some place not yett laid out for any other use soe as the same be not upon any part of Ashley River, and if the same happen upon any navigable River or any River capable of being made navigable you are to allow only the fifth part of the depth thereof by the water side, And a Certificate fully specifying the scituacon and bounds thereof you are to returne to us with all convenient speed and for your soe doeing this shall be your sufficient Warr^{t}. Given under our hands at Charles Towne this xviijth. day of Aprill 1674./

To John Yeamans Surveyo^{r}./

John Yeamans
Mau: Mathews Joseph West

Carolina./

You are forthwth to admeasure and lay out for Thomas Worme One hundred acres of land allowed to him by the Lords prop^{rs} concessions for himselfe arriveing a Servt. in the first ffleet, in such place as you shall be directed by him being not injurious to any lands heretofore laid out for any other person or use, and if the same happen upon any navigable River or any River capable of being made navigable you are to allow only the fifth part of the depth thereof by the water side And a Certificate fully specifying the scituacon and bounds thereof you are to returne to us with all convenient speed and for your soe doeing this shall be yor. sufficient warr^{t}. Given under our hands at Charles Towne this xviijth day of Aprill 1674.

To Capt^{t}: Stephen Bull Surveyor:/

John Yeamans
Mau: Mathews Joseph West

Carolina/

You are forthwth. to admeasure and lay out for Phillip Braidy Seaventy acres of land allowed to him by the lords prop^{rs}: concessions for himselfe arriveing a Servt. in December 1671./ in such place as yo^{u} shall be directed by him being not injurious to any lands heretofore laid out for any other person or use and if the same happen upon any navigable River or any River capable of being made navigable you are to allow only the fifth part of the depth thereof by the water side, And a Certificate fully specifying the scituacon and bounds thereof you are to returne to us with all convenient speed and for your soe doeing this shall be your sufficient warr^{t}. Given under our hands at Charles Towne this xviijth day of Aprill 1674./

To Capt. Stephen Bull Surveyor./ — John Yeamans, Joseph West, Mau: Mathews

Carolina/

You are forthwth to cause to be admeasured and laid out for M^{rs}. Joane Carner two hundred and seaventy acres of land allowed to her by the lords prop^{rs}: concessions for her selfe her daughter Margarett Sullivan and One Negro by name Tony arriveing in August 1672 in such place as yo^{u} shall be directed by her being not injurious to any lands heretofore laid out for any other person or use and if the same happen upon any navigable River or any River capable of being made navigable, you are to allow only the fifth part of the depth thereof by the water side, And a Certificate fully specifying the scituacon and bounds thereof you are to returne to us wth all convenient speed and for your soe doeing this shall be your sufficient warr^{t} Given under our hands at Charles Towne this xviijth. day of Aprill 1674./

To Capt: Stephen Bull Surveyo^{r}:/ — John Yeamans, Joseph West, Mau: Mathews

Carolina./

Yo^{u}. are forthwth. to cause to be admeasured and laid out for Mr Thomas Buttler fifty acres of land pursuant to an order of the Grand Councill dated the 8th day of July. 1673 in some place not heretofore laid out for any other use, and if the same happen upon any navigable River or any River capable of being made navigable you are to allow only the fifth part of the depth thereof by the water side, and a Certificate fully specifying the scituacon and bounds thereof you are to returne to us with all convenient speed and for your soe doeing this shall be your sufficient Warr[t]. Given under our hands at Charles Towne this xviij[th] day of Aprill 1674./

To Cap[t]: Stephen: Bull Surveyo[r]:/ — Mau: Mathews — John Yeamans, Joseph West

Carolina./

You[u]. are forthw[th] to cause to be admeasured and laid out for Denis Moron two hundred and tenn acres of land for himselfe his Wife and child arriveing in Aug[t]: 1672 in some place not yett laid out or marked to be laid out for any other person or use and if the same happen upon any navigable River or any River capable of being made navigable you are to allow only the fifth part of the depth thereof by the water side, And a Certificate fully specifying the scituacon and bounds thereof yo[u] are to returne to us with all convenient speed and for your soe doeing this shall be your sufficient warr[t]. Given under our hands at Charles Towne this xxx[th]. day of May 1674./

To John Yeamans Surveyo[r]:/ — Mau: Mathews — John Yeamans, Joseph West, John Godfrey

Carolina./

Yo[u]. are forthw[th]. to cause to be admeasured and laid out for William Jones two hundred and tenn acres of land for himselfe his Wife and one child arriveing in May 1673. in some place not yett laid out or marked to be laid out for any other person or use, and if the same happen upon any navigable River or any River capable of being made navigable, you are to allow only the fifth part of the depth thereof by the water side And a Certificate fully specifying the scituacon and bounds thereof you are to returne to us with all convenient speed and for your soe doeing this shall be yo[r]. sufficient warr[t]. Given under our hands at Charles Towne this xxx[th] day of May 1673./

To John Yeamans Surveyo[r]./ — Mau: Mathews — John Yeamans, Joseph West, John Godfrey

Carolina/

Yo^{u}. are forthwth. to cause to be admeasured and laid out for James Donaghoe ninety acres of land for himselfe arriveing in ffebruary 167$\frac{0}{1}$ in some place not yett laid out or marked to be laid out for any other person or use, and if the same happen upon any navigable River or any River capable of being made navigable you are to allow only the fifth part of the depth thereof by the water side, And a Certificate fully specifying the scituacon and bounds thereof you are to returne to us with all convenient speed and for your soe doeing this shall be your sufficient warr^{t}. Given under our hands at Charles Towne this xxxth. day of May 1674./

To John Yeamans Surveyo^{r}./

John Yeamans
Mau: Mathews. Joseph West
John Godfrey

Carolina./

Yo^{u} are forthwth to cause to be admeasured and laid out for Roger Hounsdon two hundred and tenn acres of land for himselfe Ann his Wife and one child arriveing in December 1671. in some place not yett laid out or marked to be laid out for any other person or use and if the same happen upon any navigable River or any River capable of being made navigable you are to allow only the fifth part of the depth thereof by the water side, And a Certificate fully specifying the scituacon and bounds thereof you are to returne to us wth. all convenient speed and for your soe doeing this shall be yor. sufficient Warr^{t}. Given under our hands at Charles Towne this xxxth day of May 1674./

To Capt^{t}: Stephen Bull Surveyo^{r}./

John Yeamans
Mau: Mathews Joseph West
John Godfrey

Carolina./

Yo^{u}. are forthwth to cause to be admeasured and laid out for John Hooper one hundred and forty acres of land allowed to him for himselfe and Esther his Wife arriveing in May 1673 in some place not yett laid out or marked to be laid out for any other person or use, and if the same happen upon any navigable River or any River capable of being made navigable you are to allow only the fifth part of the depth thereof by the water side And a Certificate fully specifying the scituacon and bounds thereof you are to returne to us with all convenient speed and for your soe doeing this shall be your sufficient Warr[t]. Given under our hands at Charles Towne this xxx[th]. day of May 1674./

To John Yeamans Surveyo[r]./ — Mau: Mathews — John Yeamans, Joseph West, John Godfrey

Carolina./

You[u]. are forthw[th] to cause to be admeasured and laid out for M[r] Thomas Lane Seaven hundred and forty acres of land for him-selfe & 7 serv[ts]. namely Mathew Harris Robert Leeds arriveing in July 1672 Trismus Morrison David Derling John Hooper Hesther Lane in May 1673 in some place not yett laid out or marked to be laid out for any other person or use and if the same happen upon any navigable River or any River capable of being made navigable yo[u] are to allow only the fifth part of the depth thereof by the water side And a Certificate fully specifying the scituacon and bounds thereof you are to returne to us with all convenient speed and for yo[r] soe doeing this shall be yo[r]. sufficient Warr[t]. Given under our hands at Charles Towne this xxx[tth]. day of May 1674./

To John Yeamans Surveyo[r]./ — Mau: Mathews — John Yeamans, Joseph West, John Godfrey

Carolina./

Yo[u]. are forthw[th] to cause to be admeasured and laid out for William Cason One hundred acres of land for himselfe arriveing in May 1673 in some place not yett laid out or marked to be laid out for any other person or use and if the same happen upon any navi-gable River or any River capable of being made navigable you are to allow only the fifth part of the depth thereof by the water side and a Certificate fully specifying the scituacon and bounds thereof yo[u]. are to returne to us with all convenient speed and for your soe doeing this shall be yo[r]. sufficient Warr[t]. Given under our hands at Charles Towne the xxx[th]. day of May 1674./

To John Yeamans Surveyo[r]./ — Mau: Mathews — John Yeamans, Joseph West, John Godfrey

Carolina

you are forthwith to cause to be admeasured & laid out for M[r]: Ralph: Marshall one hundred and forty eight acres of land for him-self arriveing in the first fleet, or soe much thereof as is between ye lands of mr: Samuel: West to ye South & Thomas: Norris to ye North, on ye Eastward side of Ashley river And a Certificate specifieing the scittuacon & full bounds thereof you are to returne to us with all convenient speed, & for yor soe doeing this shall be yor: sufficient wart: Given undr: our hands at Charles Towne this xxxth: day of May 1674.

To Capt: Stephen: Bull
Surveyor:/ Mau: Mathews John: Yeamans
Joseph: West
John: Godfrey

Carolina

you are forthwith to cause to be admeasured & laid out for Henry: Wood one hundred & eighty acres of land ye residue for himself & his wife arriveing in the first fleet in some place not yet laid out or marked to be laid out, for any other person or use, and if the same happen upon any Navigable river, or any river capable of being made Navigable you are to allow onely the fifth part of ye depth thereof by the water side, And a Certificate fully specifieing, the scittuacon & bounds thereof, you are to returne to us, with all convenient speed, And for yor: soe doeing this shall be yor: sufficient wart: Given undr: our hands at Charles Towne this xxxth: day of May 1674.

To Stephen Bull
Surveyor:/ Mau: Mathews John: Yeamans
Joseph: West
John: Godfrey

Carolina

You are forthwith to cause to be admeasured and laid out for mr: Amos: Jefford four hundred acres of land allowed for himself & 3: servts: namely Stephen: Taylor, John Mills & John: Wilkinson arriveing in December 1671. in some place not yet laid out or marked to be laid out for any other person or use, and if the same happen upon any navigable river or any river capable of being made navigable, you are to allow onely the fifth part of ye depth thereof by ye waterside, and a Certificate fully specifieing the scittuacon & bounds thereof you are to returne to us with all convenient speed & for yor: soe doeing this shall be yor sufficient warrt: Given undr: our hands at Charles Towne this xxvijth: day of June 1674.

To Capt: Stephen: Bull Mau: Mathews. John: Yeamans
Surveyor: John: Godfrey
Joseph: West

Carolina

You are forthwith to cause to be admeasured & laid out for Benjamin: Andrewes one hundred acres of land allowed for himself arriveing in November 1673. in some place not yet laid out or marked to be laid out for any other person or use, & if the same happen upon any navigable river or any river capable of being made navigable, you are to allow onely the fifth part of the depth thereof by the waterside, And a Certificate fully specifieing the scittuacon & bounds thereof you are to returne to us with all convenient speed, and for yor: soe doing this shall be yor: sufficient warr^t^: Given und^r^: our hands at Charles Towne this xxvij^th^: day of June 1674:

To Capt: Stephen: Bull Surveyo^r^: Mau: Mathews. John Yeamans
John: Godfrey
Joseph: West

Carolina

You are forthwith to cause to be admeasured & laid out for John: Mills seaventy acres of land allowed for himself arriveing a serv^t^: in December 1761 in some place not yet laid out or marked to be laid out for any other person or use, & if the same happen upon any navigable river or any river capable of being made navigable, you are to allow onely the fifth part of ye depth thereof by the waterside, and a Certificate fully specifieing the scittuacon & bounds thereof you are to returne to us with all convenient speed, And for yor: soe doeing this shall be yor: sufficient war^t^: Given und^r^: our hands at Charles Towne this xxvij^th^: day of June 1674.

To Stephen Wheelwright Surveyo^r^:/ Mau: Mathews. John Yeamans
John: Godfrey
Joseph: West

Carolina

You are forthwith to cause to be admeasured & laid out for James: Hutton seaventy acres of land allowed for himself arriveing a serv^t^: in December 1671. in some place not yet laid out or marked to be laid out for any other ℘son or use and if the same happen upon any Navigable river or any river capable of being made Navigable, you are to allow onely the fifth part of ye depth thereof by the waterside, and a Certificate fully specifieing the scittuacon & bounds thereof you are to returne to us with all convenient speed, and for yor: soe doeing this shall be yor: sufficient war^{t}: Given und^{r}: our hands at Charles Towne this xxvijth: day of June 1674

To Stephen: Wheelwright. John: Yeamans
Surveyo^{r}:/ Mau: Mathews John: Godfrey
Joseph: West

Carolina

Yo^{u}: are forthwith to cause to be admeasured & laid out for John Boon one hundred acres of land for himself arriveing in ye first fleet in some place not yet laid out or marked to be laid out for any other person or use; if ye same happen upon any navigable river or any river capable of being made navigable, yo^{u} are to allow onely the fifth part of ye depth thereof by the waterside and a Certificate fully specifieing ye scittacon & bounds therof yo^{u} are to returne to us with all convenient speed, And for yor: soe doeing this shall be yor. suff^{t}: war^{t}: Given und^{r}: our hands at Charles Towne this xxvth: Day of July 1674

To John: Yeamans: Mau: Mathews, John: Yeamans
Surveyo^{r}:/ Joseph: West
John: Godfrey

Carolina

you are forthwith to cause to be admeasured & laid out for L^{t}: Coll John: Godfrey two hundred acres of land for two serv^{ts}: namely Mathew English, & Tho: Ellis arriveing in ffebr 167$\frac{0}{1}$ in some place not yet laid out or marked to be laid out for any other ꝑson or use, and if the same happen upon any Navigable river or any river capable of being made Navigable, you are to allow onely the fifth part of ye depth thereof by ye water side, & a Certif. fully specifieing the scittuacon & bounds thereof you are to returne to us with all convenient speed & for yor: soe doeing this shall be yor suff^{t}: war^{t}: Given und^{r}: our hands at Charles Towne this xxvth: day of July 1674/

To John: Yeamans Ma: Mathews John: Yeamans
Surveyo^{r}. Will: Owen. Joseph: West
Jo

Carolina

You are forthwith to cause to be admeasured & laid out for Lieu^{t}: Coll John: Godfrey one hundred acres of land due to him for one serv^{t}. namely Henry:. Wintrop arriveing in ffebr $167\frac{0}{1}$ in some place not yet laid out or marked to be laid out for any other person or use, & if the same happen upon any Navigable river or any river capable of being made navigable, you are to allow onely the fifth part of ye depth thereof by the waterside, and a Certificate fully specifieing the scittuacon and bounds thereof you are to returne to us with all convenient speed & for yor: soe doeing this shall be yor: sufficient war^{t}: Given und^{r}: our hands at Charles Towne this xxvth. day of July. 1674./

To John: Yeamans Surveyo^{r}./

Ma: Mathews John: Yeamans
Will: Owen Jos: West

Carolina

You are forthwith to cause to be admeasured & laid out for John: Maverick one hundred acres of land for himself arriveing in ffebr $167\frac{0}{1}$ in some place not yet laid out or marked to be laid out for any ꝑson or use & if the same happen upon any navigable River or any River capable of being made navigable you are to allow only the fifth part of the depth thereof by the water side And a Certificate fully specifying the scituacon and bounds thereof yo^{u} are to returne to us with all convenient speed and for yor soe doing this shall be your sufficient warr^{t} Given under our hands at Charles Towne this 25th. day of July 1674

To John Yeamans Surveyo^{r}./

John Yeamans
Joseph West
Mau: Mathews
Willm: Owen

Carolina

You are forthwith to cause to be admeasured & laid out for Richard: Berry one hundred acres of land for himself arriveing in December 1671, in some place not yet laid out or marked to be laid out for any other person or use & if the same happen upon any navigable River or any River capable of being made navigable you are to allow only the fifth part of the depth thereof by the water side And a Certificate fully specifying the scituacon and bounds thereof you are to returne to us with all convenient speed and for your soe doeing this shall be yor sufficient warr^{t} Given under o^{r} hands at Charles Towne this 25th day of July 1674.

To John Yeamans Surveyo^{r}./

John Yeamans./
Joseph West./
Mau: Mathews./
W^{m}. Owen./

Carolina

you are forthwith to cause to be admeasured & laid out for Dennis. Mahoon two hundred acres of land for himself & his wife, in some place not yet laid out, or marked to be laid out for any other ꝑson or use, & if the same happen upon any navigable River or any River capable of being made navigable you are to allow only the fifth part of the depth thereof by the water side; And a Certificate fully specifying the scituacon and bounds thereof you are to returne to us with all convenient speed: and for your soe doeing this shall be your sufficient warr^{t}. Given under our hands at Charles Towne this 25th day of July 1674./

To John Yeamans
Surveyo^{r}./

John Yeamans./
Joseph West./
Mau: Mathews./
Will: Owen./

Carolina

you are forthwith to cause to be admeasured & laid out for George Canty one hundred & sixty acres of land for himselfe & his wife Martha in some place not yet laid out or marked to be laid out for any other ꝑson or use & if the same happen upon any navigable River or any River capable of being made navigable yo^{u}. are to allow only the fifth part of the depth thereof by the water side; And a Certificate fully specifying the scituacon and bounds thereof you are to returne to us with all convenient speed and for your soe doeing this shall be your sufficient warr^{t}. Given under our hands at Charles Towne this 25th day of July 1674./

To John Yeamans
Surveyo^{r}./

John Yeamans./
Joseph West./
Mau: Mathews./
Will: Owen./

Carolina./

You are forthwth to cause to be admeasured and laid out for Hugh Carterett one hundred and sixteen acres of land as part of a greater quantity of land due to him by the Lords Prop^{rs}: concessions in some place not yett laid out or marked to be laid out for any other person or use and if the same happen upon any navigable River or any River capable of being made navigable you are to allow only the fifth part of the depth thereof by the water side; And a Certificate fully specifying the scituacon and bounds thereof you are to returne to us with all convenient speed and for your soe doeing this shall be your sufficient warr[t]. Given under o[r] hands at Charles Towne this 5th day of September 1674./

To Cap[t]: Stephen Bull
Suveyo[r]./

Joseph West./
John Godfrey./
Mau Mathews./
Will. Owen./
Ra: Marshall./

Carolina./

You are forthw[th] to cause to be admeasured and laid out for M[r] Thomas Midwinter three hundred acres of land allowed for the arriveall of himselfe his Wife and his sone; in some place not yett laid out or marked to be laid out for any other person or use and if the same happen upon any navigable River or any River capable of being made navigable you are to allow only the fifth part of the depth thereof by the water side and a Certificate fully specifying the scituacon and bounds thereof you are to returne to us with all convenient speed and for your soe doeing this shall be yo[r] sufficient warr[t]; Given under our hands at Charles Towne this 5th. day of September 1674

To Stephen Wheelewright
Surveyo[r]./

Joseph West
John Godfrey
Mau: Mathews
Will: Owen
Ra: Marshall

Carolina,/

You are hereby required forthw[th] to cause to be admeasured and laid out for John Carrill seaventy acres of land for himselfe in some place not yett laid out or marked to be laid out for any other person or use, and if the same happen upon any navigable River or any River capable of being made navigable you are to allow only the fifth part of the depth thereof by the water side And a Certificate fully specifying the scituacon and bounds thereof you are to returne to us with all convenient speed and for your soe doeing this shall be your sufficient Warr[t]: Given under o[r]: hands at Charles Towne this 5th day of September 1674./

To Cap[t]: Stephen Bull
Surveyo[r]./

Joseph West./
John Godfrey./
Mau: Mathews./
Will: Owen./
Ra: Marshall./

Carolina./

You are forthwth. to cause to be admeasured and laid out for John Cattell seaventy acres of land for himselfe arriveing a Servt in August 1672 in some place not yett laid out or marked to be laid out for any other ꝑson or use and if the same happen upon any navigable River or any River capable of being made navigable you are to allow only the fifth part of the depth thereof by the water side; And a Certificate fully specifying the scituacon and bounds thereof you are to returne to us with all convenient speed and for your soe doeing this shall be yor sufficient Warr^{t} Given under our hands at Charles Towne this 5th day of September 1674./

To Capt^{t}: Stephen Bull
Surveyo^{r}./

Joseph West
John Godfrey
Mau: Mathews
Will: Owen
Ra: Marshall

Carolina./

You are forthwth to cause to be admeasured and laid out for the Lady Margarett Yeamans one thousand and seaventy acres of land for her selfe and soe many Serv^{ts}. and Negroes arriveing in the yeare 1671 & 1672 in some place not yett laid out or marked to be laid out for any other person or use, and if the same happen upon any navigable River or any River capable of being made navigable you are to allow only the fifth part of the depth thereof by the water side; and a Certificate fully specifying the scituacon and bounds thereof you are to returne to us with all convenient speed & for yor soe doeing this shall be yor sufficient warr^{t}. Given under o^{r} hands at Charles Towne this 5th day of September 1674

To M^{r}: John: Yeamans
Surveyo^{r}

Will: Owen
Ra: Marshall./

Jos: West
John Godfrey
Mau: Mathews

Carolina./

You are forthwth to cause to be admeasured and laid out for Mr Henry Hughes two hundred twenty five acres of land for himselfe and the halfe share of one Servt namely John Neale arriveing in the first ffleet or soe much thereof as yo^{u} shall find to be contained between the lines of the lands allotted to be laid out to Mr John Comings to the North and a certaine parcell of land allotted to be laid out for a Towne at the Oyster Poynt to the South wthout prejudicing either of the s^{d} allotted lines; And a Certificate fully specifying the scituacon and bounds thereof you are to returne to us with all convenient speed and for your soe doeing this shall be your sufficient Warr^{t}: Given under our hands at Charles Towne this 5th: day of September 1674./

To M^{r}: John Yeamans
Surveyo^{r}:

Joseph West./
John Godfrey./
Mau Mathews./
Ra: Marshall./ Will: Owen./

Carolina./

You are forthwth to cause to be admeasured and laid out for L^{t} Co^{ll}: John Godfrey two hundred acres of land for himselfe and One Servt. in some place not yett laid out or marked to be laid out for any other person or use, and if the same happen upon any Navigable river or any river capable of being made Navigable you are to allow onely the fifth part of ye depth thereof by the waterside, and a Certificate fully specifieing ye scittuacon and bounds thereof you are to returne to us with all convenient speed And for yor: soe doeing this shall be yor: sufficient war^{t}: Given und^{r}: our hands at Charles Towne this 5th day of sept^{r}: 1674./

To Capt. Stephen: Bull
Surveyo^{r}:

Jos: West
John: Godfrey
Mau: Mathews
Will: Owen
Ra: Marshall.

Carolina./

You are forthwth to cause to be admeasured and laid out for Richard Rowser six hundred and thirty acres of land two hundred and ten acres thereof for himselfe his wife and one child and fower hundred and twenty acres thereof as he is Execut^{r}. to Christopher Field deceased in some place not yet laid out or marked to be laid out for any other person or use, & if the same happen upon any Navigable river or any river capable of being made Navigable you are to allow onely ye fifth part of ye depth thereof by ye waterside, and a Certificate fully specifieing ye scittuacon and bounds thereof you are to returne to us with all convenient speed and for yor: soe doeing this shall be yor: suff^{t}. war^{t}: Given und^{r}: our hands at Charles Towne this 5th: day of sep^{t}: 1674/

To Stephen Bull
Surveyo^{r}./

Jos: West
John: Godfrey
Mau: Mathews
Will: Owen
Ra: Marshall

Carolina./

You are forthw[th] to cause to be admeasured and laid out for M[r] Simon Berringer three thousand acres of land for himselfe and soe many Servts and Negroes arriveing in the yeare 1671 & 1672. in some place not yett laid out or marked to be laid out for any other person or use and if the same happen upon any navigable River or any River capable of being made navigable you are to allow only the fifth part of the depth thereof by the water side; And a certificate fully specifying the scituacon and bounds thereof you are to returne to us with all convenient speed and for yo[r] soe doeing this shall be yo[r] sufficient Warr[t]. Given under o[r] hands at Charles Towne this 5th. day of September 1674./

To Mr. John Yeamans
Surveyo[r]

Joseph West./
John Godfrey./
Mau: Mathews./
Will: Owen./
Ra: Marshall./

Carolina./

You are forthw[th] to cause to be admeasured and laid out for Oliver Spencer three hundred & fourty acres of land for foure Serv[ts]: George Rubry, Will: Hill, Eliz: Webb, & Nich: Webb arriveing in June 1671 in some place not yet laid out or marked to be laid out for any other person or use, & if the same happen upon any navigable river or any river capable of being made navigable you are to allow onely the fifth part of ye depth thereof by ye waterside, And a Certificate fully specifieing the scittuacon and bounds thereof you are to returne to us with all convenient speed, and for yo[r]: soe doeing this shall be yo[r]: suff[t]: war[t]: Given und[r]: our hands at Charles Towne this 5th: September 1674.

To Cap[t]: Stephen Bull
Surveyo[r]

Joseph: West
Will: Owen — John: Godfrey
Ra: Marshall. — Mau: Mathews

Carolina./

You are forthw[th] to cause to be admeasured and laid out for Oliver Spencer two hundred acres of land for himselfe and One Serv[t] namely Thomas King arriveing in August 1672. in some place not yet laid out or marked to be laid out for any other person or use & if the same happen upon any navigable river or any river capable of being made Navigable, you are to allow onely ye fifth part of ye depth thereof by ye waterside, And a Certificate fully specifieing the scittuacon and bounds thereof you are to returne to us with all convenient speed and for yor: soe doeing this shall be yor: suff^t^: war^t^: Given und^r^: our hands at Charles Towne this 5th: September 1674./

To Capt: Stephen Bull
Surveyo^r^./

Will: Owen. Joseph: West
John: Godfrey
Mau: Mathews

Carolina/

You are forthw^th^ to cause to be admeasured and laid out for Thomas Machanelloe seaventy acres of land for himselfe arriveing a Servt in August 1672. in some place not yett laid out or marked to be laid out for any other person or use; and if the same happen upon any navigable River or any River capable of being made navigable you are to allow only the fifth part of the depth thereof by the water side; And a Certificate fully specifying the scituacon and bounds thereof you are to returne to us with all convenient speed; and for your soe doeing this shall be your sufficient Warr^t^. Given under our hands at Charles Towne this 5th September 1674./

To Capt: Stephen Bull
Surveyo^r^./

Joseph West./
John Godfrey./
Mau: Mathews./
Will: Owen./

Carolina./

You are forthw^th^ to cause to be admeasured and laid out for John Cole seaventy acres of land for himselfe arriveing a Servt. in February 1670. in some place not yett laid out or marked to be laid out for any other person or use, and if the same happen upon any navigable River, or any River capable of being made navigable, you are to allow only the fifth part of the depth thereof by the water side; and a Certificate fully specifying the scituacon and bounds thereof you are to returne to us with all convenient speed and for your soe doeing this shall be yor. sufficient Warr^t^. Given under our hands at Charles Towne this xxx^th^ day of May 1674./

To Capt: Stephen Bull
Surveyo^r^./

Mau: Mathews John Yeamans
Joseph West
John Godfrey

Carolina./

You are forthwth to cause to be admeasured and laid out for Mr John Berringer three thousand acres of land for himselfe and soe many Servt^{s} arriveing in the yeare 1670 and in the first ffleet, in some place not yet laid out or marked to be laid out for any other person or use, and if the same happen upon any Navigable river, or any river capable of being made Navigable you are to allow onely the fifth part of ye depth thereof by ye waterside, and a Certificate fully specifieing the scittuation and bounds thereof you are to returne to us with all convenient speed, And for yor: soe doeing this shall be yor: sufficient war^{t}: Given under our hands at Charles Towne this 5th: day of September 1674/

To Mr John Yeamans Surveyo^{r}./

Jos: West
John Godfrey
Mau: Mathews
Will: Owen
Ra: Marshall

Carolina./

You are forthwth to cause to be admeasured and laid out for Edmund Fogertee fower hundred acres of land for himselfe his Wife and three children arriveing in February 167$\frac{0}{1}$ in some place not yett laid out or marked to be laid out for any other person or use, and if the same happen upon any navigable River or any River capable of being made navigable you are to allow only the fifth part of the depth thereof by the water side, and a Certificate fully specifying the scituacon and bounds thereof you are to returne to us with all convenient speed and for your soe doeing this shall be your sufficient warr^{t}. Given under our hands at CharlesTowne this 5th. day of September 1674./

To Mr John Yeamans Surveyo^{r}./

Joseph West
John Godfrey
Mau: Mathews
Will: Owen
Ra: Marshall

Carolina./

You are forthwth to cause to be admeasured and laid out for Mrs Joan Carver one hundred acres of land bought by her of Teague Cantey deceased in some place not yet laid out or marked to be laid out for any other Ꝑson or use & if ye same happen upon any navigable river, or any river capable of being made Navigable, you are to allow onely ye fifth part of ye depth thereof by the waterside and a certificate fully specifieing the scittuacon & bounds thereof you are to returne to us with all convenient speed & for yor: soe doeing this shall be yor sufft: wart: Given und^r^: our hands at Charles Towne this 5th: day of september 1674./

To Mr: John: Yeamans Joseph West
Surveyor. Will: Owen

Carolina

you are forthwith to cause to be admeasured and laid out for Patrick Stuard Seaventy acres of land for himself arriveing in May 1673 in some place not yet laid out or marked to be laid out for any other person or use, & if the same happen upon any Navigable river or any river capable of being made Navigable, you are to allow onely the fifth part of the depth thereof by the waterside, and a Certificate fully specifieing the scittuacon & bounds thereof you are to returne to us with all convenient speed, And for yor soe doeing this shall be yor sufft: wart: Given undr our hands at Charles Towne this 15th: day of september 1674/

To Capt: Stephen: Bull Joseph: West
Surveyor./ Will: Owen. John: Godfrey
Mau: Mathews

Carolina

You are forthwith to cause to be admeasured & laid out for Mrs: Dorcas: Smith three hundred and forty acres of land for herself one Negroe man & 2 women servts: arriveing 1672 & 1673. in some place not yet laid out or marked to be laid out for any other person or use, & if the same happen upon any Navigable river or any river capable of being made Navigable you are to allow onely the fifth part of the depth thereof by ye waterside, & a cert: fully specifieing the scittuacon & bounds thereof you are to returne to us with all convenient speed & for yor soe doeing this shall be yor: sufft: wart: Given undr our hands at Charles Towne this xvth: day of Septr 1674/

To Mr: John: Yeamans Joseph: West
Surveyor:/ Will: Owen./ John: Godfrey
Mau: Mathews

Carolina./

You[u] are forthw[th] to cause to be admeasured and laid out for Mathew Smallwood one hundred acres of land for himselfe arriveing in the first ffleet in some place not yett laid out or marked to be laid out for any other person or use and if the same happen upon any navigable River or any River capable of being made navigable you are to allow only the fifth part of the depth thereof by the water side and a Certificate fully specifying the scituacon and bounds thereof you are to returne to us with all convenient speed and for yo[r] soe doeing this shall be yo[r] sufficient warr[t]. Given und[r] our hands at Charles Towne this xv[th] day of September 1674

To Cap[t]: Stephen Bull
Surveyo[r]./

Joseph West
Will Owen John Godfrey
Mau: Mathews

Carolina./

You are forthw[th] to cause to be admeasured and laid out for John Morgan Seaventy acres of land for himselfe arriveing in ffebruary 1670 in some place not yett laid out or marked to be laid out for any other person or use and if the same happen upon any navigable River or any River capable of being made navigable you are to allow only the fifth part of the depth thereof by the waterside And a Certificate fully specifying the scituacon & bounds thereof you are to returne to us with all convenient speed and for your soe doeing this shall be your sufficient warr[t]. Given under our hands at Charles Towne this 27th day of September 1674

To Cap[t]: Stephen Bull
Surveyo[r]./

Joseph West
John Godfrey
Mau: Mathews

Carolina./

You[u] are forthw[th] to cause to be admeasured and laid out for John Berton seaventy acres of land for himselfe arriveing in ffebruary 1670 in some place not yett laid out or marked to be laid out for any other person or use and if the same happen upon any navigable River or any River capable of being made navigable you are to allow only the fifth part of the depth thereof by the water side; And a Certificate fully specifying the scituacon & bounds thereof you are to returne to us with all convenient speed and for yor soe doeing this shall be yor sufficient warr^t^ Given under our hands at Charles Towne this third day of October 1674

To Capt Stephen Bull
Surveyo^r^.

Joseph West
John Godfrey
Mau: Mathews

Carolina/

You are forthw^th^ to cause to be admeasured and laid out for Henry Symonds One hundred thirty and fower acres of land for himselfe arriveing in the first Fleet and Frances his Wife arriveing in August 1671 in some place not yett laid out or marked to be laid out for any other person or use and if the same happen upon any navigable River or any River capable of being made navigable you are to allow only the fifth part of the depth thereof by the water side and a Certificate fully specifying the scituacon and bounds thereof you are to returne to us with all convenient speed and for yor soe doeing this shall be your sufficient warr^t^ Given under our hands at Charles Towne this third day of October 1674.

To Capt: Stephen Bull
Surveyo^r^:

Joseph West
John Godfrey
Mau: Mathews

Carolina./

You are forthw^th^ to cause to be admeasured and laid out for Capt: Richard Conant One hundred & fifty acres of land being the residue of the land due to him for himselfe and One Negro namely Baccus arriveing in December 1671. not some place not yett laid out or marked to be laid out for any other person or use, and if the same happen upon any navigable River or any River capable of being made navigable you are to allow only the fifth part of the depth thereof by the water side; And a Certificate fully specifying the scituacon and bounds thereof you are to returne to us with all convenient Speed; and for your soe doeing this shall be yor sufficient Warr^t^. Given under our hands at Charles Towne this tennth day of November 1674./

To Mr John Yeamans
Surveyo^r^./

Joseph West
John Godfrey
Mau: Mathews

Carolina./

Yo^u^. are forthw^th^ to cause to be admeasured and laid out for Andrew Richment ninety acres of land being the residue of the land due to him for himselfe arriveing in June 1671: in some place not yett laid out or marked to be laid out for any other person or use and if the same happen upon any navigable River or any River capable of being made navigable you are to allow only the fifth part of the depth thereof by the waterside And a Certificate fully specifying the scituacon and bounds thereof you are to returne to us with all convenient speed; and for your soe doeing this shall be your sufficient warr[t]. Given under our hands at Charles Towne this tenth day of November 1674/

To M[r] John Yeamans
Surveyo[r]./

Joseph West
Mau: Mathews
Richard Conant

Carolina./

You are forthw[th] to cause to be admeasured and laid out for John Pinckett three hundred and sixty acres of land being the residue of the land due to him for himselfe arriveing in June 1671. his Wife Mary Pinkett John Pinkett Jun[r]: his Sonne and one Serv[t]. namely James Purvys arriveing in August 1672. in some place not yett laid out or marked to be laid out for any other person or use; and if the same happen upon any navigable River or any River capable of being made navigable you are to allow only the fifth part of the depth thereof by the water side; And a Certificate fully specifying the scituacon and bounds thereof you are to returne to us with all convenient speed and for your soe doeing this shall be your sufficient Warr[t]: Given under our hands at Charles Towne this tennth day of November 1674./

To M[r] John Yeamans
Surveyo[r]./

Joseph West/
Mau: Mathews/
Richard Conant./

Carolina./

You are forthw[th] to cause to be admeasured and laid out for Thomas ffindon fower hundred and fifty acres of land being the residue of the land due to him for himselfe Mary ffindon his Wife, Thomas Findon Jun[r], John ffindon and Henry Findon his Sonnes arriveing in June 1671. in some place not yett laid out or marked to be laid out for any other ℘son or use; and if the same happen upon any navigable River, or any River capable of being made navigable you are to allow only the fifth part of the depth thereof by the water side; And a Certificate fully specifying the scituacon and bounds thereof you are to returne to us with all convenient speed and for your soe doeing this shall be yor: sufft^{t}: war^{t}: Given und^{r}: our hands at Charles Towne this tenth day of November 1674

To M^{r}: John Yeamans Surveyo^{r}:/

Joseph West
Rich: Conant
Mau: Mathews

Carolina./

You are forthwth to cause to be admeasured and laid out for Capt: Stephen Bull One hundred acres of land due to him for One Servt: namely Johnathan Barker arriveing in the first ffleet or soe much thereof as is contained between the lands of John ffaulkoner towards the South and M^{r}: Ralph Marshall towards the North; and a Certificate fully specifying the scituacon and bounds thereof you are to returne to us with all convenient speed and for your soe doeing this shall be your sufficient Warr^{t}. Given under our hands at Charles Towne this 21th: day of November 1674./

To Mr John Yeamans Surveyo^{r}./

Joseph West
William Owen
John Godfrey./

Carolina./

You are forthwth to cause to be admeasured and laid out for Nicholas Bird Seaventy acres of land for himselfe arriveing in February 1670 in some place not yett laid out or marked to be laid out for any other person or use, and if the same happen upon any navigable River or any River capable of being made navigable you are to allow only the fifth part of the depth thereof by the water side; And a Certificate fully specifying the scituacon and bounds thereof you are to returne to us with all convenient speed and for your soe doeing this shall be your sufficient warr^{t}. Given under our hands at Charles Towne this xxxth day of May 1674./

To Capt: Stephen Bull Surveyo^{r}./

John Yeamans
Joseph West
Mau: Mathews./ John Godfrey./

Carolina./

You are forthwth to cause to be admeasured and laid out for James Williams two hundred acres of land for himselfe and Martha his Wife arriveing Serv^{ts}. in the first ffleet in some place not yett laid out or marked to be laid out for any other person or use and if the same happen upon any navigable River or any River

capable of being made navigable you are to allow only the fifth part of the depth thereof by the water side and a Certificate fully specifying the scituacon & bounds thereof you are to returne to us with all convenient speed and for yo[r] soe doeing this shall be your sufficient warr[t]. Given under our hands at Charles Towne this fifth day of December 1674./[1]
To

Carolina./

You are forthw[th] to cause to be admeasured and laid out for M[r] Christopher Portman a small parcell of land lying upon the Westward side of his planting lott nere Charles Towne; granted to him upon his mocon this day made before the Grand Councill; And a Certificate fully specifying the scituacon bounds and quantity thereof you are to returne to us before the fourth day of January next ensueing the date hereof, & for your soe doing this shall be your sufficient warr[t]. Given under our hands at Charles Towne this fifth day of December 1674./

To Capt: Stephen Bull Joseph West
Surveyo[r]./ Will: Owen M Mathews Richard Conant

Carolina./

You are forthw[th] to cause to be admeasured and laid out for John Chambers Seaventy acres of land for himselfe arriveing in August 1671. in some place not yett laid out or marked to be laid out for any other person or use and if the same happen upon any navigable River or any River capable of being made navigable you are to allow only the fifth part of the depth thereof by the water side: And a Certificate fully specifying the scituacon and bounds thereof you are to returne to us with all convenient speed and for your soe doeing this shall be your sufficient Warr[t]. Given under o[r] hands at Charles Towne this xxvj[th]. day of Decemb[r] 1674./
To

Joseph West
John Godfrey
Will: Owen. Mau: Mathews./

[1]This warrant was cancelled.

Carolina./

You are forthwth to cause to be admeasured and laid out for Henry Wintrop seaventy acres of land for himselfe arriveing in Februarie $167\frac{0}{1}$. in some place not yett laid out or marked to be laid out for any other person or use and if the same happen upon any navigable River or any River capable of being made navigable you are to allow only the fifth part of the depth thereof by the waterside and a Certificate fully specifying the scituacon and bounds thereof you are to returne to us with all convenient speed and for yor soe doeing this shall be yor sufficient warr^{t}. Given under our hands at Charles Towne this xxvjth. day of December 1674

To Stephen Wheelewright
Surveyo^{r}./

Joseph West
John Godfrey
Mau: Mathews
Will Owen

Carolina./

Yo^{u} are forthwth to cause to be admeasured and laid out for John Farringdon Seaventy acres of land for himselfe arriveing in February $167\frac{0}{1}$. in some place not yett laid out or marked to be laid out for any other person or use and if the same happen upon any navigable River or any River capable of being made navigable yo^{u} are to allow only the fifth part of the depth thereof by the water-side And a Certificate fully specifying the scituacon and bounds thereof you are to returne to us with all convenient speed and for yor soe doeing this shall be yor. sufficient Warr^{t}. Given under our hands at Charles Towne this xxvjth day of December 1674./

To Stephen Wheelwright
Suryeyo^{r}./

Mau Mathews.
Will: Owen./

Joseph West
John Godfrey

Carolina./

You are forthwth to cause to be admeasured and laid out for James Powell seaventy acres of land for himselfe arriveing in June 1671 in some place not yett laid out or marked to be laid out for any other person or use and if the same happen upon any navigable River or any River capable of being made navigable you are to allow only the fifth part of the depth thereof by the water side; and a Certificate fully specifying the scituacon and bounds thereof you are to returne to us with all convenient speed and for yor

soe doing this shall be yor. sufficient warr^{t}. Given under our hands at Charles Towne this xxvjth. day of December 1674./

To M^{r}: John: Yeamans Surveyo^{r}:/

Joseph West
John Godfrey
Mau: Mathews
Will: Owen./

Carolina./

You are forthwth to cause to be admeasured and laid out for Anthony Churne and John Chambers all that parcell of ground late belonging to M^{r}. Joseph Dalton and by him voluntarily surrendered to the uses aforesaid scituate nere Charles Towne between the lands now in the possession of Capt: Maurice Mathews and the lands late belonging to Thomas Holton and now in the possession of Mr Ralph Marshall, and the said land equally to devide betweene the said Anthony Churne and John Chambers, and the severall Certificates fully specifyeing the scituacon and bounds of each part you are to returne to us wth all convenient speed; and for your soe doeing this shall be your sufficient Warr^{t}: Given under our hands at Charles Towne this twentieth day of ffebruary 1674/5./

To Capt: Stephen Bull Surveyo^{r}./

Joseph West
John Godfrey./ Mau: Mathews
Will: Owen./

Carolina./

You are forthwith to cause to be admeasured and laid out for Capt: Robert Donne Seaventy acres of land for Elizabeth his Wife arriveing in August 1671. in some place not yett laid out or marked to be laid out for any other person or use; and if the same happen upon any navigable River or any River capable of being made navigable you are to allow only the fifth part of the depth thereof by the water side and a Certificate fully specifying the scituacon and bounds thereof you are to returne to us with all convenient speed and for your soe doeing this shall be your sufficient Warr^{t}. Given under our hands at Charles Towne this xxth day of March 1674/5./

To Stephen Whelewright Surveyo^{r}./

Joseph West./
John Godfrey./
Will: Owen:
Ste: Bull./
Ra: Marshall./

Carolina./

You are forthwith to cause to be admeasured and laid out for Mr: Amos Jefford one hundred acres of land for one Servt: namely Will: Long arriveing in ffebruary 1672. in some place not yett laid out or marked to be laid out for any other person or use; and if the same happen upon any navigable River, or any River capable of being made navigable, you are to allow only the fifth part of the depth thereof by the water side, and a Certificate fully specifying the scituacon and bounds thereof you are to returne to us with all convenient speed and for your soe doeing this shall be your sufficient Warrt: Given under our hands at Charles Towne this xxth. day of March 1674/5/

To Capt: Stephen: Bull
Surveyor:/

Joseph West./
John Godfrey./
Will: Owen./
Ra: Marshall

Carolina

you are forthwith to cause to be admeasured and laid out for George: Beadon and Elizabeth his wife one hundred acres of land for ye said Elizabeth arriveing in the first fleet, in some place not yet laid out or marked to be laid out for any other person or use, and if the same happen upon any Navigable river or any river capable of being made Navigable, you are to allow onely one fifth part of the depth thereof by ye waterside, and a Certificate fully specifieing the scittuacon and bounds thereof you are to returne to us with all convenient speed, And for yor: soe doeing this shall be yor sufficient wart: Given undr: our hands at Charles Towne this xijth.. day of Aprill 1675.

To Stephen: Wheelwright
Surveyor:/

Joseph: West
John: Godfrey
Mau: Mathews
Ra: Marshall.

Carolina

you are forthwith to cause to be admeasured and laid out for Mr: Thomas: Smith one hundred and fifty acres of land for himself arriveing in ye first fleet in some place not yet laid out, or marked to be laid out, for any other person or use, and if the same happen upon any Navigable river or any river capable of being made Navigable you are to allow onely ye fifth part of ye depth thereof by y^{e}: waterside, And a Certificate fully specifieing the scittuacon and bounds thereof you are to returne to us with all cenvenient speed, And for yor: soe doeing this shall be yor: sufficient war^{t}: Given und^{r}: our hands at Charles Towne this xijth: day of Aprill 1675/

To Stephen: Wheelwright Surveyo^{r}../

Joseph: Dalton
John: Godfrey
Mau: Mathews
Ra: Marshall

Carolina

You are forthwith to cause to be admeasured and laid out for M^{r}: Thomas Smith and M^{r}: James: Smith two hundred acres of land for two serv^{ts}: namely Henry Sumpton, and Thomas: Vayle arriveing in Aug^{t}: 1671, in some place not yet laid out or marked to be laid out for any other person or use, and if the same happen upon any Navigable river or any river capable of being made Navigable you are to allow onely the fifth part of ye depth thereof by ye waterside, and a Certificate fully specifieing ye scittuacon and bounds thereof you are to returne to us with all convenient speed, And for yor: soe doeing this shall be yor.. suff^{t}. war^{t}: Given und^{r}: our hands at Charles Towne this xijth: day of Aprill 1675/

To Stephen: Wheelwright Surveyo^{r}:

Mau: Mathews
Ra: Marshall
Joseph: West
John: Godfrey

Carolina

You are forthwith to cause to be admeasured and laid out for M^{r}. Thomas Smith & M^{r}. James: Smith five hundred and fifty acres of land for four serv^{ts}: namely Henry: Jones, John: Huddleston, Hugh: Wigglesworth & Alice Rix arriveing in the first fleet, in some place not yet laid out, or marked to be laid out for any other person or use (deducting their tenn acre Lott cont: fifty acres) and if the same happen upon any Navigable river or any river capable of being made Navigable you are to allow onely the fifth part of ye depth thereof by ye waterside, And a Certificate fully specifieing ye scittuacon & bounds thereof you are to returne to us with all convenient speed and for yor, soe doeing this shall be yor: sufficient war^{t}: Given und^{r}: our hands at Charles Towne this xijth: day of Aprill 1675./

To Stephen: Wheelwright Surveyo^{r}:/

Ra: Marshall
Joseph: West
John: Godfrey
Mau: Mathews

Carolina./

You^u^. are forthw^th^. to cause to be admeasured and laid out for Leiu^t^: Coll: Godfrey three hundred acres of land for himselfe, his Wife and one serv^t^ namely John Ferrington arriveing in the yeare 1670 and 1671. in some place not yett laid out or marked to be laid out for any other person or use, and if the same happen upon any navigable River or any River capable of being made navigable, you are to allow only the fifth part of the depth thereof by the water side; and a Certificate fully specifying the scituacon and bounds thereof you are to returne to us with all convenient speed, and for your soe doeing this shall be your sufficient Warr^t^: Given under our hands at Charles Towne this xxvij^th^ day of Aprill 1675

To Stephen Wheelwright Surveyo^r^./ — Richard Conant — Joseph West, Mau:Mathews, Ste:Bull

Carolina./

You are forthwith to cause to be admeasured and laid out for Leiu^t^: Coll: John Godfrey fower hundred and forty acres of land due to him for John Godfrey Junr: Richard Godfrey and three servants namely Mathew English Thomas Ellis and George Jerman arriveing in the yeare 1670 in some place not yett laid out or marked to be laid out for any other person or use and if the same happen upon any navigable River or any River capable of being made navigable yo^u^. are to allow only the fifth part of the depth thereof by the water side, and a Certificate fully specifying the scituacon and bounds thereof yo^u^. are to return to us with all convenient speed and for yor soe doeing this shall be your sufficient Warr^t^. Given under our hands at Charles=Towne this xxvij^th^. day of Aprill 1675

To Mr John Yeamans Surveyo^r^./ — Richard Conant — Joseph West., Mau:Mathews, Ste:Bull

Carolina

You are forthwith to cause to be admeasured and laid out for M^r^: William: Morrill a certaine parcell of land lyeing to ye Eastward of ye lands of Anthony Churne, and John:Hawkes,and the Westward of wandoe river not injureing the lines of any lands lying next ye same, And a Certificate fully specifieing ye scittuacon, bounds, & quantity thereof you are to returne to us with all convenient speed, and for yor: soe doeing this shall be yor: sufficient warr^{t}: Given und^{r}: our hands at Charles Towne this xijth day of June 1675/

To M^{r}: John :Yeamans Surveyo^{r}:/ Mau :Mathews Will :Owen Jos :West John :Godfrey

Carolina

You are forthwith to cause to be admeasured and laid out for Thomas: ffluellin two hundred acres of land (deducting his Towne lott,and tenn acre lott) due for himself and Abigail his wife arriveing in December 1671 in some place not yet laid out, or marked to be laid for any other person or use,and if the same happen upon any navigable river or any river capable of being made navigable you are to allow onely the fifth part of the depth thereof by ye waterside,and a Certificate fully specifieing the scittuacon and bounds thereof you are to returne to us with all convenient speed,and for yor. soe doeing this shall be yor. sufficient warr^{t}: Given under our hands at Charles Towne this xth. day of July 1675.

To Capt^{t}: Stephen :Bull Surveyo^{r}:/ Richard Conant Maurice :Mathewes. Joseph :West John :Godfrey

Carolina./

You are forthwth. to cause to be admeasured and laid out for Jno: Fraiser One hundred acres of land for himselfe arriveing in the first ffleet in some place not yett laid out or marked to be laid out for any other person or use, and if the same happen upon any navigable River or any River capable of being made navigable yo^{u} are to allow only the fifth part of the depth thereof bÿ the water side; And a Certificate fully specifying the scituacon and bounds thereof yo^{u}. are to returne to us with all convenient speed and for your soe doeing this shall be your sufficient warr^{t}. Given under our hands at Charles Towne this tenth day of July 1675./

To Capt: Stephen Bull Surveyo^{r}./

Joseph West
John Godfrey
Mau :Mathews
Richard Conant

Carolina./

You are forthwth. to cause to be admeasured and laid out for Patrick Steward seaventy acres of land for himselfe arriveing in May 1673 in some place not yett laid out or marked to be laid out for any other person or use and if the same happen upon any navigable River or any River capable of being made navigable you are to allow only the fifth part of the depth thereof by the water side And a Certificate fully specifying the scituacon and bounds thereof you. are to returne to us with all convenient speed and for your soe doeing this shall be your sufficient Warrt: Given under our hands at Charles Towne this 5th day of September 1674./

To Capt Stephen Bull
Surveyor./

Joseph West
Richand Conant John Godfrey
Mau:Mathews[1]

Carolina./

You are forthwth to cause to be admeasured and laid out for James Williams two hundred acres of land for himselfe and Martha his Wife arriveing servts. in the first ffleet in some place not yett laid out or marked to be laid out for any other person or use and if the same happen upon any navigable River or any River capable of being made navigable you are to allow only the fifth part of the depth thereof by the water side and a Certificate fully specifying the scituacon and bounds thereof you are to returne to us with all convenient speed and for your soe doeing this shall be your sufficient warrt: Given under our hands at Charles Towne this fifth day of December 1674./

To Capt: Stephen Bull
Surveyor:/

Joseph West
John Godfrey
Mau:Mathews
Richard Conant.

Carolina./

You are forthwith to cause to be admeasured and laid out for Robert George One hundred and forty acres of land for himselfe and Izabell his Wife arriveing in ffebruary 1670/1 in some place not yett laid out or marked to be laid out for any other person or use and if the same happen upon any navigable River or any River capable of being made navigable you are to allow only the fifth part of the depth thereof by the water side and a Certificate fully specifying the scituacon and bounds thereof you are to returne to us with all convenient speed and for your soe

[1]This warrant was cancelled.

doeing this shall be your sufficient Warr^{t}: Given under our hands at Charles Towne this xth day of July 1675./

To Capt^{t}: Stephen Bull
Surveyo^{r}./

Joseph West
John Godfrey
Mau:Mathews
Richard Conant

Carolina./

You^{u} are forthwith to cause to be admeasured and laid out for Robert Thomas One hundred and forty acres of land for himselfe and Mary his Wife arriveing in February 1670/1 in some place not yett laid out or marked to be laid out for any other person or use and if the same happen upon any navigable River or any River capable of being made navigable you are to allow only the fifth part of the depth thereof by the water side and a Certificate fully specifying the scituacon and bounds thereof you are to returne to us with all convenient speed and for your soe doeing this shall be your sufficient Warr^{t}: Given under our hands at Charles Towne this tenth day of July 1675./

To Capt^{t}: Stephen Bull
Surveyo^{r}./

Joseph West
Richard Conant/ John Godfrey
Mau:Mathews

Carolina./

You are forthwth to cause to be admeasured and laid out for John Hughes seaventy acres of land for himselfe arriveing in ffebruary 1670: in some place not yett laid out or marked to be laid out for any other person or use and if the same happen upon any navigable River or any River capable of being made navigable you are to allow only the fifth part of the depth thereof by the water side and a Certificate fully specifying the scituacon and bounds thereof yo^{u} are to returne to us with all convenient speed and for yor soe doeing this shall be yor sufficient Warr^{t} Given under our hands at Charles Towne this 4th day of September 1675./

To Stephen Wheelewright
Surveyor./

Joseph West
Rich Conant
Will: Owen
Ra:Marshall

Carolina./

You^{u} are forthwth. to cause to be admeasured and laid out for John Bassett one hundred and forty acres of land for himselfe and Lidia his Wife arriveing in August 1672 in some place not yett laid out or marked to be laid out for any other person or use and if the same happen upon any navigable River or any River capable of being made navigable you are to allow only the fifth part of the depth thereof by the water side; And a Certificate fully specifying the scituacon and bounds thereof you are to returne to us with all convenient speed and for your soe doeing this shall be your sufficient Warr[t]. Given under our hands at Charles Towne this 4th. day of September 1675./

To M[r] John Yeamans
Surveyo[r]/

Will:Owen.
Joseph West
Richard Conant
Ra:Marshall/

Carolina/

You are forthw[th] to cause to be admeasured and laid out for Thomas Steere Seaventy acres of land for himselfe arriveing in August 1671. in some place not yett laid out or marked to be laid out for any other person or use and if the same happen upon any navigable River or any River capable of being made navigable you are to allow only the fifth part of the depth thereof by the water side and a Certificate fully specifying the scituacon and bounds thereof you are to returne to us with all convenient speed, and for your soe doeing this shall be your sufficient Warr[t]. Given under our hands at Charles Towne this 4th. day of September 1675./

To Cap[t]: Stephen Bull
Surveyo[r]./

Joseph West
Mau:Mathews
Will:Owen
Richard Conant
Ra: Marshall.

Carolina/

You are forthw[th] to cause to be admeasured and laid out for William Long seaventy acres of land for himselfe arriveing a Servant in ffebruary 1672 in some place not yett laid out or marked to be laid out for any other person or use and if the same happen upon any navigable River or any River capable of being made navigable you are to allow only the fifth part of the depth thereof by the water side and a Certificate fully specifying the scituacon and bounds thereof you are to returne to us with all convenient speed and for your soe doeing this shall be your sufficient Warr^t^. Given under our hands at Charles Towne this fourth day of September 1675./

To Capt: Stephen Bull
Surveyo^r^./

Joseph West
Mau: Mathews
Will:Owen
Ra' Marshall/
Richard Conant./

Carolina
You are forthwith to cause to be admeasured and laid out for John: ffaulkoner two hundred and forty acres of land for Ann his wife and John: and Henry his sonnes arriveing in March 1672. in some place not yett laid out or marked to be laid out for any other person or use; and if the same happen upon any navigable River or any River capable of being made navigable yo^u^. are to allow only the fifth part of the depth thereof by the water side and a Certificate fully specifying the scituacon and bounds thereof you are to returne to us with all convenient speed and for your soe doing this shall be your sufficient warrant Given under our hands at Charles Towne this xj^th^ day of September 1675./

Joseph West
Maurice Mathews./
Will:Owen.
Ralph Marshall

To M^r^: John: Yeamans
Surveyo^r^:

Carolina You are forthwith to cause to be admeasured and laid out for Originall Jackson one hundred acres of land for Millicent his wife arriveing in the first ffleet in some place not yett laid out or marked to be laid out for any other ℘son or use and if the same happen upon navigable River or any River capable of being made navigable you are to allow only the fifth part of the depth thereof by the water side; And a Certificate fully specifying the scituacon and bounds thereof you are to returne to us with all convenient speed and for your soe doeing this shall be your sufficient warrant; Given under our hands at Charles Towne this xj^th^. day of September 1675./

To Mr John Yeamans
Surveyo^r^./

Joseph West
Maurice Mathews
Will:Owen
Ra: Marshall

Carolina You are forthwith to cause to be admeasured and laid out for John: ffaulkoner Extor to Edward Roberts decd one hundred acres of land due for the said Edward: Roberts arriveing in ffebruary 1670 in some place not yett laid out or marked to be laid out for any other ℘son or use, and if the same happen upon any navigable River or any River capable of being made navigable you are to allow only the fifth part of the depth thereof by the water side; And a Certificate fully specifying the scituacon and bounds thereof you are to returne to us with all convenient speed and for yor soe doeing this shall be your sufficient warr^t^. Given under our hands at Charles Towne this xj^th^ day of September 1675

Joseph West
Mau: Mathews
Will:Owen
Ralph Marshall./

To Mr John:Yeamans
Surveyo^r^:

Carolina

You are forthwith to cause to be admeasured and laid out for John: ffaulkoner one hundred acres of land for himself arriveing in September 1670 (deducting his Towne lott and tenn acre lott) in some place not yett laid out or marked to be laid out for any other person or use and if the same happen upon any navigable River or any River capable of being made navigable yo^u^. are to allow only the fifth part of the depth thereof by the water side and a Certificate fully specifying the scituacon and bounds thereof you are to returne to us with all convenient speed and for yor soe doeing this shall be your sufficient Warr^t^. Given under our hands at Charles Towne this xj^th^. day of September 1675./

To M^r^: John:Yeamans
Surveyo^r^:/

Joseph West
Mau:Mathews
Will:Owen:
Ralph Marshall.

Carolina./

Yo^u^. are forthw^th^ to cause to be admeasured and laid out for the right hon^ble^: Anthony Earle of Shaftesbury one of the Ld^s^. prop^rs^: of this province twelve thousand acres of land in some place not yett laid out or marked to be laid out for any other person or use; And a Certificate fully specifying the scituacon and bounds thereof you are to returne to us with all convenient speed and for your soe doeing this shall be yor sufficient Warr^t^. Given under our hands at Charles Towne this xiiij^th^ day of September 1675./

To Capt: Stephen Bull & Joseph West
Mr Jno Yeamans Surveyo^rs^:/ W^m^.Owen
Ra: Marshall

Carolina./

You are forthw^th^ to cause to be admeasured and laid out for Jacob Wayte six hundred acres of land for himselfe his Wife, his Sonn and three Serv^ts^. namely Thomas Reed Thomas Bydall and John Willson arriveing in September 1675 in some place not yett laid out or marked to be laid out for any other person or use, and if the same happen upon any navigable River or any River capable of being made navigable yo^u^ are to allow only the fifth part of the depth thereof by the water side; And a Certificate fully specifying the scituacon and bounds thereof yo^u^ are to returne to us with all convenient speed and for yor: soe doeing this shall be yor. sufficient Warr^t^. Given under our hands at Charles Towne this xiiij^th^ day of September 1675.

To M^r^: John Yeamans Joseph West
Surveyo^r^./ Mau :Mathews
Will: Owen
Ra :Marshall./

Carolina./

Yo^u^. are forthw^th^ to cause to be admeasured and laid out for Capt fflorence ô Sullivan one thousand nine hundred acres of land (deducting soe much therefro as his Towne lott and tenn acre lott amounts to) for himselfe and twelve Serv^ts^. namely Eliz: Dimock, Rich: Alexander Stephen Wheelewright, John Dale, Jno Mare Geo: White, Wm Bevin, Brian Fitzpatrick, Dan: Sullivan, Jno. Scott, Aaron Allouron and Teigue Shugeron arriveing in the first ffleet, in some place not yett laid out or marked to be laid out for any other person or use and if the same happen upon any navigable River or any River capable of being made navigable you are to allow only the fifth part of the depth thereof by the waterside And a Certificate fully specifying the scituacon and bounds thereof you are to returne to us with all convenient speed and for yor soe doeing this shall be yor sufficient Warr^t^. Given under our hands at Charles Towne this 14th. day of September 1675./

To Stephen Wheelewright Joseph West
Surveyo^r^./ Mau :Mathews
Will :Owen
Ra :Marshall.

Carolina./

You[u] are forthwith to cause to admeasured and laid out for Capt: fflorence ô Sullivan Administrator of Michaell Moron deceased foure hundred acres of land being the full proporcon of land allowed to the said Michaell Moron for himselfe his Wife and One child arriveing in the first ffleet, by the lords prop[rs]: Concessions (deducting therefrom his Towne lott and Tenn acre lott if any he hath) in such place as you shall be directed by the said Capt: Sullivan, and if the same happen upon any navigable River capable of being made navigable you are to allow only the fifth part of the depth thereof by the waterside; and a Certificate fully specifying the scituacon and bounds thereof you are to returne to us with all convenient speed and for your soe doeing this shall be your sufficient Warrt. Given under our hands at Charles Towne this 14th day of September 1675

To Stephen Wheelewright
Surveyor./

Joseph West
Mau:Mathews
Will:Owen
Ra:Marshall

Carolina./

You are forthwth to cause to be admeasured and laid out for Capt: fflorence ô Sullivan one hundred acres of land for one Servant namely Jno. Freezer arriveing in August 1671. in some place not yett laid out or marked to be laid out for any other person or use and if the same happen upon any navigable River or any River capable of being made navigable you are to allow only the fifth part of the depth thereof by the water side And a Certificate fully specifying the scituacon and bounds thereof you are to returne to us with all convenient speed and for your soe doeing this shall be your sufficient Warrt. Given under our hands at Charles Towne this 14th day of September 1675.

To Stephen Wheelewright
Surveyor./

Joseph West
Mau:Mathews
Will Owen
Ra:Marshall.

Carolina

You are forthwith to cause to be admeasured and laid out for Mr: John: Smith eight hundred and seaventy acres of land for himselfe his wife and seaven servts: namely Violetta: Vincum, William:

fflavie, William: Westbury, Richard: Millionton Thomas: penderry John: Hawkinson & Robert Smith in some place not yet laid out or marked to be laid out for any other person or use, and if the same happen upon any Navigable river, or any river capable of being made Navigable you are to allow onely the fifth part of the depth thereof by the waterside, And a Certificate fully specifieing the scittuation and bounds thereof you are to returne to us with all convenient speed And for yor. soe doeing this shall be yor: suff^{t}: war^{t}: Given und^{r}: our hands at Charles Towne this xvjth: day of October 1675

To Capt: Stephen: Bull &
Mr John: Yeamans
Surveyo^{rs}:/ — Mau:Mathews, Joseph:West, And^{r}: percivall. John: Godfrey

You are forthwith to cause to be admeasured and laid out for M^{r}: John: Smith six hundred and thirty acres of land haveing undertaken to settle ye same with ꝑsons ꝑꝑconable to ye Lords prop^{rs}: Concessions within two yeares next comeing in some place not yet laid out or marked to be laid out for any other person or use, and if the same happen upon any Navigable river or any river capable of being made Navigable, you are to allow onely the fifth part of ye depth thereof by the waterside and a Certificate fully specifieing the scittuacon & bounds thereof you are to returne to us with all convenient speed And for yor: soe doeing this shall be yor: sufficient war^{t}: Given und^{r}. our hands at Charles Towne this xvith: day of October 1675./

To Capt: Stephen: Bull &
M^{r}: John: Yeamans
Surveyo^{rs}: — Mau:Mathews, Joseph:West, Andr: percivall, John:Godfrey

You are forthwith to cause to be admeasured and laid out for Jacob: Wayte a certaine parcell of land already laid out for him, and bounding upon a Creeke there being which is granted to him by order of the Grand Councill dated ye 16: 8^{ber}: 1675 haveing undertaken to procure soe many persons to settle the same, as shall be sufficient to take the right thereof, within three yeares next ensueing And a Certificate fully specifieing the scittuation and bounds thereof you are to returne to us with all convenient speed, And for yor:

soe doeing this shall be yor: sufficient war^{t}: Given under our hands at Charles Towne this xxxth: day of October 1675./

To M^{r}: John: Yeamans Surveyo^{rs}: | Will :Owen Richard :Conant. | Joseph :West John :Godfrey

You are forthwith to cause to be admeasured and laid out for Bartholomew Browne seaventy acres of land for himself arriveing in ffebruary 1670 in some place not yet laid out or marked to be laid out for any other person or use, and if the same happen upon any Navigable river or any river capable of being made Navigable you are to allow onely the fifth part of the depth thereof by the waterside And a Certificate specifieing the scittuation and bounds thereof you are to returne to us with all convenient speed, And for yor: soe doeing this shall be yor: sufficient war^{t}: Given under our hands at Charles Towne this second day of Nevember 1675.

To Capt^{t}: Stephen: Bull Surveyo^{r}: | Rich: Conant | Joseph :West John: Godfrey

You are forthwith to cause to be admeasured and laid out for John: Betty one hundred acres of land for himself arriveing in May 1674 in some place not yet laid out or marked to be laid out, or marked to be laid out for any other person or use, and if the same happen upon any Navigable river or any river capable of being made Navigable you are to allow onely the fifth part of the depth thereof by the waterside. And a Certificate fully specifieing the scittuation and bounds thereof you are to returne to us with all convenient speed, And for yor: soe doeing this shall be your sufficient war^{t}: Given under our hands at Charles Towne this xxxth day of October 1675./

To Stephen :Wheelwright Surveyo^{r}: | John :Godfrey Richard :Conant | Joseph :West Andr^{r} :percivall

You are forthwith to cause to be admeasured and laid out for Hugh: Wigglesworth one hundred acres of land for himself arriveing in the first fleet in some place not yet laid out or marked to laid out for any other person or use, & if the same happen upon any Navigable river or any river capable of being made Navigable you are to allow onely the fifth part of the depth thereof by the waterside, And a Certificate fully specifieing the scittuation & bounds thereof you are to returne to us with all convenient speed, And for yor. soe doeing this shall be yor: suff^{t}: war^{t}: Given und^{r}: our hands at Charles Towne this xxxth: day of October 1675/

To Stephen: Wheelwright Surveyo^{r}: John: Godfrey Rich: Conant Joseph: West Andr: percivall

You are forthwith to cause to be admeasured, and laid out for Thomas: Rowntree one hundred acres of land for himself arriveing in May 1674 in some place not yet laid out or marked to be laid out for any other person or use, and if the same happen upon any Navigable river or any river capable of being made Navigable you are to allow onely the fifth part of the depth thereof by the waterside, and a Certificate fully specifieing the scittuacon & bounds thereof, you are to returne to us with all convenient speed And for yor soe doeing this shall be yor: sufficient war^{t}: Given und^{r}: our hands at Charles Towne this xxxth: day of October 1675

To Stephen: Wheelwright Surveyo^{r}:/ John: Godfrey Rich: Conant Joseph: West Andr: Percivall

you are forthwith to cause to be admeasured and laid out for Thomas: Akin, one hundred acres of land for himself arriveing in May 1674 in some place not yet laid out or marked to be laid out for any other person or use, and if the same happen upon any Navigable river or any river capable of being made Navigable you are to allow onely the fifth part of the depth thereof by the waterside, and a Certificate fully specifieing the scittuation and bounds thereof you are to returne to us with all convenient speed And for yor soe doeing this shall be yor. suff^{t}: war^{t}: Given und^{r}: our hands at Charles Towne this xxxth. day of October 1675

To Stephen: Wheelwright Surveyo^{r}: Rich: Conant Andr: percivall./ Joseph: West John: Godfrey

You are forthwith to cause to be admeasured & laid out for Thomas: Dickison two hundred acres of land for himself and one man servant namely Morgan: Owen arriveing in Sept: 1675 in some place not yet laid out or marked to be laid out for any other person or use and if the same happen upon any Navigable river or any river capable of being made Navigable you are to allow onely the fifth part of the depth thereof by the waterside, and a Certificate fully specifieing the scittuacon & bounds thereof, you are to returne to us with all convenient speed, and for yor: soe doeing this shall be yor:

sufficient war[t]: Given und[r]. our hands at Charles Towne this xxvij[th]: November 1675./

To M[r]. John:Yeamans Surveyo[r]: | Andr:percivall Will:Owen | Joseph:West Rich:Conant

You are forthwith to cause to be admeasured & laid out for Thomas: Hunt one hundred and forty acres of land for himself and Jane his wife arriveing in May & November 1673 in some place not yet laid out or marked to be laid out for any other person or use, and if the happen upon any Navigable river or any river capable of being made Navigable you are to allow onely the fifth part of the depth thereof by the waterside, and a Certificate fully specifieing the scittuacon and bounds thereof you are to returne to us with all convenient speed, And for yo[r]: soe doeing this shall be yo[r]: sufficient war[t]: Given und[r]: our hands at Charles Town this xxvij[th]: November 1677./

To Cap[t] Morris Mathews surveyr: | Will:Owen. | Joseph:West Richard:Conant Jo[n] Godfrey:[1]

You are forthwith to cause to be admeasured and laid out for John: Hartley seaventy acres of land for himself arriveing in Aug[t]: 1671. in some place not yet laid out or marked to be laid out for any other person or use, and if the same happen upon any Navigable river or any river capable of being made Navigable you are to allow onely the fifth part of the depth therof by the waterside, And a Certificate fully specifieing the scittuacon and bounds thereof you are to returne to us with all convenient speed, And for yo[r]: soe doeing this shall be yo[r]: sufficient warr[t]: Given under our hands at Charles Towne this xxx[th]: day of October 1675./

To Capt: Stephen:Bull Surveyo[r]./ | Andr: percivall Will: Owen. | Joseph:West Richard: Conant

You are forthwith to cause to be admeasured and laid out for priscilla: Bourke two hundred and ninety acres of land allowed for herself, and John Bourke and and Michael Burke arriveing in ffebruary 1670 (deducting her Tenn acre lott) in some place not yet laid out or marked to be laid out for any other person or use,

[1]This warrant was first dated 1675, but a 7 was written over the 5 and the name of Andrew Percival, which had been put down as one of the deputies signing it, was scratched out and John Godfrey's name was added.

and if the same happen upon any Navigable river or any river capable of being made Navigable you are to allow onely the fifth part of the depth thereof by the waterside: And a Certificate fully specifieing the scittuacon and bounds thereof you are to returne to us with all convenient speed, And for yor: soe doeing this shall be yor: sufficient war^{t}: Given under our hands at Charles Towne this xxxth: day of October 1675

To Stephen:Wheelwright Surveyo^{r}./ John:Godfrey Richard:Conant/ Joseph:West Andr:percivall

You are forthwith to cause to be admeasured and laid out for M^{r}: Robert Browne five hundred acres of land for his wife and 4: serv^{ts}: namely Robert: pett Edward Huggin Hugh Magrady and peter a Negroe arriveing in Aug^{t}: 1672 in some place not yet laid out or marked to be laid out for any other person or use; and if the same happen upon any Navigable river or any river capable of being made Navigable you are to allow onely the fifth part of the depth thereof by the waterside, and a Certificate fully specifieing the scittuation and bounds thereof you are to returne to us with all convenient speed and for yor: soe doeing this shall be yor: sufficient war^{t}: Given und^{r}: our hands at Charles Towne this xth. December 1675./

To Stephen:Wheelwright Surveyo^{r}:/

Joseph:West
John: Godfrey
Andr:percivall
Ste: Bull.

You are forthwith to cause to be admeasured and laid out for M^{r}. John: Smith three hundred acres of land haveing undertaken to settle the same with ℘sons pro℘conable to the Lords prop^{rs}. Concessions within two yeares next comeing in some place not yet laid out or marked to be laid out for any other person or use, and if the same happen upon any Navigable river, or any river capable of being made Navigable you are to allow onely the fifth part of the depth thereof by the waterside, and a Certificate fully specifieing the scittuacon and bounds thereof you are to returne to us with all convenient speed And for yor: soe doeing this shall be yor: sufficient war^{t}: Given und^{r}: our hands at Charles Towne this xth: December 1675/

To Capt: Stephen:Bull & M^{r}: John: Yeamans Surveyo^{rs}:/

Mau:Mathews Joseph:West
John:Godfrey
Andr:percivall.

You are forthwith to cause to be admeasured and laid out for Robert: Layton seaventy acres of land for himself arriveing in August 1671 in some place not yet laid out or marked to be laid out for any other person or use, and if the same happen upon any Navigable river or any river capable of being made Navigable, you are to allow onely the fifth part of the depth thereof by the waterside, and a Certificate fully specifieing the scittuacon & bounds thereof you are to returne to us with all convenient speed And for yo[r]. soe doeing this shall be yo[r]: suff[t]: war[t]: Given und[r]: our hands at Charles Towne this x[th]: December 1675./

To Cap[t]:Stephen:Bull
&
M[r]:John: Yeamans
Surveyo[rs]:/

Mau:Mathews.
Joseph:West
John:Godfrey
Andr:percivall.

You are forthwith to cause to be admeasured and laid out for Joseph: pendarvys seaventy acres of land for himself arriveing in Aug[t]. 1671 in some place not yet laid out or marked to be laid out for any other person or use and if the same happen upon any Navigable river, or any river capable of being made navigable you are to allow onely the fifth part of the depth thereof by the waterside, and a Certificate fully specifieing the scittuacon and bounds thereof you are to returne to us with all convenient speed and for yo[r]: soe doeing this shall be yo[r]: sufficient war[t]: Given und[r]: our hands at Charles Towne this x[th]: December 1675

Joseph:West
John:Godfrey
Andr:percivall
Mau:Mathews

You are forthwith to cause to be admeasured and laid out for Joseph: pendarvys and Elizabeth his wife one hundred twenty and three acres of land being the residue of two hundred and fifty acres which should have been laid out for them on the Oyster point) in some place not yet laid out or marked to be laid out for any other person or use, and if the same happen upon any Navigable river or any river capable of being made Navigable you are to allow onely the fifth part of the depth thereof by the waterside, And a Certificate fully specifieing the scittuation and bounds thereof you are to returne to us with all convenient speed and for yo[r]: soe doeing this shall be yor. sufficient war^t^: Given under our hands at Charles Towne this x^th^: December 1675/

To M^r^: John: Yeamans Surveyo^r^:/ — Andr: percivall./ Joseph: West, John: Godfrey, Mau: Mathews

You are forthwith to cause to be admeasured and laid out for Thomas: Butler four hundred and tenn acres of land for Sarah his wife two children Shem and Ann, two serv^ts^: Edward:Perry & John: Hofford arriveing in September 1675 in some place not yet laid out or marked to be laid out for any other person or use, & if the same happen upon any Navigable river or any river capable of being made Navigable you are to allow onely the fifth part of the depth thereof by the waterside, and a Certificate fully specifieing the scittuacon & bounds thereof, you are to returne to us with all convenient speed, And for yor: soe doeing this shall be yor: sufficient war^t^: Given und^r^: our hands at Charles Towne this x^th^: December 1675/

To Capt: Stephen: Bull
Surveyo^r^:/

You are forthwith to cause to be admeasured and laid out for Margaret Lady Yeamans widdow one thousand and seaventy acres of land, eight hundred and eighty acres whereof is for her self and eight of her own proper Negroes namely Hannah, Jone, Jupiter, Rentee, Gilbert, Resom, Jossee & Simon, and one man servant John: Hopkins arriveing in Aug^t^: 1672, and ffebruary 1674, and one hundred and ninety acres the residue thereof haveing undertaken to transport soe many persons more to settle the same as shall be sufficient for that Appropriation, according to the Lords proprieto^rs^: Concessions in some place not yet laid out or marked to be laid out for any other person or use, and if the same happen upon any Navigable river or any river capable of being made Navigable you are to allow onely the fifth part of the depth thereof by the water side, And a Certificate fully specifieing the scittuation, and bounds thereof you are to returne to us with all convenient speed, And for yor: soe doeing this shall be yor: sufficient war^t^: Given und^r^: our hands at Charles Towne this fifth day of September 1674/

To M^r^: John: Yeamans Surveyo^r^:/ — Mau: Mathews, Andr: percivall, Joseph: West, John: Godfrey

You. are forthwth to cause to be admeasured and laid out for Mr: Edward Mathews five hundred and seaventy acres of land for himselfe and 5 Servants namely Hugh Lewis, Robert Layton Randall Evans, Thomas Steeres and Judith Pocock arriveing in August 1671. in some place not yett laid out, or marked to be laid out for any other person or use, and if the same happen upon any navigable River, or any River capable of being made navigable you. are to allow only the fifth part of the depth thereof by the water side, and a Certificate fully specifying the scituacon and bounds thereof you. are to returne to us with all convenient speed, and for your soe doeing this shall be yor. sufficient Warrt. Given under our hands at Charles Towne this xixth. day of February 1675./

To Mr: John Yeamans
Surveyor:/

Will:Owen
Mau:Mathews./

Joseph West
Ste.Bull
John Godfrey

You. are forthwth to cause to be admeasured and laid out for Mr: Christopher Portman foure hundred and seaventy acres of land for himselfe Nicholas Holford, John Hartley, Edward Haward and Elizabeth Norris arriveing in August 1671 in some place not yett laid out or marked to be laid out for any other person or use, and if the same happen upon any navigable River or any River capable of being made navigable you are to allow only the fifth part of the depth thereof by the water side and a Certificate fully specifying the scituacon and bounds thereof you are to returne to us with all convenient speed and for your soe doeing this shall be your sufficient Warrt. Given under our hands at Charles Towne this xixth day of February 1675./

To Mr John Yeamans
Surveyor./

Joseph West.
Mau: Mathews./
John Godfrey./
Will:Owen./

You are forthwith to cause to be admeasured and laid out for Mr: William Thomas eight hundred and tenn acres of land for himself, and eight servants namely William: Jones,Ann: Jones,one infant William: Cason,William: Jackson,Thomas:Hunt,and Richard: and Salisbury two Negroes, arriveing in May 1673 in some place not yet laid out,or marked to be laid out for any other person or use, and if the same happen upon any Navigable river, or any river capable of being made Navigable, you are to allow onely the fifth part of the depth thereof by the water side,and a Certificate fully specifieing the scittuation and bounds thereof,you are to returne to us with all convenient speed, and for yor: soe doeing this shall be yor: sufficient war^{t}: Given under our hands at Charles Towne the xviijth: day of March 1675./

To Stephen :Wheelwright Surveyo^{r}:/

Richard Conant Joseph :West
Mau :Mathews
Stephen :Bull John :Godfrey

You are forthwith to cause to be admeasured and laid out for M^{r}: Robt: Browne seaven hundred and seaventy acres of land for himself his wife & six serv^{ts}: namely Robert :pett Edward Huggin,Hugh Magrady,peter a Negroe,John fforgison,& Joan Bayly arriveing before June 1675 in some place not yet laid out,or marked to be laid out for any other person or use, and if the same happen upon any Navigable river or any river capable of being made Navigable you are to allow onely the fifth part thereof by the waterside And a Certificate fully specifieing the scittuacon and bounds thereof you are to returne to us with all convenient speed And for yor: soe doeing this shall be yor: sufficient warr^{t}: Given under our hands at Charles Towne this xth: day of June 1676/.

To M^{r}: Stephen: W,heelwright Surveyo^{r}: These./

Will :Owen Joseph :West
Mau :Mathews

You are forthwith to cause to be admeasured and laid out for M^{r}: Robert: Browne two hundred and thirty acres of land haveing undertaken to settle the same with persons proporconable to the Lords proprieto^{rs}: Concessions within two yeares next ensueing in some place not yet laid out or marked to be laid out for any other person or use, and if the same happen upon any Navigable river, or any river capable of being made Navigable you are to allow onely the fifth part of the depth thereof by the waterside and a Certificate fully specifieing the scittuacon and bounds thereof you are to returne to us with all convenient speed, and for yor: soe doeing this shall be yor: sufficient war^{t}: Given und^{r}: our hands at Charles Towne this xth: day of June 1676./

To Mr Stephen :Wheelwright Surveyo^{r}:/

Joseph :West
Will :Owen Mau: Mathews

You are forthwith to cause to be admeasured and laid out for Evan Jones seaventy acres of land for Jone his wife arriveing a serv^{t}: in

March 1672 in some place not yet laid out or marked to be laid out for any other person or use and if the same happen upon any Navigable river or any river capable of being made Navigable you are to allow onely the fifth part of ye depth thereof by the waterside And a Certificate fully specifieing the scittuacon and bounds thereof you are to returne to us with all convenient speed and for yor: soe doeing this shall be yor: sufficient wart: Given undr: our hands at Charles Towne this xvijth day of June 1676

To Mr: John: Yeamans Surveyor./

Mau: Mathews Joseph: West John: Godfrey Andr percivall

You are furthwth to cause to be Admeasured and layd out for mr Edmund Gibbons one hundred and thirtie acres of land in som place not yet layd out or marked to be layd out for any other person or use and if ye same happen upon any navigable river or river capable of being made navigable you are onlye to allowe ye fifth part of ye depth thereof by ye waterside and a Certificat fully specifyeing ye scituacon and ye bounds thereof you are to returne to us with all Convenient speede and for yor soe doeing this shalbe yor sufficient warrt Given undr or hands att Charles Towne this 28° day of June 1676:

To Mr Jon Yeamans Surveyor:

In pursuance of an order of Councill dated ye 2° day of septr Instant you are furthwth to cause to be admeasured and layd out for Steven Clay marriner foure hundred acres of land in som place not yet layd out or marked to be layd out for any other person or use and if ye same happen upon any Navigable river or any river capable of being made Navigable you are to allowe onlie ye 5th part of ye depth thereof by the water side And a Certificat fully specifyeing the scituacon and bounds thereof you are to returne to us with all Convenient speed And for yor soe doeing this shalbe yor sufficient Warrt Given undr or hands att Charles Towne this 10th day of September 1676:

Joseph West

To Capt Steven Bull: Surveyr:

Jon Godfrey

Will: Owen: Andrew piercevall:

In pursuance of an order of Councill dated ye 2d Instant you are furthwth to cause to be admeasured and layd out for Wm: Brockhurst marriner foure hundred acres of land in som place not yet layd out or marked to be layd out for any other person or use And if ye Same happen upon any navigable river or any river capable of being made navigable you are to allowe onlie the 5th part of ye depth thereof be ye waterside And a Certificat fully specifyeing ye Scituacon and bounds thereof you are to returne to us with all Convenient speede and for yor soe doeing this shalbe yor Sufficient Wart Given undr or hands att Charles Towne this 10th day of Sept: 1676

To Capt Steven Bull Surveyr: Jon Godfrey Joseph West
And :piercevall :
Will :Owen :

You are furthwth to cause to be Admeasured and Layd out for Jon Lorrisson marriner one of ye settlers of and in this provinc twoe hundred and fiftie acres of Land it being for himself and one man servant Arived in ye yeare 1672 and yt in som place not yet Layd out or marked to be Layd out for any other person or use and if ye same happen upon any Navigable river or capable to be made navigable you are onlie to allowe ye 5t part of ye depth thereof by ye water side and a Certificat fully specifyeing ye Scituacon and bounds thereof you are to returne to us with all Convenient speede And for yor soe doeing this shalbe yor Sufficient Warrt Given undr or hands att Charles Towne ye 10th Day of 7ber ano 1676

To Capt Steven Bull Surveyr: Joseph West

Carolina SS

You are forthwth to Admeasure & Lay out for Coll Jo Godfrey one hundred Acres of Land in Some Place nott yett Layed out or Marked to bee Layed out for any other ꝑsonn or ꝑsonns or use & if the Same happen upon any Navigable or river Capable of being made navigable you are to allow only the 5h ꝑte of the depth by the water side & A Certificate fully specifyinge the boundes & scittuacon thereof to returne to us wth all Convenient speed & for soe doinge this shalbee yor sufficient warrt given under our hands att Charles Towne ye 30th Daye of September 1676

To Capt Ste: Bull
Surveyor

Joseph West
Andrew Percivall
Jo Godfrey
Maurice Mathewes

Carolina SS.

Yo^{u} are forthwth to Admeasure & Lay out for Coll J^{o} wade one of the ffreemen of this setlem^{t} one hundred Acres of Lande in some place nott yett Layed out nor marked to bee Layed out for any other ꝑsonn or ꝑsonns or use & if the same happen upon any Navigable or river Capable of beinge made Navigable yo^{u} are to allow onely the 5^{h} ꝑte of the depth by the water side & A Certificate fully specifyinge the boundes & Scittuacon thereof to returne to us wth all Convenient speed & for yor soe Doinge this shalbee yor sufficient warr^{t} given under our hands att Charles Towne the 30th Daye of September 1676

To Capt Ste: Bull
Surveyo^{r}/

Joseph west
Andrew Percivall
John Godfrey
Maurice Mathewes

Carolina SS

Yo^{u} are fforthwth to Admeasure and Lay out for Walter Darby one of the freemen of this province one hundred acres of Land in som place not yet Layd out or markt to bee Layed out for any other ꝑson or ꝑsonns or use & if the same happen upon any navigable or river Capable of being made Navigable river yo^{u} are to allow onely the 5^{h} ꝑte of the depth to the water side & A Certificate fully specifyinge the boundes & scittuacon thereof to returne to us wth all Convenient speed & for yor soe Doinge this shalbee yor sufficient warr^{t} given under our hands att Charles Towne this 30th of September 1676./

To Capt Ste: Bull
Surveyo^{r}/

Joseph west
Andrew Percivall
John Godfrey
Maurice Mathews

You are furthwth to Admeasure and Lay out for Robert George one of the freemen of this province one hundred acres of Land in som place not yet Layd out or marked to be Layd out for any other person or ꝑsons or use and if ye same happen upon any Navigable river or river capable of being made Navigable you are to allowe only the fifth part of ye depth by ye water side, and a Certificat fully specifyeing the bounds and Scituacon thereof to returne to us with all Convenjent speede and for soe doeing this shalbe your Sufficient Warr^{t} Given und^{r} o^{r} hands att Charles Towne ye 10th day of No^{br}: 1676:

Jo: West
J: Godfrey Andrew P:
M: Mathews:

Carolina SS:
You are furthwth to Admeasure and Lay out for Anthonie Churne one of ye freemen of this provinc one hundred acres of Land in som place not yet Layd out or marked to be Layd out for any other person or use and if ye same happen upon any Navigable river or river capable of being made Navigable you are to allowe onlie ye fifth part of ye Depth by ye water side and a Certificat fully specifyeing ye bounds and scituacon thereof you are to returne to us with all Convenjent speed and for soe Doeing this shalbe yor Warr^{t} Given und^{r} our hands att Charles Towne ye 10th Day of No^{br} 1676
To Capt Maurice Mathews Survey^{r}:

Joseph West
Rich: Conant: And^{r} Percivall
Will: Owen:

Carolina/
You are forthwith to Cause to be Admeasured and Layd out for mrs Jane Rixam one of ye settlers of this province three hundred and forty Acres of Land being the proportion due to her selfe Daughter one woeman servant & one man servant all whom Arrived in the yeare 1676 in some place not yet layd out or marked to be Layd out for any other ꝑson or use and if ye same happen upon any navigable River or any River Capable of being made Navigable you are to Allow only ye fifth part of the depth by the water side & Certificate fully specyfying the scituation and bounds thereof you are to Returne to us with all Convenient speed & for soe doeing this shall be your warrant given under our hands at Charles Towne ye 10th day of November 1676:
To Steph: Whelewright; Surveyour

Mau: Mathews Joseph West
Rich Connant

Carolina/
You are forthwith to Cause to be Admeasured & layd out for Tho Williams one of the freeman of this province one hundred & seaventy Acres of Land being the proportion allowed to him for himselfe & Ellinor Burnet his wife deducting always wt quantity of

Land he or she hath taken up for their or any of their towne lott or ten Acre lotts in some place not yet layd out or marked to be layd out for any other person or use and if ye same happen to be upon any Navigable river or river capable of being made Navigable you are to allowe onlje ye fifth part of ye depth thereof by ye water side and a Certificat fully specifyeing ye scituacon thereof and bounds alsoe you are to returne to us with all Convenjent speede & for yor soe doeing this shalbe yor Warr^t^ Given und^r^ o^r^ hands att Charles Towne ye 10th 9^ber^ 1676:

To Capt Steven Bull Surveyr:

Joseph West:
M:Matthews:
Rich: Conant:
Andr:piercevall

Carolina

You: are forthwth: to Admeasure & Lay out for ye Right Honoble: Anthoney Earle of Shaftesbury one of ye Lords proprietors of ys ℘vince four hundred & ninety Acres of Land being part of a greater quantity in Some place not yett Layd out or marked to be Layd out for any other person or use; And if ye: same happen upon any navigable River or River Capable of being made navigable; you: are to allow onely ye: fifth part of ye: Depth by ye: water side & a Certifycate fully specifying ye: bounds & Scituation thereof to Return to us wth: all Convenient speede & for yor: soe doeing this shall be yor: warrant Given under our hands at Charles Towne ye twenty Eight Day of Octobr: 1676/

Richard Conant Robert Donne
To Capt: Maurice Mathewes Will: Owen
Surveyr:/

Joseph West
Stephen Bull

Carolina

You: are forthwth: to Admeasure & Lay out for ye Right Honoble: Anthoney Earle of Shaftesbury one of ye Lords Proprietors: of ys Province nine hundred Acres of Land being Part of a greater Quantety in some place not yett Layd out or Marked to be Layd out for any other Person or use & if ye same happen upon any navigable River or River Capable of being made navigable; you: are to allow onely ye fifth ℘t: of ye Depth by ye water side & a Certifycate fully specifying ye bounds & Scituation thereof to Returne to us wth: all Convenient speede & for soe doeing this shall be yor: Warrent Given under our hands at Charles Towne ye Twenty Eight day of 8^ber^: 1676/

To Capt: Maurice Mathewes Surveyo^r^: } Richard Conant Robt: Donne Joseph West William Owin Stephen Bull

Carolina

Yo^u^: are forthw^th^: to Admeasure & Lay out for ye Right Hono^ble^: Anthoney Earle of Shaftesbury one of y^e^: Lords Proprieto^rs^: of y^s^: Province three hundred twenty & five Acres of Land being part of a greater Quantety in some place not yett Layd out or Marked to be Layd out for any other Person or use & if y^e^. same happen upon any Navigable River or River Capable of being made Navigable yo^u^: are to allow onely ye fifth part of y^e^: Depth by y^e^: water side and a Certificate fully specyfying y^e^: bounds & scituation thereof to Return to us w^th^: all Convenient speede & for soe doeing this shall be yor: warrant Given under our hands at Charles Towne the Twenty Eight Day of 8^ber^: 1676/

To Capt: Maurice Mathewes Surveyo^r^:/ William Owen Joseph West Stephen Bull Robt: Donne

Carolina

Yo^u^: are forthw^th^: to Admeasure & Lay out for John Maverick one of ye settlers of y^s^: province One hundred acres of Land in some place not yett Layd out or Marked to be Layd out for any other person or use; and if y^e^. same happen upon any navigable River or River Capable of being made navigable yo^u^: are to allow onely y^e^: fifth ꝑ^t^: of y^e^: Depth upon y^e^: River Side, and a Certificate fully specifying y^e^. bounds and Scituation thereof yo^u^: are to Return to us w^th^: all Convenient speede hereof fayle not Dated y^e^: 2^d^: Decemb^r^: 1676/

To Capt: Stephen Bull Surveyo^r^:/

Carolina

You are forthwith to Admeasure and lay out for m^r^ John Clutterbuck one of the settlers of this province one hundred and seaventy acres of land in some place not yet layd out or marked to bee layd out for any other person or use And if the same happen upon any Navigable river or river capable of beinge made Navigable you are to allowe only ye fifth part of ye depth upon ye river side and a Certificate fully specifying ye boundes and scituation thereof you are to returne to us with all convenient speede hereof faile not Dated ye 1st: Decemb^{r}: i676/

Joseph: West

you are alsoe to deduct hereout the quantity of land heretofore layd out for m^{r} Clutterbuck for his tenn acres or towne lott/

And: Percival Will: Owen
Richard Conant

Carolina
you are forthwith to admeasure & lay out for James Greene one of ye settlers of this Province one hundred Acres of land in some place not yet laid out or marked to bee layd out for any other person or use and if ye same happen on any Navigable river or River Capable of being made navigable you are to allow only the fifth part of ye depth upon ye river side and a Certyficate fully specyfinge the boundes and scituation thereof, you are to returne to us wth all convenient speede hereof fayle not Dated ye 30th: Decem: i676/

To Capt: Maurice Matthewes Surveyr^{r}: — Joseph: West.

Richard Conant And: Percivall Will: Owen

Carolina./
You are forthwith to cause to be admeasured & laid out for Hen: Wood One hundred & Eighty acres of land, thee residue for himself & his wife arivinge in ye first fleett in some place not yet laid out or marked to bee laid out for any other person or use, and if ye same happen upon any Navigable river or capable of being made Navigable you are to allow only ye fifth part of ye depth thereof by ye watter side, and a Certyficate fully specifyinge the scituation & boundes thereof you are to returne to us wth. all convenient speed, and for yr soe doing this shall bee yr sufficient warr^{t}. given under our handes this 30th: day of Decemb^{r}: i674/

To Capt. Maurice Matthewes Survey^{r}. — Joseph West

And: Percivall
Richard Conant
Will Owen

Carolina/
You are forthwith to admeasure and lay out for John Boone one of ye settlers of this province One hundred Acres of Land in some place not yet Laid out or marked to bee Layd out for any other person or use, and if ye same happen upon any Navigable river or river capable of beinge made Navigable you are to allow only ye fifth part of ye depth upon ye river side, and a Certifycate fully specifyinge the boundes and Scituation thereof you are to returne to us wth all convenient speede hereof fayle not Dated ye 30th. Decm: i676

To Capt. Maurice Matthewes
Surveyr.

Joseph: West
And. Percivall
Richard Conant
Will:Owen

Carolina/
You are forthwith to admeasure & lay out for John Boone, one of ye settlers of ys. province, One hundred acres of land in some place not yet layd out or marked to be layd out for any other person or use. And if ye same happen upon any navigable river or River capable of beinge made Navigable you are to allow only the fifth part of ye depth upon ye River side, and a certifycate fully speecifyinge ye boundes and Scituation thereof; you are to returne to us wth all convenient speede hereof fayle not Dated ye 30th: Decemr: i676/

Joseph: West

To Capt. Maurice Matthewes
Surveyr:

And: Percivall
Richard Conant
Wm: Owen

Carolina/
You are forthwith to cause to be admeasured and layd out for Thomas Stanyan nine hundred & fifty Acres of land for himself his wife five children & foure servants arriving in May i675 in some place not yet laid out, or marked to bee layd out for any other person or use, and if ye saime happen on any Navigable river or any river capable of beinge maide Navigable, you are to allow only ye fifth part of ye depth thereof by ye watter side And a certifycate fully specifyinge the scituation and bounds thereof you are to returne to us wth: all convenient speed. And for yr so doinge this shall bee yr sufficient warrt. given under our hands at Charles Towne this thirteenth Jan: i676/

To Capt. Stephen: Bull
Surveyr

Carolina/
You are forthwith to admeasure and lay out for mr Peter Herne one of ye settlers of ye province seaven hundred & eighty acres of land in some place not yet layd out or marked to be laid out for any other person or use, and if ye same happen upon any Navigable River or River capable of being made Navigable you are to allow only ye fifth part of ye depth on ye river side, and a certifycate fully specifyinge ye boundes & scituation thereof you are to returne to us wth: all convenient speede, hereof fayle not Dated: 30 Decemb^{r}: i676

Carolina/ you are forthwith to admeasure & lay out for mr W^{m}: Murrell one of the settlers of this province hundred acres of land in some convenient place not yet laid out or marked to bee laid out for any other person or use, and if ye same happen upon any Navigable River or River capable of being made Navigable you are to allow only ye fifth part of ye depth on ye River side, and a certifycate fully specifying ye bounds & scituation thereof you are to returne to us wth— all convenient speed hereof fayle not Dated ye 30th— Decemb: i676/
To Capt. Maurice Matthewes
Survey^{r}

Carolina
Yo^{u}: are forthwth: to admeasure and Lay out for M^{r}: Morris Mathewes one of y^{e}: settlers of y^{s}: ꝑvince seaven hundred & fifty acres of Land in some place not yett Layd out or marked to be Layd out for any other ꝑson or use, And if y^{e}: same happen upon any navigable River or River Capable of being made navigable; yo^{u}: are to allow onely ye fifth ꝑ^{te}: of y^{e}: Depth upon y^{e}: River side; and a sertificate fully specifying y^{e}: bounds & scituation thereof; yo^{u}: are to Returne to us wth: all Convenient speede hereof fayle not Dated y^{e}: 30th: Day of December 1676/
To M^{r}: Stephen Bull
Surveyo^{r}:/

Joseph West
Richard Conant
Andrew Percivall
W^{m}: Owen

Carolina
Yo^{u}: are forthwth: to Admeasure and Lay out for M^{r}: Thomas Eakins one of ye settlers of y^{s}. ꝑvince one hundred acres of Land in some place not yett Laid out or Marked to be Laid out for any other ꝑson or use; And if y^{e}: same happen upon any navigable

River or River Capable of being made navigable, yo^{u}: are to allow onely y^{e}: fifth ꝑ^{te}: of y^{e}: Depth upon y^{e}: River side; and a Certificate fully specifying y^{e}: bounds and scituation thereof; yo^{u}: are to Return to us. wth: all Convenient speede hereof fayle not Dated ye 30th: Decemb^{r}: 1676/

To Capt: Stephen Bull
Surveyo^{r}:

Joseph West
Andrew Percivall
Richard Conant
Will: Owen:

Carolina

Yo^{u}: are forthwth: to Admeasure and Lay out for Barnaby Bull one of y^{e}: settlers of y^{s}: ꝑvince One hundred & fifty acres of Land in some place not yett Layd out or marked to be Layd out for any other ꝑson or use; And if y^{e}: same happen upon any Navigable River or River Capable of being made Navigable yo^{u}: are to allow onely ye fifth ꝑ^{te}. of y^{e}: Depth upon ye River side; And a Certivicate fully specyfying y^{e}: bounds & scituation thereof; yo^{u}: are to Return to us wth: all Convenient speede; hereof fayle not Dated y^{e}: 30th Day of January 1676/7

To Capt: Maurice Mathewes
Surveyo^{r}.//

Joseph West
Andrew Percivall Richard Conant
Will: Owen:

Carolina

Yo^{u}: are forthwth: to Admeasure & Lay out for Tho: Turpin one of ye settlers of y^{s} ꝑvince for himselfe & one Servt: by name Philly White one hundred & seaventy acres of Land in Some place not yet Layd out or marked to be Layd out for any other ꝑson or use And if ye same happen upon any Navigable River or River Capable of being made navigable yo^{u}: are to allow onely y^{e}: ffifth ꝑ^{t} of ye Depth upon y^{e}: River side; And a Certificate fully specifying ye bounds & scituation thereof, yo^{u}: are to Return to us wth: all Convenient speede hereof fayle not Dated y^{e}: 30th: Day of January 1676/7

To M^{r}: Stephen Bull
Surveyo^{r}:/

Richard Conant Joseph West
Andrew Percivall

Carolina

Yo^{u}: are forthwth: to Admeasure and Lay out for Capt: Hen: Bryan one of ye settlers of y^{s} ꝑvince Eleaven hundred acres of Land in Some place not yett Layd out or marked to be Layd out for a other ꝑson or use; And if ye same happen upon any navigable River or River Capable of being made navigable yo^u: are to allow onely ye fifth ꝑ^{te}: of ye Depth upon ye River side; and a Certificate fully Specyfying y^e: bounds and Scituation thereof yo^u: are to Return to us w^{th}: all Convenient speede; hereof fayle not Dated y^e: 30th: Day of January: 1676/7

To Capt: Maurice Mathewes Surveyo^r/

Joseph West

W^m: Owen Richard Conant

Ste: Bull

Carolina

Yo^u: are $forthw^{th}$: to Admeasure and Lay out for M^r: Nicholas Carteret one of y^e settlers of y^s ꝑvince Seaven hundred acres of Land in Some place not yett Layd out or marked to be Layd out for any other ꝑson or use; And if y^e: Same happen upon any navigable River or River Capable of being made navigable yo^u: are to allow onely y^e: fifth ꝑ^{te}: of ye Depth upon y^e: River side, and a Certificate fully specifying y^e: bounds & scituation thereof yo^u: are to Return to us w^{th}: all Convenient speede, hereof fayle not Dated y^e: 30th: day of Janua^{r}y: 1676/7

To Capt: Maurice Mathewes Surveyo^r./

Joseph West

Richard Conant

Wm Owen Ste: Bull

You are $forthw^{th}$ to Admeasure and lay out for Margret White one of the free persons of this provinc seaventy acres of Land in som place not yet Layd out or m^{r}ked to be Layd out for any other person or use alloweing only the fifth part thereof by ye waterside if it happen to be upon any Navigable river or river Capable to be made Navigable, and a Certificat fully specifyeing ye bounds and scituacon thereof to returne to us with all Convenjent speede Dated y^e 30th day of Novemb^r. i676:

To Capt Steven Bull Surveyr:

Joseph West

Mauric Mathews

Robt Donn:

And^{r}w piercevall

Will: Owen

You are $furthw^{th}$ to Admeasure and lay out for Andrew piercevall Esqr fi̊ve hundred acres of Land in part of a greater Quantitie due to him in som place not yet Layd out or marked to be Layd out for any other person or use and if it shall happen upon any Navigable river or river capable to be made Navigable you are to allow onlie the fift part of ye depth thereof by ye waterside and a Certificat fully speci fyeing ye bounds and Scituacon thereof you are to returne to us wit all Convenient speed Given undr or hands att Charles Towne ye 27t Day of Janry i676:

To mr Maurice Mathews
Surveyr/

Joseph West
Step: Bull
Robt Donne
Will: Owen

Carolina SS:

You are forthwith to admeasure & lay out for Edward Evans on of the ffreemen of this Province Seaventy Acres of Land in som place not yet laid out or marked to be laid out for any other Persoı or use; And if it shall happen upon any Navigable River or Rive to be made Navigable you are to allow only the fifth part of th depth thereof by ye waterside, & a certificate fully specifying th bounds & situation thereof you are to returne to us with all Con venient speed. Given under our hands at Charles Towne ye 24t Mar: i677:

To Capt Morris Mathews Surveyr:

Joseph West
Robt Donne
Rich: Conant
Will: Owen

Carolina: SS:

You are forthwith to admeasure & lay out for Richard Hill one o the ffreemen of this Pvince one hundred Acres of Land in some place not yet laid out or marked to be laid out for any other Persor or use, & if it shall happen upon any Navigable River or River capa- ble to be made navigable, you are to allow only ye fifth part of y depth thereof by the waterside, & a Certificate fully specifying the situation thereof you are to returne to us with all Convenient speed Given under our hands at Charles Towne ye 24° Mar :1677:

To Capt Morris Mathews Surveyr:

Carolina SS:

You are forthwith to admeasure & Lay out for Willm Chambers one of the ffreemen of this Pvince one hundred Acres of Land in some place not yet laid out or marked to be laid out for any other Persor or use, & if it shall happen upon any Navigable River, or River capa- ble to be made Navigable you are to allow only ye fifth part of y depth thereof by ye waterside, & a Certificate fully specifying the bounds & situation thereof you are to returne to us with all Convenient speed Given under our hands at Charles Towne ye 3th

To Capt. M: Mathews Survey^r

Joseph West:
Will: Owen: Richard Conant:
Robt Donne:

Carolina SS:

You are forthwith to admeasure & lay out for mr Tho: Stanjon one of the ffreemen of this Province foure hundred & fiftie acres of land in some place not yet laid out or marked to be laid out for any other Person or use; & if it shall happen upon any Navigable River, or River capable to be made Navigable you are to allow only ye fifth part of ye depth thereof by ye waterside, & a certificate fully specifying the bounds & situation thereof you are to returne to us with all Convenient speed. Given under our hands at Charles Towne ye 31th of Mar: i677:

To Capt Maurice Mathews Survey^r:

Joseph West
R Donn
Rich Connant
Will: Owen:

Carolina SS:

You are forthwith to admeasure & lay out for m^r Tho: Stanjon one of ye ffreemen of this Province five hundred acres of land in some place not yet laid out or marked to be laid out for any other Person or use; & if it shall happen upon any Navigable River or River capable to be made Navigable y^u are to allow only ye fifth part of ye depth thereof by ye waterside, & a certificate fully specifying the bounds & situation thereof you are to returne to us with all Convenient Speed Given under our hands at Charles Towne ye 31th day of Mar i677:

To Capt Morris Mathews: Survey^r

Joseph West
Robert Donn:
Will: Owen Rich Connant

Carolina SS:

You are forthwith to admeasure & lay out for John Huddleston one of ye ffreemen of this Province One hundred acres of Land: in some Place not yet laid out or marked to be laid out for any other Person or use; & if it shall happen upon any Navigable River or

River capable to be made Navigable you are to allow only ye fifth part of ye depth thereof by ye waterside; & a certificate fully specifying the bounds & situation thereof y^u are to returne to us withall Convenient speed. Given under our hands at Charles Towne ye 31th of Mar: i677:

To Capt Morris Mathews Survey^r:

J West
Robt Donne
Rich Connant
Will: Owen.

Carolina

You are forthwith to admeasure & lay out for John Sympson one of the ffreemen of this Province five hundred & fiftie acres in some place not yet laid out or marked to be laid out for any other Person or use, & if it shall happen upon any Navigable River or River capable to be made Navigable y^u are to allow only ye fifth part of the depth thereof by the water side & a Certificate fully specifying the bounds & situation thereof you are to returne to us with all Convenient speed Given under our hands at Charles Towne ye 31th of Mar i677:

To Capt Steven Bull Surveyr:

Joseph West
Rich Conant
M :Mathews: Will :Owen:

Carolina

You are forthwith to admeasure & lay out for Morgan Morris one of the ffreemen of this Province seaventie acres of land in some place not yet laid out or marked to be laid out for any other Person or use, & if it shall happen upon any Navigable River, or River Capable to be made Navigable you are to allow only ye fifth part of the depth thereof by ye waterside, & a Certificate fully specifying the bounds & situation thereof you are to returne to us with all Convenient speed. Given under our hands at Charles Towne ye 31th of Mar: 1677:

To Capt Steven Bull Surveyr

Carolina

Y^u are forthw^th to admeasure & lay out for John Mells one of the ffreemen of this Pvince seaventie acres of land in some place not yet laid out or marked to be laid out for any other Person or Use, & if it shall happen upon a Navigable River, or River Capable to be made Navigable y^u are to allow only ye fifth part of the depth thereof by the waterside, & a Certificate fully specifying the bounds & situation thereof you are to returne to us wth all Convenient speed. Given under our hands at Charles Towne ye 31 of mar 1677

To Capt Steven Bull

Jo: West:

M Mathews

Will: Owen

Rich: Connant:

Carolina SS:

Y^u are forthw^th to admeasure & lay out for Timothie Biggs one of the ffreemen of this Pvince three hundred acres of Land in some place not yet laid out or marked to be laid out for any other Person or use & if it shall happen upon any Navigable River or River Capable to be made Navigable you are to allow only the fifth part of ye depth thereof by the water side, & a Certificate fully specifyyng the bounds & situation thereof y^u are to returne to us with all Convenient speed. Given under our hands at Charles Towne.

To Capt Maurice Mathews: Survy^r:

Joseph West

Will: Owen: Rich Conant:

Robt Donn:

Carolina SS:

Y^u are forthw^th. to admeasure & Lay out for Tho: Rose One of ye ffreemen of this Pvince five hundred acres of land in some place not yet Laid out or marked to be Laid out for any other Person or Use; & if it shall happen upon any Navigable River, or River Capable to be made Navigable you are to allow only ye fifth part of the depth thereof by ye water side, & a Certificate fully specifying the bouds & situation thereof y^u are to returne to us wth all Convenient speed. Given under our hands at Charles Towne

To Capt Steven Bull, Survey^r:

Joseph West

Mau Mathews

Rob: Done

Will Owen

Carolina SS

Y^u are forthw^th to admeasure and lay out for Cri: Portman Gen^tle: One of ye ffreemen of this Pvince seaven hundred & sixty acres of Land in some place not yet laid out or marked to be laid out for any other Person or Use; & if it shall happen upon any Navigable River or River Capable to be made Navigable, y^u are to allow only ye fifth

part of ye depth thereof by ye waterside, & a Certificate fully specifying the bounds & situation thereof y^u^ are to returne to us w^t^ all Convenient Speed. Given under our hands at Charles Towne this 21 day of Ap^l^: 1677—
To Capt: Maurice Matthewes
Suryey^r^

Carolina/
You are forthwith to admeasure and lay out for Hamlett Kemp one of the freemen of this province one hundred acres of Land in some place not yet laid out or marked to bee laid out for any other person or use, and if it shall happen upon any Navigable River or River capable of being maide Navigable, you are to allow only the fifth part of ye depth theirof by ye watterside, and a certificate fully specifyinge the boundes & scituation theirof you are to returne to us, wth all convenient speed Given under our handes at Charles Towne this 2i day of Ap^r^: 1677/
Neverthes you are thereout to deduct y^t^ part or portion allowed unto him as a Towne Lott.—
To Capt Steven Bull: Survey^r^:

Jo: West:
Robt Donn:
M: Mathews
Richd Connant

Carolina/
You are forthwith to measure and laye out for John Stevenson freeman of this province one towne lott in ye Oyster point observinge the forme & method established and designed for the buildinge of the towne y^r^: and not prejudicinge the lines of any lands lying next ye said lott and a certyficate fully specifying the scituation and boundes thereof you are to returne to us wth all convenient speed Given under our handes at Charles Towne this 2i^st^ day of Ap^r^: 1677/
To Capt: Mau: Matthews
Capt Ste: Bull
& Ste: Wheelewright
} suryey^r^s: W^m^. Owen: Joseph: West
Richard Conant
Ro Donne

Carolina/
You are forth with to admeasure and lay out for Mary Benson one Towne lott in ye Oyster point observinge the forme and method established and designed for ye buildinge of ye towne their and not prejudicinge ye lines of any lands lying next the said lott, And a

certyficate fully specifyinge the scituation and boundes theirof you are to returne to us wth all convenient speed, Given under our handes at Charles Towne this 2ist: day of Apr: i677/

To

Carolina./
You are forthwith to admeasure and lay out for Hamlett Kemp one of thee freemen of this province one towne lott in ye Oyster pointe observinge ye forme & method established & designed for ye buildinge of ye towne their, and not prejudicinge the lines of any lands lyinge next ye said lott and a certyficate fully specifyinge the scituation and boundes theirof you are to returne to us wth: all convenient speed given under our hands at Charles Towne this 2ist. day of Apr: i677/

To Capt M: Mathews: Capt Steven Bull and Steven Wheelewright	Surveyrs	Jo: West: M: Mathews Rich Conant Ro. Donn

Carolina/
You are forthwith to admeasure and lay out for Dan: Lacey one of thee freemen of this province two hundred and forty acres of Land beinge the proportion allotted bye ye Lords: Concesss: for himself his wife and child, in some place not yet laid out or marked to be laid out for any other person or use and if it shall happen upon any Navigable River or River capable of being maid Navigable you are to allow only ye fifth part of ye depth theirof by ye watter side and a certyficate fully specyfinge the boundes & scituation theirof you are to returne to us wth. all convenient speed, Given under our handes at Charles Towne this 2ist: day of Apr: i677/
To Capt: Ste: Bull
Surveyr

Carolina/: You are forthwth: to admeasure & lay out for Jno: Mavericke one of the ffreemen of this province two hundred & forty Acres of Land in some place not yet layd out or marked to bee layd out for any other person or use & if it shall happen upon any Navigable River, or River capable to be made Navigable you are to allow only ye fifth part of ye depth theirof by ye watter side & a certyficate specifying the bounds & scituation yrof you are to returne to us w^{th}: all convenient speed, Given under our handes at Charles Towne this 2ist: day of Ap^{r}: i677/

To

Carolina:/ pursuent to an ord^{r}: of councill Dated ye 24° March: Last you are to admeasure and lay out for mr Tim^{o}: Biggs all y^{t} vacant Land scituate upon Ashley river and lyinge betweene ye land of Tho: Hunt to ye South eastward and the plantation and Land of W^{m}: Murrell to ye Northward Contayninge about 300 acres of Land be it more or less and a certifycate fully specifyinge y^{e} marks boundes and exact scituation thereof to returne to us with all convenient speed Given under our handes this 2ist: Day of Ap^{r}: i677/

Joseph West
Ro: Donne Ste: Bull
And^{r}: Percivall

To Capt: Ma: Matthewes
$Survey^{r}$/

Carolina/ you are forthwith to admeasure and lay out for Robt. Daniell $gent^{le}$: one of thee freemen of this province fifteene hundred Acres of Land in some place not yet laid out or marked to bee laid out for any other person or use and if it shall happen on any Navigable River or River capable of being made Navigable you are to allow only y^{e} fifth part of y^{e} depth theirof by the watter side, and a certyficate fully specifyinge the boundes and scituation y^{r} of you are to returne to us w^{th}: all convenient speed, given under our handes at Charles Towne this 2ist: day of Ap^{r}: i677:—

To mr Jno Yeamans
Suryeyr:

Joseph West
Ste: Bull
Mau: Mathews Rich Conant

Carolina/ you are forthwith to admeasure and lay out for $m^{r}s$: Mary Benson one of y^{e} setlers of this province two hundred and seaventy Acres of land in some place not yet laid out nor marked to bee laid out for any other person or use, and if y^{e} same happen upon any Navigable River or River Capable of being maide Navigable you are then to allow only the fifth part of ye depth to ye watterside and a certyficate fully specifyinge the boundes and scituation thereof to returne to us w^{th}: all convenient speed: Given under our hands at Charles towne y^{e} 28th: of Ap^{r}: i677/

To Steven Wheelewright
$Suryey^{r}$/

Carolina/: You are forthwith to admeasure and lay out for W^m: Jackson one of the freemen of this province seaventy Acres of land in some place not yet laid out or marked to bee laid out for any other person or use, and if y^e same happen upon any Navigable River or River capable of being maide Navigable you are to allow only ye fifth part of ye depth y^rof by ye watterside, and a certyficate fully specifyinge ye scituation and boundes theirof you are to returne to us wth all Convenient speed given under our handes at Charles Towne this 28th Ap^r: i677/
To Step: Wheelewright
Suryer^r./

Carolina/ You are forthwith to admeasure and lay out for Mary: MacMarvill and her sonn one of the setlers of this province one hundred and seaventy Acres of land in some place not yet laid out or marked to bee laid out for any other person or use, and if ye same happen upon any Navigable river or river capable of being maide Navigable you are to allow only ye fifth part of ye depth yrof by ye watter side, and a certyficate fully specifyinge ye scituation and boundes theirof you are to returne to us w^th: all Convenient speed. Given under our handes at Charles Towne this 28th: Ap^r: i677/
To Step. Wheelwright
Suryev^r/

Carolina/ you are forthwith to admeasure and lay out for Mary M^c:Marvill one Towne Lott in ye Oyster point observinge the forme and method Established and designed for ye buildinge of ye towne their and not prejudicinge the lines of any Land lying next ye said lott and a certyficate fully specifyinge the scituation and boundes y^rof you are to returne to us w^th: all convenient speed, Given under our hands at Charles Towne this 28th: of Ap^r: i677:—
To: Capt^t: Mau: Matthews }
Capt: Step: Bull } Suryev^rs
& Step: Wheelwright }

Carolina/ you are forthwith to admeasure and lay out for Jno: Harteley one towne lott in ye Oyster pointe observinge ye forme and method Established and designed for ye buildinge of ye Towne y^r: and not prejudicinge ye lines of any Lands lyinge next ye said lott and a certyficate fully specifyinge the scituation and boundes thereof you are to returne to us w[th]: all convenient speed Given under our handes at Charles Towne this 28[th]: day of Ap[r]: i677—

To Cap[t]: Mau: Mathews
Cap[t] Step. Bull
& Step: Wheelwright } Suryev[r]s

Carolina: you are forthwith to admeasure and lay out for Tho: ffluelline one of the Inhabitants of this province seaventy Acres of Land in in y[e] right of his wife Jane in some place not yet laid out or marked to bee laid out for any other person or use and if y[e] same happen upon any Navigable River or River capable of being made Navigable you are to allow only y[e] fifth part of y[e] depth thereof by y[e] watter side and a certyficate fully specifyinge the scituation and boundes thereof you are to returne to us w[th]: all Convenient speed: Given under our hands at Charles Towne this 28th: Ap[r]: i677/

To Step: Wheelwright
Suryev[r].

Carolina—In pursuance to an order of Councell bearing date the 2i[st] of Aprill 1677 you are forthwith to Admeasure and lay out for Tho: Stevenson: one of the setlers of the province six hundred Acres of Land in some place not yet Layd out or marked to be Layd out for any other person or use and if the same happen upon any navigable River or any River Capable of being made Navigable you are to Allow only the fifth part of the depth thereof by the water side and a Certyficate fully the scituation and bounds thereof you are to Returne to us with all Convenient speed Given under our hands at Charles Towne this xxviiith of Aprill 1677:/

To M[r] John Yeamans
Surveyo[r]:

Carolina/ You are forthwith to admeasure and lay out unto Rob[t]: Lewis and Mary his wife the Quantity of one hundred Acres of Land beinge y[e] right & proper dew of y[e] said Mary Arivinge here in y[e] yeare i675 in some place not yet laid out or marked to bee laid out for any other person or use and if y[e] same happen upon any Navigable River or River capable of being maide Navigable you are to allow only y[e] fifth part of y[e] depth by ye watter side, and a Certyfycate fully specyfying the boundes and scituation theirof you are to returne to us w[th]: all convenient speed, Given under our handes at Charles Towne y[e] 4th: May: i677

To Cap[t] Maurice Matthews
Sury[r]/

Richard Conant Joseph West
Ste: Bull John Godfrey

Carolina/ you are forthwith to admeasure and lay out for Roger Nicolls one of thee freemen of this province five hundred & tenn Acres of Land in some place not yet laid out or marked to bee laid out for any other person or use, and if ye same happen on any Navigable river or River capable of being maid Navigable you are to allow only ye fifth part of ye depth theirof by ye watter side, and a certyficate fully specifyinge ye boundes & scituation yrof you are to returne to us wth. all convenient Speed Given under our handes at Charles Towne this i9^th^ may: i677/

To Capt. Maurice Mathews Suryey^r^

Joseph West
Mau: Mathews John Godfrey
Richard Conant

Carolina/ you are forthwith to admeasure and lay out for Jno: Hooper & Hester his wife in ye right of Tho: Ingram in ye Right of Tho: Laine ffreemen of this province one hundred and fifty Acres of Land in some place not yet laid out or marked to be laid out for any other person or use and if ye same happen on any Navigable River or River capable of being maid Navigable you are to allow only ye fifth part of ye depth theirof by ye watter side and a certyficate fully specifying the boundes and scituation yrof you are to returne to us w^th^: all convenient speed. Given under our handes at Charles Towne this i9 day of May i677/

To Capt Maurice Mathews Suryeyr

Wm Owen Joseph West
Richard Conant John Godfrey

Carolina/ you are forthwith to admeasure and lay out for W^m^: Cooke one of thee ffreemen of this province seaventie acres of Land in some place not yet laid out or marked to bee laid out for any other person or use, and if ye same happen on any Navigable River or River capable of being maide Navigable you are to allow only ye fifth part of ye depth yrof by ye watter side and a certyficate fully specifying ye boundes and scituation yrof you are to returne to us wth all convenient Speed Given under our handes at Charles Towne this i9^th^: May: i677/

To mr Ste: Wheelewright Suryey^r^

Joseph West
Wm Owen: Richard Conant
Ste: Bull

Carolina/ you are forthwith to admeasure and lay out for Phill Orrill one of ye freemen of this province seaventie Acres of Land, in some place not yet laid out or marked to bee laid out for any other person or use, and if ye same happen on any Navigable River or River capable of being maid Navigable you are to allow only ye fifth part of ye depth yrof by ye watterside and a certyficate fully specyfyinge ye boundes and scituation yrof you are to returne to us w^th^: all convenient speed, Given under our hands at Charles Towne this i9 day of May i677

To Capt Ste: Bull Suryey^r^: | Mau: Mathews Joseph West Richard Conant John Godfrey

Carolina:/ you are forthwith to admeasure and lay out for James Jones one of thee freemen of this Province in ye right of his wife eightie Acres of Land in some place not yet laid out or marked to bee laid out for any other person or use, and if ye same happen on any Navigable River or River capable of being maid Navigable you are to allow only ye fifth part of ye depth yrof by ye watterside, and a certyficate fully specyfying ye bounds and scituation yrof you are to returne to us wth all Convenient speed Given under our handes at Charles Towne this i9 May: i677/

To mr. John Yeamans Suryey^r^ | Mau: Mathews Joseph West Richard Conant John Godfrey

Carolina/ you are forthwith to admeasure and lay out for Jno: Collins one of thee freemen of this province one hundred and fifty Acres of Land in some place not yet laid out, or marked to bee laid out for any other person or use, and if ye same happen on any Navigable River or River capable of being maid Navigable you are to allow only ye fifth part of ye depth yrof by ye watter side, and a certyfycate fully specyfying ye boundes and scituation yrof you are to returne to us w^th^: all convenient speed Given under our hands at Charles Towne this i9^th^: day of May: i677/

Capt. Mau: Mathewes Suryey^r^. | And^r^ Percivall Joseph West Richard Conant John Godfrey

Carolina/ persuant to an order of Councill Dated ye 30th: Ap^r^: i677 you are forthwith to admeasure and lay out for Jonah Lynch one of thee freemen of this Province six hundred Acres of Land in some place not yet laid out or marked to bee laid out for any other person or use, and if ye same happen on any Navigable River or River capable of being maid Navigable you are to allow only ye fifth part of ye depth yrof by ye watter side, and a certyfycate fully specyfyinge ye boundes and scituation yrof you are to returne to us w^th^:

all convenient speed Given under our handes at Charles Towne this 21st: May: 1677/

To Capt: Ste: Bull
Suryeyr:

Andr. Percivall Joseph: West
Richard Conant
John Godfrey

Carolina You are forthwith to Admeasure and Lay out for Tho: ffluellin one of the freemen of this province one hundred Acres of Land in in the right of Jane his wife Executrix to the last will and testament of James Birch deceased in some place not Layd out for any other person or use and if ye same happen upon any navigable River or any River Capable of being made navigable you are to allow only the fifth part of the depth to be ye breadth by the water side and a Certyficate fully specyfing the scituation and bounds therof you are to returne to us with all convenient speed Given under our hands at Charles Towne this 16th of June 1677

To Steph: Whelewright
Surveyor

Joseph West
Mau: Mathews John Godfrey
Rich Connant Step: Bull

Carolina: You are forthwith to Admeasure and Lay out for Mr Tho Smyth[1]— —one of the freemen of this province one hundred Acres in some place not yet Layd out or marked to be Layd out for any other person or use and if the same happen upon any navigable River or any River capable of being made Navigable you are to allow only only allow ye fifth part of the depth to be the breadth by the water side and a Certyficate fully specyfying the scituation and bounds therof you are to returne to us with all Convenient speed Given under our hands at Charles Towne this xvith day of June: 1677

To Capt Steph Bull
Surveyor

Mau: Mathews Joseph: West
Rich: Conant John: Godfrey

Carolina

You are forthwith to Admeasure and Lay out for Jno: Carrell one of the freemen of this province in right of his wife 70 Acres—of Land in some place not yet Layd out or marked to be Layd out for any other person or use and if the same happen upon any navigable River or any River Capable of being made Navigable you are to allow only one fifth part of the depth to be the breadth by the water

[1]The index to the volume gives him as "Doctor Tho: Smyth".

side and a Certyficate fully specyfying the scituation and bounds therof you are to Returne to to us with all Convenient speed Given under our hands at Charles towne this 16 day of June 1677

To Steph Whelewright, Surveyo[r] Rich Conant Joseph West John: Godfrey

Carolina—You are forthwith to Admeasure and Lay out for Edward Wilson one of ye freemen of this province seaventy Acres of Land in some place not yet Layd out or marked to be Laid out for any other person or use and if the same happen upon any Navigable River or any River Capable of being made Navigable you are to allow only the fifth part of the depth therof by the water side and a Certyfycate fully specyfy the scituation and bounds therof you are to returne to us with all Convenient speed Given under our hands att Charles towne this ii[th] day of August 1677/

To Steph: Whelewright Surveyo[r] Rich: Connant Jos: West Mau: Matthews John: Godfrey

Carolina You are forthwith to Admeasure and lay out for Leiu[t] Coll John Godfrey one of ye settlers of this province five hundred Acres of Land in some place not yet Layd out or marked to be Layd out for any other ꝑson or use and if ye same happen upon any Navigable River or any River Capable of being made Navigable you are to allow only one fifth part of ye depth therof by ye water side and a Certyfycate fully specyfying the scituation and bounds therof you are to returne to us with all Convenient speed Given under our hands at Charles towne this ii[th]. day of August 1677/

To Steph: Whelewright Surveyo[r] Joseph: West Rich: Connant Mau: Matthews

Carolina You are forthwith to Admeasure and Lay out for Robt George in y[e] right of Isabell his wife seaventy Acres of Land in some place not yet Layd out or marked to be laid out for any other person or use & if the same happen upon any Navigable River or any River Capable of being made Navigable you are to allow only ye fifth part of the depth therof by the water side and a Certyfycate fully specyfy y[e] scituation and bounds therof you are to returne to us with all Convenient speed Given under our hands at Charles Towne this ii[th] day of August 1677/

To Steph: Whelewright Surveyo[r] Richard: Connant Joseph: West Mau: Matthews John: Godfrey

Carolina: You are forth with to Admeasure and Lay out for Rich Morgan one hundred Acres of Land, one of the freemen of this province, in some place not yet Layd out or marked to be Laid out for any other person or use and if the same happen upon a Navigable River or a River Capable of being made Navigable you are to allow only one fifth part of ye depth therof by ye water side and a Certyfycate fully specyfying ye scituation and bounds therof you are to returne to us with all Convenient speed Given under our hands at Charles Towne this iith day of August 1677/

To Steph: Whelewright Surveyor: — Mau Matthews, Jos: West, Will: Owen, John: Godfrey

Carolina/You are forthwith to Admeasure and Lay out for Thomas Thompson one of ye first settlers of this province four hundred fifty and Nine Acres of Land in some place not yet Layd out or marked to be Layd out for any other person or use and if the same happen upon a Navigable River or a River Capable of being made Navigable you are to allow only ye fifth part of the depth therof by the water side and a Certyfycate fully specyfying ye scituation and bounds therof you are to returne to us with all convenient speed Given under our hands at Charles Towne this iith day of August 1677

To Mr Steph: Whelewright Surveyor — Rich Connant, Jos: West, Will Owen, John: Godfrey

Carolina/You are forthwith to Admeasure and Lay out for Jno Bullen one of the freemen of this province one hundred Acres of Land in some place not yet Layd out or marked to be Layd out for any other ꝑson or use and if the same happen upon a Navigable River or a Rive— Capable of being made Navigable—you are to allow only ye fifth part of ye depth therof by the water side and a Certyfycate fully specÿfÿing the scituation and bounds therof you are to returne to us with all convenient speed Given under our hands at Charles towne this iith day of August: 1677

To Mr Steph: Whelewright Surveyor — Rich Conant, Jos West, Will Owen, John: Godfrey

Carolina/ You are forthwith to Admeasure and Lay out for Matthew English thirty Acres of Land in some place not yet Layd out or marked to be Layd out for any other person or use & if the same happen upon a Navigable River or a River Capable of being made Navigable you are to allow a fifth part of the depth therof by the water side and a Certyfycate fully specyfying the scituation and bounds therof you are to returne to us with all Convenient Speed Given under our hands this iith day of August 1677/

To Mr Steph: Whelewright Surveyor — Rich Connant, Will Owen, Joseph West, John Godfrey

Carolina: You are forth with to Admeasure and Lay out for Edmund Aggis one of the freemen of this province one hundred Acres of Land in some convenient place not yet Layd out or marked to be Laid out for any other person or use and if the same happen upon a Navigable River or a River Capable of being made Navigable you are to allow only ye fifth part of ye depth therof by the water side & a Certyfycate fully specyfying ye situation and bounds therof you are to returne to us with all convenient speed; Given under our hands at Charles towne this iith day of August 1677/

To Mr Steph: Whelewright Surveyor — Richard Connant, Will: Owen, Joseph: West, John: Godfrey

Carolina: You are forthwith to Admeasure and Lay out for Robert Tomes one of the Settlers of this province two Hundred Acres of Land being in right of himselfe and his wife in some convenient place not yet Layd out or marked to be Layd out for any other person or use; & if the same happen upon a Navigable River or any River capable of being made navigable you are to allow only the fifth part of the depth bÿ ye water side and a Certyfycate fully specyfying the scituation and boundes therof you are to returne to us with all Convenient speede Given under our handes att Charles Towne this iith Day of August 1677

To Mr Steph: Whelewright, Surveyor — Rich: Connant, Will Owen:, Jos: West, John: Godfrey

Carolina

You are forthwith to Admeasure and Lay out for Tho: Holton one of the freemen of this province fifty Acres of Land in some place not yet Layd out or marked to be Layed out for any other person or use and if the same happen upon a Navigable River or a River Capable of being made Navigable you are to allow only one fifth part of the depth therof by the water side and a Certyfycate fully specyfying ye scituation and bounds therof you are to returne to us with all Convenient speede Given under our hands at Charles Towne this iith day of August 1677

To Capt Morrice Matthews Surveyor — Rich Connant, Andrew percivall:, Jos: West, John: Godfrey

Carolina/ You are forthwith to Admeasure and Lay out for Robt Hunt one of the freemen of this province one hundred Acres of Land in some place not yet Layd out or marked to be Layd out for any other person or use and if the same happen upon any Navigable River or any River Capable of being made Navigable you are to Allow only ye fifth part of ye depth by the water side and a Certify-cate fully specyfying the scituation and bounds therof you are to returne to us with all Convenient speed Given under our hands at Charles Towne this iith day of August 1677/

To Capt Morrice Matthews Surveyor — Rich Connant, Mau: Matthews, Jos: West, John: Godfrey

Carolina. You are forthwith to Admeasure and Lay out for Abraham Smith one of the freemen of this province one hundred Acres of Land in some place not yet Layd out or marked to be Layd out for any other person or use and if the same happen upon a Navigable River or a River Capable of being made Navigable you are to allow one fifth part of the depth therof by the water side and a Certyficate fully Specyfying the scituation and bounds therof you are to returne to us with all Convenient Speed Given under our hands att Charles Towne this iith day of August 1677/

To Capt Morrice Matthews Surveyor — Rich Connant, Andrew percivall, Joseph West, John: Godfrey

Carolina:/ You are forthwith to Admeasure and Lay out for Hugh Lewes one of the freemen of this province seaventy Acres of Land in some place not yet Layd out or marked to be Layd out for any other person or use and if the same happen upon a Navigable River or a River Capable of being made Navigable you are to allow only the fifth part of the depth therof by ye water side and a Certyfycate fully specyfying the scituation and bounds therof you are to returne to us with all Convenient speed Given under our hands at Charles towne this iith day of August 1677

To Capt Morrice Matthewes Surveyor — Rich: Connant, Mau: Matthews, Jos: West, John: Godfrey

Carolina—You are forthwith to Admeasure and Lay out for Tho Hunt & Jane his wife one hundred and forty Acres of Land in some place not yet Layd out or marked to be Layd out for any other person or use and if the same happen upon a Navigable River or a River Capable of being made Navigable you are to allow only one fifth part of the depth therof by the water side and a Certyficate fully specyfying ye scituation and bounds therof you are to returne to us with all Convenient speed Given under our hands at Charles Towne this ii^th day of August[1] 1677/

To Capt Morrice Matthewes Surveyo^r — Richard Connant, Andrew percivall, Jos West, Jo: Godfrey

Carolina You are forthwith to Admeasure and Lay out for Jno Horton in ye right of his wife Mary seaventy Acres of Land in some place not yet Layd out or marked to be Layd out for any other person or use and if the same happen upon a Navigable River or a River capable of being made Navigable you are to to allow only ye fifth part of ye depth by water side and a Certyfycate fully specyfying the scituation and bounds therof you are to returne to us with all convenient speed Given under our hands at Charles Towne this ii^th day of August 1667[2]

To Capt Morrice Matthews — Jos: West

Carolina/ You are forthwith to Admeasure and Lay out for Stephen Whelewright one of ye freemen of this province one hundred Acres of Land in some place not yet Layd out or marked to be Layd out for any other person or use and if the same happen upon a Navigable River or a River Capable of being made Navigable you are to allow only ye fifth part of ye depth therof by the water side and a Certyfycate fully specyfying ye scituation and bounds therof you are to returne to us with all Convenient speed Given under our hands at Charles Towne this ii^th day of August 1677

To Capt Morrice Matthewes — Rich: Connant, Andrew percivall, Jos West, John: Godfrey

Carolina: You are forthwith to Admeasure and Lay out for Jno Horton one of ye settlers of this province one hundred Acres of Land in some place not yet Layd out or marked to be Layd out for any other ꝑson or use and if the same happen upon a Navigable River or a River Capable of being made Navigable you are to allow only one fifth part of ye depth therof by ye water side and a Certyficate fully specyfying ye scituation and bounds therof you are to

---

[1] "30th day of Oct" is written over "iith day of August."

[2] A slip of the pen for 1677, of course.

returne to us with all Convenient speed Given under our hands at Charles Towne This iith day of August 1677/

To Capt Morrice Matthew Surveyor — Andrew percivall, Jos: West, Jno: Godfrey, Jon Godfrey

Carolina/You are forthwith to Admeasure and Lay out for John: Williams one of the freemen of this province one hundred Acres in some place not yet Layd out or marked to be Layd out for any other person or use and if the same happen upon a Navigable River or a River Capable of being made Navigable you are to allow only ye fifth part of ye depth therof by the water side and a Certyfycate fully specyfying ye scituation and bounds therof you are to returne to us with all Convenient speed Given under our hand at Charles Towne this iith day of August 1677/

To Capt Morrice Matthews Surveyor — Will Owen, Jos: West, Richard Connant, Jno Godfrey

Carolina/ You are forthwith to Admeasure and Lay out for Jno Hoppins one of ye freemen of this province one hundred Acres of Land in some place not yet Layd out or marked to be Layd out for any other ℘son or use and if the same happen upon any Navigable River or a River Capable of being made Navigable you are to allow only ye fifth part of the depth by the water side and a Certyfycate fully specyfying ye scituation and bounds therof you are to returne to us with all Convenient Speed Given under our hand at Charles Towne this iith day of August 1677

To Capt Morrice Matthews Surveyor — Rich Connant, Jos: West, Will Owen, Jno Godfrey

Carolina/

Pursuant to the Earl of Shaftsburyes lettr: dated ye 10th: Aprill i677: You are forthwith to admeasure and lay out for Robt: Smith mercht: six hundred acres of land in some place not yet laid out or marked to bee laid out for any other person or use, and if the same happen upon any Navigable River or River capable of being maid Navigable you are only to allow the fifth part of the depth theirof by ye watter side, and a certyficate fully specyfyinge the boundes and scituation theirof you are to returne to us wth: all convenient speed Dated at Charles Towne this 25th: day of August i677—

To Capt Step: Bull Suryevr — Joseph West, Rich Connant, Will: Owen, John Godfrey

Carolina/ You are forthwith to Admeasure & Lay out Mau: Matthewes gent: of this province one hundred and seaventy Acres of Land in some place not yet layd out or marked to be layd out for any other person or use and if the same happen on any navigable River or a river capable of being made navigable you are to allow only the fifth part of ye depth therof by the water side and a certyfycate fully specyfying the scituation and bounds therof you are to returne to us with all convenient speed: Given under our hands at Charles Towne this 8th of 7ber: 1677

To Mr John: Yeamans Surveyor: — Ste: Bull, Joseph: West, Will: Owen, John: Godfrey

Carolina/ you are to admeasure and lay out for the honrbl: Sr: Peter Colleton Barrt: one of the Lords Proprietors of this province Tho: Colleton & James Colleton esqrs: all yt quantity and proportion of land belonging to their plantation called Wahiwah together wth: the said plantation and Improved or manured Landes in such manner as you shall bee directed theirin by them or one of them or their assignes not Injuringe the line or lines of any person whose land Adjoyne thereunto, and a certificate of the boundes and scituation thereof you are to returne wth: all convenient speed Dated ye 8th of 7ber: 1677

To Capt: Mau: Mathews Surveyr/ — Joseph West, Wm: Owen/, Richard Connant, Ste: Bull

Carolina/ you are forthwith to admeasure & lay out for mr Paul Parker one of the ffreemen of this province three hundred and fortie Acres of Land in some place not yet laid out or marked to bee laid out for any other person or use and if the same happen on any Navigable river or river capable of being maid Navigable you are to allow only the fifth part of the depth theirof by the watter side and a certificate fully specifyinge the boundes and scituation theirof you are to returne to us wth: all convenient speed Given under our hands at Charles Towne this 8th: Septbr: 1677

To mr Jno: Yeamans Surveyr: — Joseph: West, Richard Conant, Mau: Mathews

Carolina/

You are forthwith to admeasure and lay out for mr: Peirce Woodward one of the ffreemen of this province one hundred Acres of land in some place not yet laid out or marked to bee laid out for any other person or use and if the same happen upon any Navigable river or river capable of being maid Navigable you are to allow only y[e] fifth part of the depth theirof by the watter side and a certificate fully specifyinge y[e] boundes & scituation theirof you are to returne to us wth all convenient speed: Given under our handes at Charles Towne this 8th Sept[br]: i677

To mr Ste: Wheelwright
Suryev[r]

Mau: Mathews Joseph: West
W[m]. Owen Rich Conant

Carolina/ By y[e] Govern[r]: by and with y[e] Advice and Consent of y[e] Councill:

You are furthw[th] to cause to be Admeasured and Layd out for Leiu[t] Coll, Jn[o] Godfrey three hundred acres of land in such place as you shalbe directed by y[e] said Leiu[t] Coll John Godfrey soe as y[e] same be not upon land laid out or marked to be layd out for any other person or use and if y[e] same happen upon any Navigable river or any river capable to be made Navigable you are to allow onlie y[e] fifth part of y[e] Depth by y[e] water side and a Certificat fully specifyeing ye scituacon and bounds thereof you are to returne to us with all Convenjent speed Given und[r] our hands att Charles towne in this province this 6[t] day of Oct[r]: i677:

To Cap[t] steven Bull:
Surveyr:/

Joseph West
Will: Owen:
Steven Bull:

Carolina ss You are forthwith to Admeasure and Lay out for George Lisster one hundred Acres of Land in Some Place not layd out nor marked to be layd out for any other person or use, & if the same happen upon any Navigable River or River capable to be made Navigable you are to Allow only the fifth part of the depth by the water side and a certificate fully specifying the bounds & situation thereof you are to return to us with all Convenient speed Given under our hands at Charles Towne

Carolina ss. You are forthwith to lay out and Admeasure unto Peter Hern Junior mary Hern Bridget Hern and Richard Hern Two hundred and eighty Acres of Land in some place not yet layd out for any other Person or use, & if the same happen upon any Navigable River you are to allow only the fifth part of the Depth thereof by the water side, and a certificate fully specifying the bounds and situation thereof you are to return to us with all Convenient speed. Given under our hands at Charles Towne Septembr.

Carolina ss. You are forthwth to cause to bee admeasured and laid out for Ralph Marshall gent fifty foure Acres of Land beinge ye remainder of 150 Acres of Land due to him by vertue of ye fundamentall Constitucons of this province in some place not yett laid out or marked to be laid out for any other ꝑson or use and if ye same happen upon any Navigable River or any River capable of being made Navigable, you are to allow onely the fifth parte of ye depth thereof by the waterside and a Certificate fully specifieing the scituacon & bounds thereof you are to returne to us wth all convenient speed and for yor soe doeinge this shall be yor sufficient warrt. Given undr our hands att Charles Towne this 5th day of Novembr 1677/

Jo: West
Ste: Bull
Ric: Conant
Will Owen

Carolina ss. You are forthwith to Admeasure and lay out for John Donohee one of the ffreemen of this Province one hundred Acres of Land in some Place not yet layed out or marked to be layed out for any other Person or use; And if the same happen upon a Navigable River, or a River Capable of being made Navigable you are to Allow only the fifth part of the depth by the water side, and a certificate fully specifying ye situation and bounds thereof you are to returne to us with all convenient speed Given under our hands at Charles Towne this third day of November 1677

To Captain maurice matthews
Surveyor Generall

Carolina ss. You are forthwith to Admeasure and lay out for William Batty one of the ffreemen of this Province seaventy Acres of Land in some place not yet layed out or marked to bee layed out for any other Person or use; And if the same happen upon any Navigable River or River capable to be made Navigable you are to allow only the fifth part of the depth by the water side; And a certificate fully specifying the situation and bounds thereof you are to return to us with all convenient speed. Given under our hands at Charles Towne this third day of November 1677

To Capt. Maurice Mathews
Surveyr. Generall

Carolina ss. You are forthwith to admeasure and lay out for Richard Batten and Rebecka his wife in the right of Richard Cole deceased one hundred Acres of Land in some place not yet layd out or marked to be layd out for any other Person or use, and if the same happen on any Navigable River or River capable of being made Navigable you are to allow only the fifth part thereof by the water side, and a certificate fully specifying the bounds and situation thereof you are to returne to us with all convenient speed. Given under our hands at Charles Towne 3° day of 9^{ber}: i677:
To Capt: maurice matthews
Survey^{r}. Generall.

Carolina ss You are forthwith to Admeasure and lay out for matthew Smallwood and Anne his wife Seventy Acres of Land not yet layd out nor marked to be layed out for any other Person or use and if the same happen upon any Navigable River or River capable to be made Navigable you are to allow only the fifth part of the depth thereof by the waterside and a Certificate fully specifying the bounds thereof you are to return to us with all Convenient speed Given under our hands at Charles Town 3° day of 9^{ber} i677:
To Capt. maurice matthews
Survey^{r}. Generall.

Carolina ss You are forthwith to admeasure and lay out for Edward Wallington one of the ffreemen of this Province two hundred & forty Acres of Land in Some place not yet layed out or marked to be layed out for any other Person or use and if the same happen on any Navigable River, or River capable of being made Navigable you are to allow only the fifth part of the depth thereof by the water side, and A Certificate fully specifying the bounds and situation thereof you are to return to us withall Convenient Speed. Given under our hands at Charles Towne 3° 9^{ber} i677
To Capt: maurice matthews
Survey^{r}. Generall.

Carolina
You are furthwth to lay out and admeasure unto Joane pulford and Edward Westbury foure hundred acres of land in som place not yet layd out for any other person or use and if ye same happen upon any navigable river or river capable of to be made navigable you are to allow onlie ye 5^{t} part of ye Depth by ye water side and a Certificate

fully specifyeing ye bounds and scituation thereof you are to returne to us with all Convenient speede Given und^r our hands att Charles Towne Dated ye 1° of Dec 1677

To Capt M: Mathews Surveyr: generall. . . . . .

Joseph West
Rich: Conant
Will: Owen:

Carolina: You are furthw^th to run out and admeasure unto Oliver Spencer one hundred acres of Land in som place not layd out nor m^rked to be layd out to any other person or use and if ye same happen upon any navigable river or river capable to be made navigable you are to allowe onlie ye fifth part of ye depth thereof by ye water side and a Certificate fully specifyeing ye bounds & scituacon thereof you are to returne to us with all Convenient speede Dat ye 1° Dec 1677:

To Capt M: Mathews Survey^r gen^rall St: Bull Jo: West:
Will: Owen: Rich: Conant:

Carolina ss: You are forthwith to lay out & admeasure unto Robert Gough & for Elizabeth his wife & two serv^ts: namely Robert Leeds & John Robry foure hundred acres of land in some place not yet laid out for any other person or use, & if the same happen upon any navigable River, or River capable of being made navigable, you are to allow onely the fifth part of y^e: depth by the water side, & a Certificate fully specifying the bounds & situacon thereof you are to return to us with all convenient speed. Given under our hands at Charles Towne X^ber 1°:
1677

To Capt: M: Mathewes Surveyo^r gen^ll:

Jos: West
Rich: Conant
Will: Owen

you are to admeasure and Lay out for Henry Woodward gen^t. in ye Right of him selfe and of Margaret his wife two hundred and fiftye acres of Land in some place not yet Laid out nor marked to be Laid out for any other person or use and if ye same happen upon any Navigable River or River Capable to be maid Navigable you are to allow only ye fifth part of the Debth thereof by the water side and a Certificate fully specifiing the bounds and sittuation thereof you are to returne to us with all Convenient speed dated ye 3^d Jan^ry 1677}

To Capt: Mauris Mathews Survey^r generall

Joseph West
Richard Conant John Godfrey
Steven Bull

Carolina ss: you are pursuant to a Lre of ye rt honrble Anthony Earle of Shaftesbury one of the Lords and absolut propritors of this province Dated ye 10th day of Aprill 1677 to Lay out and admeasure unto Henry Woodward gent. Two Thousand acres of Land in some place not yet Laid out or marked to be Laid out for any other person or use and if the same happen upon any Navigable River or River Capable to be maid Navigable you are to allow only ye fifth part of ye Depth thereof by ye watter side and a Certificat ffully specifiing ye bounds and sittuation thereof you are to returne to us with all Convenient speede dated ye 3d of January 1677

To Capt Mauris Mathews
Survey generall

Joseph West
Richard Conant John Godfry
Steven Bull

Carolina ss: you are to admeasure & Lay out unto Tho Shaw gent one of ye ffreemen of this province one hundred & twenty Acres of Land in some place nott yett Layd out or Marked to bee Layd out for any other ℘son or use & if the same happen upon any Navigable river or river Capable of being made Navigable you are onely to allow ye 5h ℘te of the Depth thereof by the water side & A Certificate fully specifying the boundes and scittuacon thereof you are to returne to us wth all Convenient speed given under our hands this xxth of January 1677 att Charles Towne

To Capt Maurice Mathewes Surveyor
Genall

Jos: West
John Godfrey
Wm: Owen: Stephen Bull

Carolina ss

You are forthwith to admeasure and lay out for John Jefforde one of the freemen of this province Eleaven hundred and seventy Accres of land in sume plase not yett layd out or marked to be layed out for any other persons use and if the same happen on any navigable river or river Capible of being made navigable you are to allow only a fifth parte of the depth therof by the water side And a Certificat fully specifieing the bounds and situation therof you are to return to us with all Convenient speed Given under our hands this xx of January 1677

To Capt Maurice Mathewes
Surveyor Genall

Jos: West
John Godfrey
Will Owen: Ste: Bull.

Carolina
You are required to admeasure & lay out for James Colleton Esqr & Landgrave of this Province a Barrony of twelve thousand acres of Land in some place not yet taken up by any other person or persons and a Certificate fully specifying the situacon & bounds thereof you are to returne to us with all convenient speed, Dated the 23th of ffebruary 1677./

To Capt: Maurice Mathewes Surveyor: genll: — Jos: West, Will: owen: John Godfrey, Ste: Bull.

Carolina :/
You are forthwith to admeasure & lay out for John ffoster Cassique of this Province, One thousand acres of Land in some place not yet layd out or marked to be layd out for any other person or use, & if the same happen upon any Navigable River, or River capable of being made Navigable, you are to allow onely the fifth part of the depth thereof by the water side, & a Certificate fully specifying the bounds & situacon thereof you are to returne to us with all convenient speed, Given under our hands at Charles Towne the 23th day of ffebr 1677/8

To Capt: Maurice Mathewes Surveyor: genll: — Joseph West, Will: Owen: John Godfrey, Ste: Bull

Carolina/
You: are forthwth: to admeasure and lay out for Daniell Smethwick one of the freemen of this ℘vince two hundred accres of land in some place not ÿett laid out or marked to be laid out for anÿ other ℘son or use and if the same happen on anÿ Navigable river or River capable of being made Navigable you. are to allow only a fifth ℘te of the depth therof by the water side, and a Certificat fullÿ specifiing the bounds & sittuation therof you. are to returne to us wth. all Convenient speed given under our hands this 26 of January 167/8 at Charlestown

To Capn— Maurris Mathews Surveyor. generall — Joseph West, Richd Connat, John Godfrey, Stephen Bull

Carolina/
You[u] are forw[th]: to admeasure, and laÿ out for Robert Smethwick one of the freemen of this ℘vince two hundred accres of land in some place not ÿett laid out or marked to be laid out for anÿ other ℘son or use & if the same happen on anÿ Navigable River or River capable of being Made Navigable ÿou are to allow onlÿ a fifth ℘te of the depth therof bÿ the water side and A Certificate fullÿ specifieing the bounds and sittuation therof yo[u].. are to returne to us w[th].. all Convenient speed Given under our hands this 26th. daÿ of Januarÿ 167/8: at Charles Towne

To Cap[n] Maurris Mathews
Surveyo[r]: Gennerall

Joseph West
Rich[d]: Conant
John: Godfrey
Ste: Bull

Carolina/
You are forthw[th]: to admeasure and lay out for Henrÿ Sumpton and Susanah his wife of this provinc one hundred & seaventÿ accres of land in some place not ÿett laid out or marked to be laid out for anÿ other person or use, and if the same happen on anÿ Navigable River or River capable of being made Navigable yo[u]. are to allow onlÿ a fifth ℘te of the depth therof by the water side, and a Certificat fullÿ specifieing the bounds and sittuation therof you are to returne to us wth. all Convenient speed, Given under our hands 21th of febr: 167/8 att Charles Town

To Capt[tt] Marris Mathews
Surveyo[r]: Generall

Joseph West
Rich: Connat
John Godfry

Carolina/
You[u]: are forth with to admeasure and laÿ out for John Boydÿcott one of the freemen of this ℘vince one hundred accres of land in some place not ÿett laid out or marked to be laid out for anÿ other ℘son or use and if the same happen on any Navigable River or River capable of being made Navigable ÿo[u]: are to allow onlÿ the fifth ℘te therof bÿ the water side and a Certificat fullÿ specifing the bounds & sittuation thereof ÿo[u]: are to returne to us withall convenient speed: Given under our hands at Charles Town

To Cap[n]— Mauris Mathews
Surveyo[r]

Joseph West
Richd Connat
John Godfrey

You are forthwth: to Admeasure and laÿ out to David Dupeth and Enoch dupis Two hundred accres of land in some place not ÿett laid out or marked to be layed ou^{t} for anÿ other ꝑson or use & if the same happen on any navigable River or River Capable to be made navigable you are to allow onlÿ the fifth ꝑte of the depth therof bÿ the water side and a Certificat fullÿ specifieing the bounds and sittuation therof ÿo^{u}: are to returne to us wth:all Convenient speed Given under our hands this 21th febr 1677/8 at Charles Town

To Cap^{n}.. Mauris Mathews
Surveyo^{r}: Generall

Joseph West
Rich^{d}: Connot
W^{m}: Owen

Yo^{u}: are forthwth to admeasure and laÿ out for Richard Butler Cicilÿ his wife and Mary his Daughter one of the freemen of this province two hundred and tenn accres of land in some place not ÿet laid out or marked to be laÿd out for anÿ other ꝑson or use and if the same happen uppon anÿ River or River Capable of being made Navigable yo^{u}.. to allow onlÿ the fifth ꝑte of the depth therof bÿ the water side and a Certificat fullÿ specifiing the bounds and sittuacon therof ÿo^{u} are to return to us wth.. all Convenient speed Given under our hand this 4th daÿ of march 167/8 at Charles Town

To Cap^{n}. Mauris Mathews
Surveÿo^{r} Generall

Joseph West
John Godfrey
Stephen Bull
W^{m}.. Owen

Carolina/
Yo^{u}. are forthwth: to admeasure and laÿ out for Lawrence Sanders one of the freemen of this ꝑvince one hundred accres of land in some place not yet laid out or marked to be laid out for anÿ other ꝑson or use, and if it shall happen uppon anÿ Navigable River or River capable of being made Navigable you are only to allow in breath the fifth ꝑte therof and a Certifiecat fullÿ specifieing the bounds & sittuation therof, ÿo^{u} are to returne to us wth: all Convenient speed, given under our hands this 22th febr 167/8

To Cap^{n}— Morris Mathews
Surveÿo^{r} Generall/

Joseph West
John Godfrey
Stephen Bull
W^{m}: Owen[1]

---

[1]This warrant has been scratched out.

Carolina:
You are forthwith to Admeasure and lay out for Laurence Sanders: freeman: of this province one hundred Acres of land in some place not yett layd out or marked to be layd out for any other person or use And if ye same happen on any navigable river or River Capable of being made navigable you are to alow only a a fifth part of the depth thereof by the water side and a Certificate fully specifieing the bounds and scituation thereof you are to returne to us with all Convenient speed Given under our hands this 23th: day of March 1677: att Charles towne

To: Capt: Morris: Mathews
Surveyor:: Generall::

Joseph West:
Richard Conant:
John: Godfrey
Andrew: Percivall
Stephen Bull:

Carolina:
You are by vertue hereof to Admeasure and lay out for Mr. Peter Herne one towne lott in the oyster pointe observing the rules established in reference to the building of a towne there and a sertificate fully specifinge the metes bounds and situation: thereof to returne to us Given under our hands this 23th: of March: 1677:/

To: Capt: Morris Mathews
Surveyor:: Generall::

Joseph: West:
Richard Conant:

Carolina: You are by vertue hereof to admeasure and lay out for: John: Bullen: one towne lott in the oster point observing the rules established in reference to the building of a towne theire and a certificate fully specifinge the metes bounds and situation thereof to returne to us Given under our hands this 23th: of March 1677:

To: Capt: Morris Mathews
Surveyor Generall::

Joseph: West:
Richard Conant:

Carolina You are by vertue hereof to admeasure and lay out for Timothy Bushell one towne lott in the oster point observing the rules established in reference to the buildinge of a Towne and a certificate fully specifinge the metes bounds and situation thereof to returne to us Given under our hands the 23th of March 1677:

To Capt: Morris Mathews:
Surveyor: Generall::

Joseph West:
Richard Conant:

Carolina
You are by vertue hereof to admeasure and lay out for Oliver Spencer one towne lott in the oster point observing the rules established in reference to the buildinge of a Towne and a certificate fully specifinge the metes bounds and situation thereof to returne to us Given under our hands the 23th: of March 1677:

To Capt: Morris Mathews
Surveyor Generall:::

Joseph West:
Richard Conant:

You are forthwth to Lay out and admeasure unto Jonathan ffitz eleaven hundred and tenn acres of Land in som place not yet Layd out nor marked to be Layd out for any other person or use and if ye same happen upon any Navigable river or river capable to be made navigable you are to allow onlie ye fifth part of ye depth by ye water side and a Certificat fully specifyeing ye bounds and scituation thereof you are to returne to us with all Convenient speed Given undr or hands this 29th Day of Aprill 1678:

To Capt M Mathews Surveyr

Joseph West:
St Bull: Jno Godfrey:
Will: Owen:

Carolina: You are furthwth to lay out and Admeasure unto Jonathan ffitz one towne lot in ye Oyster point observeing ye rules and methods alreadie established for ye building of a towne there and not injureing ye lines of any other person or persons and a Certificat fully specifyeing ye metes bounds and scituacon thereof you returne to us with all Convenient speed Dat ye 23° Aprill 1678:

To Capt Maurice Mathews:
Surveyr generall:

Ste: Bull: Joseph West
Will: Owen: Jno Godfrey

You are furthwth to lay out and Admeasure unto Richard Dymond one towne lot in ye Oyster point observeing ye rules and method alreadie established for ye building a towne there & not injureing ye lines of any other person or persons and a Certificat fully specifyeing ye metes bounds and scituacon thereof you returne to us with all Convenient speede Dated ye 23° of Aprill 1678:

To Capt Maurice Mathews
Surveyr generall:

St: Bull: Jo: West:
Will: Owen: Jno Godfrey:

You are furthwith to lay out and Admeasure unto Nicholas Lockwood one towne lot in ye Oyster point observeing ye rules and method alreadie established for ye building of a towne there and not Injureing ye lines of any other person or persons and a Certificat fully specifyeing ye bounds and scituacon thereof you returne to us with all Convenient speede Dat ye 23° Aprill 1678:

To Capt Maurice Mathews Surveyr generall/ St: Bull: Jo: West: Will: Owen: Jno Godfrey:

You are furthwth to lay out and admeasure unto Edward Mayoh one towne lot in ye Oyster point observeing ye rules & method alredy established for ye Building of a towne there & not Injureing ye lines of any other person or persons and a Certificat fully specifyeing ye metes bounds and scituacon thereof you returne to us with all Convenient speed Dated ye 23° of Aprill: 1678:

To Capt M: Mathews Surveyr generall: Ste: Bull Jo: West: Will Owen: Jno Godfrey:

Carolina

In pursuance to an order of Councill of the first of May 1677 you are to admeasure and Lay out for Sr Petr Colleton Barrt one of the Lords & absolute Proprs of this Province Twelve thousand acres of Land as a Signiorie upon the Wando River & that Tract of Land called the Mulbery plantacon and a Certificate fully specifieing the Boundes and Scituacon thereof you Retourne to us wth all convenient speede Dated the 18th of May 1678/

To Capt Maurice Mathewes Surveyor Genll— } Joseph West John Godfrey Stev: Bull

Carolina—

You are forthwith to admeasure and Lay out unto mr wm Clark one Towne Lott in the oyster Point observing the Rules and method already established for the building a Towne there & not injureing the Lines of any other ꝑson or ꝑsons and a Certificate fully specifieing the metes Bounds and Scituacon thereof, you are to Retourne to us with all Convenient speede Dated the 23th of Aprill 1678/

To Capt Maurice Mathewes Surveyor Gen'll— } Jos West John Godfrey Wm Owen Steven Bull—

Carolina
You are forthwith to lay out & admeasure unto Tho Serles gent: one Towne Lott in the oyster point observing the Rules and method already established for the building a Towne there & not iniureing the Lines of any other ꝑson or ꝑsons & a Certificate fully specifieing the metes Bounds & Scituacon thereof you Retourne to us wth all Convenient speede: Dated the 23th of Ap^ll^ 1678/

To Capt Maurice Mathewes
Surveyo^r^ Genll—

Jo: West
John Godfrey
Wm Owen
Stev: Bull:

Carolina/
You are forthwith to lay out & admeasure unto Theophilus Paty one Towne lott in the oyster Point observing the Rules & method already established for the building a Towne there & not iniureing the Lines of any other ꝑson or ꝑson & a Certificate fully specifieing the metes bounds & scituacon thereof—you retourne to us with all convenient speede Dated the 23th day of Aprill 1678/

To Capt Maurice
Mathewes Surveyo^r^ Gen^ll^:

Jos: West
Rich Connant
Jno Godfrey:

Carolina—
You are forthwith to admeasure and Lay out for George Conway & John Conway freemen of this Province Two hundred acres of Land in some convenient place not yet layd out or marked to be Layd out for any other ꝑson or use & if the same happen on any navigable River or River capable of being made navigable, you are to allow onely a fifth part of the depth thereof by the water side & a certificate fully specifieing the Bounds and Scituacon thereof you are to retourne to us with all Convenient speede Given under our hands this 20th of Ap^ll^ 1678/

To Capt Maurice Mathewes
Surveyo^r^ Genll—

Carolina—
You are forthwith to admeasure and lay out unto Thomas Swaine one Towne Lott in the oyster Point observing the Rules & method already established for the building a Towne there & not iniureing the Lines of any other ꝑson or ꝑsons and a Certificate fully speci-

fieing the metes bounds and scituacon thereof you retourne to us with all Convenient speede Dated the 23th Aprill 1678/

To Capt Ma: Mathewes Surveyor Genll:

Jo: West
And— Percivall
Wm. Owen
Steven: Bull

Carolina— — You are forthwith to admeasure and Lay out unto Jno Suilivan in the Right of Racholl his wife seaventie acres of Land not yet Laid out or marked to be laid out for any other ꝑson or use And if the same happen upon any navigable River or River capable to be made navigable you are to allow onely the fifth part of the depth by the water side and a Certificate fully specifieing the bounds and scituacon thereof you are to Retourne to us wth all convenient speede Given under our hands this 20th day of Aprill 1678/

To Capt Ma: Mathewes:: Surveyor Genll—

Jo: West
Richard Conant
Wm: Owen
Ste: Bull—

Carolina — —

You are forthwith to lay out & admeasure unto Jacob Wayte one Towne Lott in the oyster Point observing the Rules & method already established for the building of a Towne there & not iniureing the Lines of any other ꝑson or ꝑsons & a Certificate fully specifieing the metes bounds & scituacon thereof you retourne to us wth all convenient speede dated the 23th of Ap'll 1678/

To Cap Ma: Mathewes Surveyor Genll—

Jo: West
John Godfrey
Wm Owen
Ste: Bull

Carolina—

You are forthwith to admeasure and Lay out unto Phillip & Charles Bulkley one Towne Lott in the Oyster Point observing the Rules and method already established for the Building a Towne there & not injureing the Lines of any other ꝑson or ꝑsons And a Certificate fully specifieing the metes Boundes and Scituacon thereof you Retourne to us wth all convenient speede Dated the 23th of Aprill 1678

To Capt Ma: Mathewes Surveyor Genll—

Jos: West
Will: Owen John Godfrey

Carolina—

You are forthwith to admeasure & lay out unto John Stevenson a hundred Acres of Land in some place not yet laid out or marked to be laid out for any other ꝑson or ꝑsons use And if the same happen upon any navigable River or River capable to be made navigable you are to allow onely the fifth part of the depth by the water side and a Certificate fully specifieing ye Bounds & Scituacon thereof, you are to retourne to us with all convenient speede Given under our hands this 18th Day of May 1678/

To Capt Mau: Mathewes
Surveyo^{r} Genll

Jos: West
John Godfrey
And: Percivall
Wm Owen—

Carolina—

You are forthwith to admeasure and lay out unto Michal Henshaw a hundred Acres of Land in some place not yet laid out or marked to be laid out for any other ꝑson or ꝑsons or use: and if the same happen upon any navigable River or River Capable to be made navigable you are to allow onely the fifth part of the depth by the water side and a Certificate fully specifieing the Bounds and scituacon thereof you are to Retourne to us with all Convenient speede Given under our hands this 18th Day of May 1678

To Capt Mau: Mathewes
Surveyo^{r} Genll—

Jos: West
Rich Conant
John Godfrey
W^{m}: Owen—

Carolina—

You are forthwith to Lay out & admeasure unto Robt Mayoh one Towne Lott in the oyster Point observing the Rules & method already established for the building a Towne there and not injureing the lines of any other ꝑson or ꝑsons and a Certificate fully specifieing the metes Bounds and scituacon thereof—you retourne to us wth all Convenient speede Dated the 18th day of May 1678

Capt Mau: Mathewes
Surveyo^{r} Genll:

Jos: West
Wm Owen:
Steven Bull—

Carolina/

You are forthwith to admeasure & lay out unto Jno Stevenson ffowre hundred & fforty acres of Land in some Convenient place not yet laid out or marked to be laid out for any other ℘son or ℘sons use And if the same happen upon any navigable River or River capable to be made navigable you are to allow onely the fifth part of the depth by the Water side and a Certificate fully specifieing the Bounds & Scituacon thereof you are to Retourne to us wth all Convenient speede Given under our hands this 18th day of May 1678/

To Cap[t] Ma: Mathews
Survey: Genll—

Jos: West
John Godfrey
And: Percivall
W[m] Owen

Carolina — —

You are forthwith to admeasure and lay out unto Tho Drayton Two hundred acres of Land in some place not yet laid out or marked to be laid out for any other ℘son or ℘sons use And if the same happen upon any navigable River or River capable to be made navigable you are to allow onely the fifth part of the depth by the water side & a certificate fully specifieing the Bounds & Scituacon thereof you are to Retourne to us wth all convenient speede Given under our hands this 18th day of may 1678/

To Cap Mau: Mathewes
Survey Genll—

Jos West
Richard Conant
John Godfrey
W[m] Owen—

Carolina — —

You are forthwith to lay out & admeasure unto Jno Wade one Towne Lott in the oyster Point observing the Rules & method already established for the building a Towne there and not injureing the lines of any ℘son or ℘sons & a Certificate fully specifieing the metes Bounds & Scituacon thereof you Retourne to us wth all Convenient speede Dated the 18th day of may 1678

To Cap[t]. Mau: Mathewes
Surveyo[r] Genll—

Joseph West
John Godfrey
Rich Conant

Carolina — —

You are forthwith to lay out & admeasure unto Phillip & Charles Bulkeley one Towne Lott in the oyster-Point observing the Rules & method already established for the building a Towne there and not iniureing the Lines of any other ℘son or ℘sons & a certificate fully specifieing the metes & bounds & scituacon thereof you retourne to us wth. all convenient speede Dated y[e] 18 day of may 1678

Joseph West:
John Godfrey
Rich Conant

Carolina
You are forthwith to admeasure & lay out unto Andrew Percevall Esq[r] three hundred acres of Land in some convenient place not yet laid out or marked to be laid out for any other ꝑson or use And if the same happen upon any navigable River or River capable to be made navigable, you are to allow onely the fifth part of the depth by the water side and a Certificate fully specifieing the Bounds & scituacon thereof you are to Retourne to us with all Convenient speede given under our hands this 18th day of May 1678

To Capt Maurice Mathewes Surveyo[r] Genll — — —

Joseph West
John Godfrey:
Rich Conant—

Carolina — — You are forthwith to lay out & admeasure unto Jos Varbin Six hundred acres of Land in some convenient place not yet laid out or marked to be Laid out for any other ꝑson or use & if the same happen upon any Navigable River or River capable to be made navigable you are to allow onely the fifth part of the depth by the water side & a a Certificate fully specifieing the bounds & Scituacon thereof you are to Retourne to us wth all convenient speede Given under our hands this 18th day of may 1678

To Capt Mau: Mathewes Surveyo[r] Genll—

Jos: West
Jno Godfrey
Rich Conant—

Carolina—
You are forthwith to Lay out & admeasure unto Pe[tr] Herne one hundred & forty acres of Land in some place not yet laid out or marked to be laid out for any other ꝑson or use And if the same happen upon any navigable River or River capable to be made navigable you are to allow onely the fifth part of the depth by the waters side & a Certificate fully specifieing the bounds and scituacon thereof you are to Retourne to us wth. all convenient speede Given under our hands this 18th Day of May 1678/

To Cap: Mau: Mathews Surveyo[r] Genll

Jos: West
Jno Godfrey
Rich Conant

Carolina—You are forthwith to lay out & admeasure unto Peleg Whithington fowre hundred acres of Land yet laid out or marked to be laid out for any other ꝑson or use & if the same happen upon any navigable River or River capable to be made navigable you are to allow onely the fifth part of the depth by the waters side and a Certificate fully specifieing the bounds & scituacon thereof you are to Retourne to us wth all convent speede Given under our hands this 18th day of may 1678./

To Capt Ma: Mathewes
Surveyor Genll—

Jo West
Jno Godfrey
Rich Conant

Carolina./

You are forthwith to Lay out & admeasure unto Theophilus Paty one Towne Lott in the Oyster Point observing the Rules & method allready established for the building a Towne there & not injureing the lines of any other ꝑson or ꝑsons and a Certificate fully specifieing the metes Bounds and Scituacon thereof you Retourne to us wth all Convenient speede Dated the 18th day of May 1678

To Capt Ma: Mathewes
Surveyor Genll—

W Owen
Josep West
Jno Godfrey
Rich Conant

You are forthwith to lay out & admeasure unto Ant: Shoris one Towne Lott in ye Oyster Point observing the Rules & method already established for the building a Towne there & not injureing the Lines of any ꝑson or ꝑsons and a Certificate fully specifieing the meetes Boundes and scituacon thereof you Retourne to us wth all Convenient speede Dated the 18th Day of may 1678/

To Capt: Maurice
Mathewes Surveyor Genll

Joseph West
John Godfrey
Rich Conant

Carolina—You are forthwith to admeasure & lay out for Jno Slilivan & Rachell his wife Seaventie acres of Land in some place not yet laid out or marked to be laid out for any other ꝑson or use & if the same happen on any Navigable River or River Capable to be made navigable you are to allow onely a fifth part of the depth thereof by the water side and a Certificate fully specifieing the bounds &

scituacon thereof you are to Retourne to us wth all Convenient speede Given under our hands this 20th of Apll 1678

To Cap Mau Mathewes
Survey Genll—

Joseph West
Jno Godfrey
Rich Conant

Carolina—You are forthwith to Lay out and admeasure unto John Stevenson acres of Land in some place not yet laid out nor marked to be layd out for any other ℘son or use And if the same happen upon any navigable River or River capable to be made navigable you are to allow onely the fifth part of the depth by the water side and a Certificate fully specifieing the Boundes & scituacon thereof you retourne to us wth all convenient speede Given under our hands this 20th day of Aprill 1678/

To Capt Mau Mathewes
Survey: Genll

Joseph West
Steven Bull
Wm Owen

Carolina

You are forthwith to admeasure and lay out unto John Godfrey Gent one hundred acres of Land in some place not yet laid out or marked to be laid out for any other ℘on or ℘sons use and if the same happen upon any navigable River or River capable to be made navigable you are onely to allow the fifth part of the depth by the water side and a Certificate fully specifieing the bounds and scituacon thereof you are to retourne to us wth all Convenient speede Given under our hands this 18th day of May 1678/

To Capt Maurice Mathewes
Surveyor Genll—

Joseph West
Richard Conant
Wm Owen—

Carolina—You are forthwith to admeasure & Lay out unto John Godfrey Gent one hundred Acres of Land in some place not yet Laid out or marked to be laid out for any other ℘son or ℘sons use. And if the same happen upon any navigable River or River capable to be made navigable you are to allow onely the fifth part of the depth by the water side and a Certificate fully specifieing the Boundes and Scituacon thereof you are to Retourne to us wth all Convenient Speede Given under our hands this 18th day of May 1678

To Capt Maurice Mathewes
Surveyor Genll—

John West*
Rich Conant
William Owen

*Evidently a slip of the pen for Joseph West.

Carolina:

You are to Admeasure and lay out forth for Mr Alexand^{r} mercer one of ye freemen of this province foure hundred acres of Land in som place not yet Laid out nor marked to be Layd for any other ꝑson or use and if ye same happen upon any Navigable river or river capable to be made navigable you are to allowe onlie ye fifth ꝑte of ye Depth thereof by ye water side & a Certificat fully Specifyeing ye bounds and scituacon thereof you retorne to us with all Convenjent speede Dat ye 13^{h} Day of July 1678

To Capt^{t} Maurice Mathews— }
Survey^{r} generall }

Joseph West
Rich: Conant Ste: Bull:
Will: Owen:

Carolina/

.You are forthwith to admeasure and lay out unto Jno Foster gent one Towne Lott in the Oyster Point observeing the Rules and method already established for the building a Towne there & not injureing the Lines of any other ꝑson or ꝑsons & a Certificate fully specifieing the metes Bounds & scituacon thereof you Retourne to us wth all Convenient speede Dated the third of June—1678/

To Capt Maur. Mathewes }
Surveyo^{r} Genll— }

Joseph West
Rich Conant
And Percivall
Wm Owen

Carolina/

You are forthwith to admeasure & lay out unto John Hartley one towne Lott in the oyster Point observing the Rules & method already established for the building a Towne there & not injureing the Lines of any other ꝑson or ꝑsons & a Certificate fully specifieing the metes Bounds & scituacon thereof you Retourne to us wth all Convenient speede Dated ye 3d of June 1678/

To Capt Mau^{r}. Mathewes
Surveyo^{r} Genll—

Josep: West
Rich Conant
Wm Owen

Carolina/

You are forthwith to admeasure & lay out unto George Cantey one towne Lott in the oyst^{r} Point observeing ye Rules & method already established for the building a Towne there & not injureing the Lines of any other ꝑson or ꝑsons & a Certificate fully specifieing the metes Bounds & scituacon thereof you retourne to us wth all Convent speede Dated the third of June—1678/

To Capt Mau^{r}: Mathewes
Surveyo^{r} Genll—

Josep West
Rich Conant
W^{m} owen

Carolina/

You are forthwith to admeasure & lay out unto James Donogho one towne Lott in the oyst^{r} Point observeing the Rules & method already established for the building a towne there & not injureing the Lines of any other ꝑson or ꝑsons & a Certificate fully specifieing the metes Bounds & scituacon thereof you retourne to us wth all Conv^{t} speede Dated the third of June 1678/

To Capt Mau^{r}: Mathewes
Surveyo^{r} Genll—

Joseph West
Rich Conant

Carolina/

You are forthwth to admeasure & lay out unto Jonathan Bounden one towne Lott in the oyst^{r} point observeing ye Rules & method already established for the building a towne there & not injureing the Lines of any other ꝑson or ꝑsons & a Certificate fully specifieing the metes bounds & Scituacon thereof you retourne to us wth all Conv^{t} speede Dated the third of June 1678/

To Capt Mau^{r}: Mathewes
Surveyo^{r} Genll—

Joseph West
Rich Conant
Wm Owen

Carolina/

You are forthwith to admeasure & lay out unto Sr Peter Colleton Barrt &c Two sevall towne lotts in the oyster point observeing the Rules & method already established for the building a Towne there & not injureing the Lines of any other ꝑson or ꝑsons & a Certificate fully specifieing the metes Bounds & scituacon thereof you retourne to us wth all Convenient speede Dated the third of June 1678/

To capt Mau^{r}: Mathewes
Survey— Genll—

Joseph West
Rich Conant
Wm Owen

Carolina/

You are forthwth to admeasure & Lay out unto William Walley Esqr— one Towne Lott in the oyster Point observeing the Rules &

method already established for the building a Towne there & not injureing the Lines of any other ꝑson or ꝑsons & a certificate fully specifieing the metes Bounds & scituacon thereof you retourne to us wth all Convenient speede Dated the third of June 1678./

To Capt Mau^r: Mathewes
Surveyo^r Genll

Joseph West
Rich Conant
W^m owen

Carolina/
You are forthwth to admeasure & Lay out unto Robt Daniel one towne Lott in the oystr Point observeing the Rules & method already established for the building a towne there & not iniureing the lines of any other ꝑson or ꝑsons & a certificate fully specifieing the metes Bounds & scituacon thereof you Retourne to us wth all Convt speede Dated the third of June 1678/

To Capt Mau^r:—
Mathewes: Survey^r Genll

Joseph West
Rich Conant
W^m. owen

Carolina
You are furthwith to Admeasure and Lay out unto Robt Smethwick one towne lot in ye oyster point observeing ye rules and methode already established for ye building a towne there and not Injureing ye Lines of any other ꝑson or ꝑsons and a Certificat fully specifyeing ye metes bounds and Scituacon thereof you retourne to us with all Convenjent speed Dated ye 16° June i678

To Capt Maurice Mathews
Survey^r genall

Joseph West
Will: Owen:
Rich: Conant
Ste: Bull:

Carolina/ you are forthwith to admeasure and lay out for Anthony Shorie one of the settlers of this Province two hundred — — in some convenient place not yet laid out or marked to bee laid out for any other person or use and if the same happen upon any Navigable River or River Capable of being maid Navigable you are to allow only the fifth part of ye depth upon ye River side and a certyficate fully specifinge the boundes and scituation yrof you are to returne to us with all convenient speed Dated the 15th: June i678/

To Capt: Mau: Mathewes
Sury^r Genr^ll/

John Godfrey
Will: Owen:
Joseph West
Richard Conant

Carolina/ you are forthwith to admeasure and lay out for Robt: Mayoh one of the settlers of this Province three hundred — — acres of Land In some convenient place not yet laid out or intended to bee laid out for any other person or use and if the saime happen upon any Navigable River or capable of being maid Navigable you are to allow only ye fifth part of ye depth yrof by ye watterside and a certyficate fully specifing the bounds & scituation yrof you are to returne to us wth all convent speed Dated i5th day of June i678/

Joseph West
Richard Conant

To Capt Mau: Mathews   John Godfrey
Survey^{r} Genr^{ll}/   Will: Owen

Carolina/ You are forthwith to admeasure and lay out for Theo: Paty one of the settlers of this province four hundred and seaventy: acres of land in some convenient place not yet laid out or marked to bee laid out for any other person or use and if the saime happen on any Navigable River or River capable of being maid Navigable you are to allow a fifth part of ye depth yrof by the watter side & a certyficate fully specifiing the boundes and scituation yrof you are to returne to us wth all convenient speed Dated this 15th June i678/

To Capt. Mau: Mathewes   John Godfrey   Joseph West
Survey^{r} Genrall/   Will: Owen   Richard Conan^{t}.

Carolina pursuant to an order of Councill you are to run out and Admeasure unto Thomas Midwinter a certaine quantitie of Land upon ye seamens point neere Charles towne being about an acre and you are to take care you ℘^{r}iudice not ye right of any other person or persons there and a Certificat of ye bounds and scituacon thereof you returne to us with all Convenjent speede Dated ye 16 June i678:

To Capt Maurice Mathews   Steven Bull   Joseph West
Survey^{r} generall: W: Owen   Jno Godfrey

Carolina

You are furthwth to Admeasure and lay out for Jno Greene one of ye settlerss of this province one hundred acres of Land in som Convenjent place not yet layd out or marked to be laid out for any other ℘son or use and if it happen upon any Navigable river or river capable of being made Navigable you are to allowe onlje ye fifth part of ye depth by ye water side and a Certificat fully specifyeing y^{e}

bounds and scituacon thereof you are to Retourne to us with all Convenjent speed hereof faile you not Dated ye 15° Day of June 1678:

Joseph West
To Capt Maurice Mathews Ste: Bull: Rich:Conant
Surveyr generall: Jno Godfrey Will: Owen:

Carolina/
You are forthwith to admeasure & lay out for ffrancis Jones, one of the settlers of this province nine hundred & forty acres of Land in some convenient place not yet laid out, or ordered to be laid out, And if the same happen upon any Navigable River, or River capable of being made navigable, you are to allow onely the fifth part of the depth upon y^e^: River side, & a Certificate fully specifying the bounds & situacon thereof you are to returne to us wth all Convenient speed Dated the 13th: day of July 1678/

To Capt: Mau: Mathews survey^r^ gen^ll^: Joseph West
Rich: Conant Jos Godfrey
W^m^: Owen Ste: Bull.

You are furthw^th^ to admeasure & lay forth for m^r^ Peter Bodit one of ye freemen of this province six hundred acres of Land in som place not yet laid out nor marked to be laid out for any other person or use and if ye Same happen upon any navigable river or river capable to be made Navigable you are to allowe only the fifth part of ye depth there by ye waters side and a Certificat fully specifyeing ye bounds & scituation to returne to us with all Convenient speede Dated ye 13° July 1678:

Capt Maurice Mathews Surv^e^y^r^ generall } Ste: Bull: Jo: West
Will: Owen: Rich: Conant

Carolina./
You^u^. are to admeasure and lay out for Richard Meadlin one of the freemen of this province and Rachell his Wife two hundred acres of land in some place not yett layd out nor marked to be laid out for any other person or use and if the same happen upon any navigable River or River capable to be made navigable yo^u^. allow only the fifth part of the depth to the waterside and a Certificate fully specifying the bounds and scittuacon thereof you returne to us with all convenient speed Dated the 10th: day of August 1678.—/

To Capt: Maurice Mathews Surveyo^r^ Generall— } Joseph West
John Godfrey
Richard Conant— Will: Owen./

Carolina

You are to Admeasure and lay out for Jn° Stevens one of the freemen of this province three hundred and Seaventie acres of land in som place not yet laid out nor marked to be laid out for any other ꝑson or use and if ye same happen upon any navigable river or river capable to be made navigable you allowe onlje ye 5h part of ye depth by ye waterside and a Certificat fully specifyeing ye bounds and Scituacon thereof you retorne to us with all Convenjent speede Dated ye 10th Day of August 1678:

To Capt M: Mathews Surveyr generall — — — — — —

Jo: West:
Rd: Conant Jn° Godfrey
Wm: Owen

Carolina

You are to admeasure and lay out for willm Davies and wm Brockus twoe of ye settlers of this province five hundred acres of Land in som place not yet laid out nor marked to be laid out for any other person or use and if ye same happen upon any Navigable river or river capable to be made Navigable you are to allowe onlje the 5h part of the depth thereof by ye waterside and a Certificat fully specifyeing ye bounds and scituacon thereof you retorne to us with all Convenient speede Dated ye 10th day of August 1678:

To Capt Maurice Mathews surveyr generall:

Jo West
Jn° Godfrey
Rich: Conant: Will: Owen:

Carolina

You are to Admeasure and lay out for Edward Mayo one of the freemen of this province Seaven hundred and fiftie acres of land in som place not yet laid out nor marked to be laid out for any other person or use and if the same happen upon any Navigable river or river capable to be made Navigable you are to allowe onlje the fifth part of the depth thereof by by ye water side and a Certificat fully specifyeing ye bounds and scituacon thereof you are to retorne to us with all Convenjent speed Dated ye 10th day of August 1678:

To Capt M: Mathews Srveyr: genrall:

Jo: West:
Rich: Conant: Jn° Godfrey
Wm: Owen:

Carolina ss./

You are to admeasure and lay out for Christopher Swaine one of the freemen of this province One hundred acres of land in some place not yet laid out nor marked to be laid out for any other person or use and if the same happen upon any navigable River or River capable to be made navigable you. are to allow only the fifth part of the depth thereof to the water side and a Certificate fully specifying the bounds and scituation thereof you are to returne to us with all convenient speed Date ye 10th: day of August 1678

To Capt: Maurice Mathews
Surveyor: Generall

Joseph West./
John Godfrey
Richard Conant./ Wm: Owen./

Carolina

You: are to admeasure and lay out for Richard Trad one of the freemen of the province three hundred acres of land in some place not yett laid out nor marked to be laid out for any other person or use and if the same happen upon any navigable River or River capable to be made navigable you. are to allow only the fifth part of the depth to the water side and a certificate fully specifying the bounds and scittuacon thereof you. are to returne to us with all convenient speed; Dated the 10th: day of August 1678—

To Capt: Maurice Mathews
Surveyor: Generall./

Richard Conant
Will: Owen
Joseph West
John Godfrey

Carolina ss/

You. are to admeasure and lay out for Alexander Sympson One of the freemen of this province one hundred acres of land in some place not yett laid out or marked to be laid out for any other person or use, and if the same happen upon any navigable River or River capable to be made navigable you. are to allow only the fifth part of the depth thereof to the water side and a Certificate fully specifying the scituacon and bounds thereof you. are to returne to us with all convenient speed Dated the 10th: day of August 1678—

To Capt: Maurice Mathews
Surveyor: Generall./

Joseph West
John Godfrey
Will: Owen.
Richard Conant.

Carolina/

You. are forthwth: to admeasure and lay out for Robert Smethwick One of the Settlers of this province fower hundred acres of land in some convenient place not yett laid out nor marked to be laid out for any other person or use and if the same happen upon any navigable River or River capable of being made navigable you. are to allow only the fifth part of the depth thereof from the water side and a Certificate fully specifying the bounds & scittuacon thereof you. are to returne to us with all convenient speed hereof fayle not Dated the 10th: day of June 1678

To Capt: Maurice Mathews Surveyor Generall — Richard Conant Joseph West John Godfrey

Carolina/

You. are forthth: to admeasure and lay out unto James Colleton Esqr: and Landgrave one Towne lott in the Oyster poynt observeing the Rules and method allready established for the building a Towne there and not injureing the lines of any other person or persons and a Certificate fully specifying the metes bounds and scituacon thereof you. returne to us with all convenient speed dated the 10th: day of June 1678

To Capt: Maurice Mathews Surveyor Generall— } Richard Conant. Joseph West John Godfrey

Carolina/

You. are forthwth to admeasure and lay out unto Theophilus Paty One Towne lott in the Oyster poynt observeing the rules and method allready established for the building a Towne there and not injuring the lines of any other person or persons and a Certificate fully specifying the method bounds and scituacon thereof you. returne to us with all convenient speed Dated the 13° July 1678

To Capt: Maurice Mathews Surveyor Generall— } Richard Conant Will: Owen } Joseph West John Godfrey }

Carolina/

You. are forthwith to admeasure and lay out unto Maurice Mathews Gent one Towne lott in the Oyster poynt observeing the Rules and method allready established for the building a Towne there and not injuring the lines of any other person or persons and a Certificate fully specifying the metes bounds and scituacon thereof you returne to us with all convenient speed Dated the 13th: day of July 1678./

To Capt: Maur: Mathews Surveyor: Generall } Richard Conant Stephen Bull } Joseph West John Godfrey }

Carolina

You[u] are forthw[th]: to admeasure and lay out unto John Godfrey Gent One Towne lott in the Oyster poynt observing the Rules and method allready established for the building a Towne there and not injuring the lines of any other person or persons and a Certificate fully specifying the metes bounds & scituation thereof yo[u]. returne to us with all convenient speed dated the 13° July 1678

To Cap[t]: Maurice Mathews
Surveyo[r]: Generall—

Joseph West
Richard Conant
Will: Owen./
Ste: Bull

Carolina/

You[u]: are forthw[th]: to admeasure and lay out unto Tho[s]: Colleton Esq[r]: one Towne lott in the Oyster poynt observeing the rules & method allready established for the building a Towne there & not injureing the lines of any other person or persons and a Certificate fully specifying the metes bounds and scittuacon thereof yo[u]. returne to us with all convenient speed Dated the 13° July 1678

To Cap[t]: Maur Mathews
Surveyo[r] Generall

Richard Conant
Joseph West
John Godfrey

Carolina/

You[u]: are forthw[th]: to admeasure and lay out for Ralph Davies One of the settlers of this province One hundred acres of land in some convenient place not yett laid out nor marked to be laid out for any other person or use and if the same happen upon any navigable River or River capable of being made navigable you are to allow onely the fifth part of the depth thereof upon the River side & a Certificate fully specifying the bounds and scittuation thereof you are to returne to us with all convenient speed hereof fayle not Dated the 15th: day of June 1678—

To Cap[t]: Maur Mathews
Surveyo[r]: Generall.

Will: Owen.
Stephen Bull.
Joseph West
John Godfrey
Richard Conant

Carolina/

You[u]: are forthw[th]: to admeasure and lay out for Teague Cantey one of the Settlers of this province five hundred and fiftie acres of land in some convenient place not yett laid out or marked to be laid out for any other person or use and if the same happen upon any navigable River or River capable of being made navigable you^{u} are to allow only the fifth part of the depth upon the River side and a Certificate fully specifying the bounds and scituacon thereof you^{u}. are to returne to us with all convenient speed hereof fayle not dated the 15th: day of June 1678./

To Capt: Maur Mathews
Surveyor: Generall.

Will Owen. Joseph West
Ste: Bull./ John Godfrey
Richard Conant

Carolina/

You^{u}: are to admeasure and lay out for Will: Wilkinson one of the freemen of this province seaventie acres of land in some place not yett laid out nor marked to be laid out for any other person or use and if the same happen upon any navigable River or river capable to be made navigable you^{u} are to allow only the fifth part of the depth thereof by the water side and a Certificate fully specifying the bounds and scittuacon thereof you returne to us with all convenient speed; Dated the 10th: day of August Ano 1678.

To Capt: Maurice Mathews
Surveyor Generall./

Richard Conant, William Owen, Joseph West, John Godfrey

You are to admeasure and layd out for Paule Parker gent three hundred and seaventie acres of land in Some place not yet laid out nor marked to be laid out for any other person or use and if ye same happen upon any Navigable river or river capable to be made Navigable you are to allowe onlie ye fifth part of ye Depth by ye waterside and a Certificat fully specifyeing ye bounds and scituacon thereof you are to returne to us with all Convenjent speede Dated ye 7° Sept: i678:

To Capt Maurice Mathews Srveyr
generall:

J: West: J: Godfrey
Rich: Conant:
Ste: Bull:
W: Owen:

Carolina/

You are furthwith to admeasure and lay out for Isack Newton seaventie acres of land in som place not yet laid out or marked to be laid out for any other person or use and if ye same happen upon any Navigable river or river capable to be made Navigable you are to allow onlje ye 5th part of ye depth by ye water side and a certificat fully specifyeing ye bounds and scituacon thereof you are to retorne to us with all Convenjent speede and for soe doeing this shalbe you sufficient warr^{t} Dated ye 7° Day of sept: i678:

To Capt Maurice Mathews:
S^{r}vey^{r}: generall:

Rich: Conant J: West
J: Godfrey:
W: Owen:

Carolina

You are to Admeasure and lay out for Jn° Bottiley one of ye freemen of this province seaventie acres of land in some place not yet layd out, or marked to be layd out for any other person or use, and if the same happen, upon any Navigable River, or capable to be made Navigable you are to allow only the fifth part of the depth, by the water side, and a Certificate specifying the bounds & scituation thereof, you are to returne to us with all Convenient speed. And for so doeing this shall be yor sufficient warrant. Dated ye 7th day of Sep^{tr}. 1678/

To Capt Maurice Matthews
Survey^{r} Gen^{r}all.

Joseph: West
Jn° Godfrey
R: Conant:
Steven Bull:

Carolina

You are to admeasure and lay out for Edwd Middleton & Arthur Middleton, Gen^{t}. Seventeen hundred & Eighty Acres of land in some place not yet layd out, or marked to be layd out, for any other person or use, and if the same happen upon any Navigable River, or capable to be made Navigable, you are to allow only the fifth part of the depth by the wat^{r} side, and a Certificate specifying the bounds and Scituation thereof, you are to returne to us, with all convenient speed, And for yor so doeing this shall be yor sufficient warr^{t} Dated ye 7th day of Sep^{t}. 1678

To Capt Maurice Matthews
Survey^{r} generall.

Joseph West
Rich^{d}. Conant. Jn° Godfrey
Will^{n}. Owen Step^{n}. Bull

Carolina You are forthwith to admeasure & lay out for Christoph^{r} Edwards & Anne his wife One hundred Acres of land in some place not yet layd out or marked to be layd out for any other person or use, and if the same happen upon any Navigable River, or Riv^{r} capable to be made Navigable, You are to allow onely the fifth part of the depth thereof by the wat^{r} side, and a Certificate fully specifying, the Scituation & bounds thereof You are to returne to us with all convenient speed, And for so doeing this shall be yo[r] sufficient warr[t]. Dated the 7[th] day of Sept[r]. 1678

To Cap[t]. Maurice Matthews
Survey[r] Gen[r]all.

Joseph West
Rich[d]. Conant. Jn[o] Godfrey
Ste. Bull. Will[m]. Owen

Carolina

You are forthwith to admeasure & lay out for Jn[o] Jifford twoe hundred * * * * * * Acres of land in some place not yet layd out or marked to be layd out for any other person or use & if the same happen upon any Navigable River, or Riv[r] capable to be made Navigable, You are to allow onely the fifth part of the depth thereof by the wat[r] side, & a Certificate fully specifying, the scituation and bounds thereof, you are to returne to us with all convenient speed. Dated the 7th day of Sep[tr]. 1678

To Cap[t]. Maurice Matthews
Survey[r] Generall.

Joseph West
Rich[d] Conant. Jn[o] Godfrey
Ste. Bull. Will. Owen

Carolina

You are forthwith to Admeasure & lay out for Anne Perriman and Augustine Perriman three hundred and forty Acres of land, in some place not yet layd out, or marked to be layd out for any other person or use, & if the same happen upon any Navigable River, or Riv[r] capable to be made Navigable, you are to allow onely the fifth part of the depth there of by the wat[r] side, & a Certificate fully specifying the scituation & bounds thereof, you are to return to us with all convenient speed Dated the 7th day of Sep[t]. 1678/

Joseph West
Rich[d] Conant, Jn[o] Godfrey
Ste. Bull. Will. Owen

To Cap[t]. Maurice Matthews
Survey[r] Generall.

Carolina/

You are to admeasure & lay out for Elizabeth Davis, and Sarah Youngborne Settlers of this province two hundred Acres of land, in some place not yet layd out or marked to be layd out, for any oth[r] person or use, and if the same happen upon any Navigable River, or Riv[r] capable to be made Navigable, you are to allow onely the fifth part of the depth thereof by the water side, and a Certificate fully specifying the situation and bounds thereof, you are to returne to us with all Convenient speed Dated ye 7th day of Sep^t^. 1678.

To Capt. Maurice Matthews
Surveyo^r^ Generall.

Joseph West
Rich^d^. Conant. Jno Godfrey
Will Owen Ste. Bull

Carolina

You are to Admeasure and lay out for Nathaniell Jones one of ye freemen of this province two hundred Acres of land, in some place not yet layd out, or marked to be layd out for any other person or use And if the same happen upon any Navigable Riv^r^, or Riv^r^ capable to be made Navigable, you are to allow only the fifth part of the depth thereof by the wat^r^side, and a Certificate full specifying ye Scituation and bounds thereof, you are to return to us with all Convenient Speed. Dated ye 7th day of Sep^t^. 1678

To Capt. Maurice Matthews
Survey^r^ Generall.

Joseph West
Richd Conant. Jno Godfrey
Will Owen. Ste. Bull.

Carolina

You are to Admeasure and lay out for Lydia Barnett one of the settlers of this province One hundred Acres of land in some place not yet layd out, or marked to be layd out for any oth^r^ person or use And if the same happen upon any Navigable River, or River capable to be made Navigable, you are to allow only the fifth part of the depth thereof by the water side, and a Certificate full specifying ye scituation and bounds thereof, you are to returne to us with all Convenient Speed. Dated ye 7th of Sep^t^. 1678

To Capt Maurice Matthews
Surveyo^r^ Gen^r^all.

Joseph West
Richd Conant. Jno Godfrey
Ste. Bull. Will Owen.

Carolina

You are forthwith to Admeasure & lay out for Thomas Swain One hundred Acres of land, in some place not yet layd out or marked to be layd out for any other person or use, and if the same happen upon any Navigable River, or Riv^r^ capable to be made Navigable you are to allow onely a fifth part of the depth by the water side, and a Certificate fully specifying the scituation and bounds thereof you are to returne to us with all Convenient Speed Dated the 7th day of Sep^t^. 1678.

To Capt. Maurice Matthews
Survey^r^ Gen^r^all.

Joseph West
Richd Conant Jno Godfrey
Will Owen Ste. Bull

Carolina
You are to Admeasure & lay out for Thomas Turpin one of the Settlers of this Province One hundred Acres of land in some place not yet layd out or marked to be layd out for any other person or use, And if the same happen upon any Navigable Riv^{r} or River capable to be made Navigable, you are to allow onely a fifth part of the Depth by the wat^{r} side, and a Certificate fully specifying the scituation & bounds thereof, you are to return to us with all convenient speed Dated the 7th day of Septr. 1678

To Capt. Maurice Matthews
Survey^{r} Generall.

Joseph West
Rich^{d}. Conant. Jno. Godfrey
Will. Owen. Ste. Bull.

Carolina.
You are to Admeasure & lay out for Thomas Colleton Esqr & Comp^{a}. five hundred & Seventy Acres of land, in some place not yet layd out or marked to be layd out for any oth^{r} person or use, And if the same happen upon any Navigable Riv^{r}, or Riv^{r} capable to be made Navigable you are to allow only a fifth part of the Depth by the wat^{r} side and a Certificate fully Specifying the scituation and bounds thereof, you are to returne to us with all convenient speed. Dated the 7th day of Sep^{t}. 1678

To Capt. Maurice Matthews
Survey^{r} Generall.

Joseph West
Richd Conant Jno Godfrey
Will Owen

Carolina.
You are to Admeasure & lay out for Thomas Colleton Esqr and Comp^{a}. five hundred & Seventy Acres of land in some place not yet layd out, or marked to be layd out for any other person or use, and if the same happen upon any Navigable Riv^{r} or Riv^{r} Capable to be made Navigable you are to allow onely the fifth part of the depth by the water side, & a Certificate fully specifying the scituation and bounds thereof you are to return to us with all convenient speed. Dated ye 7th day of Sep^{t}. 1678

To Capt. Maurice Matthews
Survey^{r} Generall.

Joseph West
Richd Conant Jno Godfrey
Will Owen

Carolina
You are to Admeasure & lay out for Clement Brown a freeman of this province Seven hundred & ten Acres of land in some place not

yet layd out, or marked to be layd out for any oth[r] person or use, and if the same happen upon any Navigable River, or River capable to be made Navigable you are to allow onely the fifth part of the depth by the wat[r] side, and a Certificate fully specifying the scituation & bounds thereof you are to return to us with all convenient speed. Dated y[e] 7th day of Sep[t]. 1678

To Cap[t]. Maurice Matthews
Survey[r] Generall.

Joseph West
Rich[d] Conant Jn[o] Godfrey
Ste. Bull

Carolina

You are to Admeasure & lay out for Edw[d]. Love one of the freemen of this province one hundred Acres of land in some place not yet layd out or marked to be layd out for any oth[r] person or use, and if the same happen upon any Navigable River, or Riv[r] capable to be made Navigable, you are to allow only the fifth part of the depth by the wat[r] side, & a Certificate fully specifying the scituation & bounds thereof you are to return to us with all convenient speed. Dated y[e] 7th. of Sep[t]. 1678.

To Cap[t]. Maurice matthews
Survey[r] Generall

Joseph West
Rich[d] Conant Jn[o] Godfrey
Ste. Bull

Carolina.

You are to Admeasure & lay out for Thomas Colleton Esq[r] & Comp[a]. One thousand Acres of land, in some place not yet layd out or marked to be layd out for any oth[r] person or use, And if the same happen upon any Navigable Riv[r] or Riv[r] capable to be made Navigable you are onely to allow the fifth part of the depth by the wat[r] side, & a Certificate fully Specifying the Scituation & bounds thereof, you are to return to us with all Convenient speed Dated y[e] 7th day of Sep[t]. 1678.

To Cap[t]. Maurice Matthews
Survey[r] Gen[rll].

Joseph West
Rich[d] Conant Jn[o] Godfrey
Will Owen

Carolina

You are to Admeasure & lay out for W[m]. Brockhurst one of the freemen of this province a Town lott in the Oyst[r] poynt observing the rules & method already Established, for the building a Town there, & not injuring the lines of any other person or persons, & a

Certificate fully specifying the meets, bounds, and scituation thereof, your are to return to us with all convenient speed. Dated ye 7th day of Sep^{t}. 1678.

To Capt. Maurice Matthews Joseph West
Survey^{r} Generall. Will Owen Jno Godfrey

Carolina

You are forthwith to Admeasure and lay out for Jno Bezant & Lydia his wife, one hundred & forty acres of land, in some place not yet layd out or marked to be layd out for any oth^{r} person or use, And if the same happen upon any Navigable Riv^{r}, or Riv^{r} capable to be made Navigable, you are onely to allow a fifth part of the depth by the wat^{r}side, and a Certificate fully specifying the scituation and bounds thereof, you are to return to us with all Convenient Speed. Dated ye 7th day of Sep^{t}. 1678

To Capt. Maurice Matthews Joseph West
Survey^{r} Gen^{r}all. Will. Owen Jno Godfrey

Carolina

You are forthwith to Admeasure, & lay out for Robt Lewis in the right of Charles Bickerstaffe deceas^{d}. one hundred Acres of land in some place not yet layd out or marked to be layd out for any other person or use, And if the same happen upon any Navigable river, or river capable to be made Navigable you are to allow onely the fifth part of the depth thereof by ye water side, & a Certificate fully specifying ye scituation & bounds thereof you are to returne to us with all convenient speed. Dated this 7th day of Sept. 1678.

To Capt. Maurice Matthews Joseph West
Survey^{r} genra^{l}: Jno Godfrey

Carolina

You are to Admeasure and lay out for Jno Mauley three hundred & Seventy Acres of land in some place not yet layd out or marked to be layd out for any other person or use, & if the same happen upon any Navigable River, or Riv^{r} capable to be made Navigable you are to allow onely the fifth part of the depth thereof by ye wat^{r} side, & a Certificate fully specifying the scituation & bounds thereof, you are to return to us with all convenient speed. Dated this 7th day of Sep^{t}. 1678.

To Capt. Maurice Matthews Joseph West
Survey^{r} Generall. Richd Conant. Jno Godfrey

Carolina
You are to admeasure & lay out for Jnº Walker one of the freemen of this Province seventy Acres of land in some place not yet layd out or marked to be layd out for any othʳ person or use, & if the same happen upon any Navigable rivʳ or rivʳ capable to be made Navigable you are to allow onely the fifth part of the depth thereof by the watʳ side, & a Certificate fully specifying the scituation & bounds thereof, you are to returne to us with all convenient speed Dated this 7ᵗʰ day of Sepᵗ. 1678.

To Capt Maurice Matthews
Surveyʳ Generall.

Joseph West.
Richᵈ Conant. Jnº Godfrey.
Ste. Bull. Will Owen.

Carolina
You are to Admeasure & lay out for Vera Aurora Peper one of the settlers of this province One hundred Acres of land in some place not yet layd out or marked to be layd for any othʳ person or use, And if the same happen upon any Navigable river, or river capable to be made Navigable you are to allow onely the fifth part of the Depth by the watʳ side, & a Certificate, fully specifying the scituation & bounds thereof, you are to returne to us with all Convenient speed Dated this 7ᵗʰ day of Sepᵗ. 1678

To Capᵗ. Maurice Matthews
Surveyʳ. Generaˡˡ:

Joseph West
Richᵈ Conant Jnº Godfrey
Ste. Bull

Carolina
You are to Admeasure & lay out for Robᵗ Collins & Elizabeth his wife & Elizabeth his daughter three hundred Acres of land in Some place not yet layd out or marked to be layd out for any othʳ person or use, And if the same happen on any Navigable River or Rivʳ capable to be made Navigable you are to allow onely the fifth part of the depth thereof by the water side, & a certificate fuˡly specifying the scituation and bounds thereof you are to returne to us with all convenient speed. Dated this 7ᵗʰ day of Sepᵗ. 1678

To Capᵗ. Maurice Matthews
Surveyʳ Generall

Joseph West
Richᵈ Conant Jnº Godfrey
Stephen Bull.

Carolina:
You are forthwᵗʰ to admeasure and lay out for Paule Newball and Jnº Michell twoe of yᵉ free persons of this province twoe hundred

acres of land in som place not yet laid out or marked to be laid out for any other ℘son or use and if ye same happen upon any navigable river or river capable to be made navigable you are to allow onlie ye 5th part of ye Depth thereof by ye water side and a Certificat fully specifyeing ye scituacon and bounds thereof you are to returne to us with all Convenient speed Dated this 7th Day of 7^ber i678:

To Capt Maurice Mathews Survey^r: gen^rall: J: West: Jno Godfrey Rich Conant Steven Bull:/

Carolina:

You are forthw^th to lay out and admeasure for Henry Leigh one hundred acres of land in som place not yet laid out or marked to be laid out for any other ℘son or use and if ye same happen upon any Navigable river or river capable to be made navigable you are to allowe onlie ye 5^h part of ye Depth thereof by ye water side and a Certificat fully specifyeing ye scituacon and bounds thereof you are to returne to us with all Convenjent speed Dated this 7th day of 7^ber i678:/

To Capt Maurice Mathews Surveyr generall: J: West Jno Godfrey Rich: Conant: Steven Bull

You are forthw^th to admeasure and lay out for wentworth Bazden one of ye freemen of this province one hundred acres of land in som place not yet Layd out or marked to be laid out for any other person or use and if ye same happen upon any Navigable river or river capable to be made navigable you are to allowe onlie ye 5th part of ye Depth thereof by ye waterside and a Certificat fully specifyeing ye bounds & scituacon thereof you are to returne to us with all Convenient speede Dated ye 7° Day of September i678/

To Capt Maurice Mathews Survey^r generall:/ Joseph West: Rich Conant: J Godfrey Steven Bull

Carolina

You are to Lay out and Admeasure unto Edward Musson and Miriam his wife two hundred Acres of Land in some place not yett Layd out nor marked to be Layd out for any other person or use, and if be upon any Navigable River or River capable to be made Navigable yo^u are onely to allow the fifth part of the Depth thereof by the water side and a Certificate fully specifinge the bounds and scituacon thereof you[u] returne to us wth all convenient Speed Given und[r] our hands att Charles Towne the 5th day of October: 1678:/

To Cap[t] Maurice
Surveyr[r] generall:

Joseph West
Rich: Conant
Andrew piercevall:
Will Owen

You are to lay out and Admeasure unto Robt Cole one of ye freemen of this province one hundred acres of land in som place not yet laid out nor marked to be laid out for any other person or use and if it be upon any Navigable river or river capable to be made Navigable you are to allow onlie y[e] 5[h] part of ye Depth thereof by y[e] waterside and a Certificat fully specifyeing ye bounds and scituacon thereof you are to retorne to us with all Convenjent speede Dated y[e] 5[h] Day of October i678:

To Cap[t] Maurice Mathews
Survey[r] generall:

J West:
R: Conant
Will: Owen
Andrew Piercevall

Carolina/

You are to Admeasure and lay out for David Maybanck senr and David Maybanck Junior one hundred and fforty acres of Land in some place not yet layd out nor marked to be layd out for any other ꝑson or use And if it be upon any navigable River or River capable to be made navigable you are onely to allow the fifth pte of the depth thereof by the water side & a certificate fully Specifieing the bounds & scituacon thereof you retourne to us wth all Convenient Speede Given under our hand at Charles towne the 5th day of october 1678/

J West
Robt Conant
Wm Owen
And Peircevall

Carolina/

You are tô lay out & admeasure unto Jno Watkins one of the ffreemen of this Province in the right of Ann his wife seaventy acres of Land in some place not yet layd out nor mked to be layd out for any other ꝑson or use & if it happen upon any navigable River or River capable to bee made navigable you are onely to allow one fifth ꝑte of the depth thereof by the water side and a Certificate fully specifieing the bounds and scituacon thereof you retourne to us wth all Convenient speede Given under our hands at Charles Towne the 5th. day of October 1678

To Capt Maur Matthewes Survey^{r} generall/

Jo West
Rich Conant
Wm Owen
And Peircevall/

You are to lay out and admeasure unto James Witter one of the ffreemen of this Province & Mary his wife two hundred acres of Land in some place not yet layd out nor mked to be layd out for any other ꝑson or use And if it ly upon any navigable River or River capable to be made navigable you are onely to allow one fifth ꝑte of the depth by the water side & a certificate fully specifieing ye bounds & scituacon thereof you retourne to us wth all Convenient speede Given under our hands at Charles Towne ye 5th day of octob^{r} 1678

To Capt Maur: Mathewes Survey^{r} generall—

W^{m}: Owen/
Jos: West
Rich Conant
And: Peircevall

You are to lay out & admeasure unto Elizabeth Davis & Sarah youngbone two hundred acres of Land in some place not yet layd out nor m^{r}ked to be layd out for any other ꝑson or use & if it happen upon any navigable River or River capable to be made navigable you are onely to allow one fifth part of the depth by the water side & a certificate fully specifieing the bounds & scituacon thereof you retourne to us wth all Convenient speede Given under our hands at Charles Towne the 5th day of octob^{r} 1678/

To Capt maur. Mathewes Surveyor Generall/

Jo. West
Rich Conant
W^{m}Owen—And— Peircevall

Carolina:—

You are furthwth to Admeasure and lay out for Roger Smith Carpenter one of ye free persons of this province twoe hundred acres of Land in som place not yet laid out or marked to be laid out for any other ꝑson or use and if ye same should happen upon any Navigable river or river capable to be made Navigable you are to allowe onlje ye fifth part of ye Depth thereof thereof by ye waterside and a Certificate fully specifyeing ye S̄cituacon and bounds thereof you are to returne to us with all Convenjent speede Dated this 2° Day of 9ber i678

To Capt M: Mathews— Surveyr generall

Jo: West
R. Connant Jon Godfrey
Andr. Piercevall
Will: Owen:

Carolina

You are forthwith to admeasure and lay out for Robert Cole one of the ffreeholders of this Province in the right of Susannah his wife one hundred Acres of Land in some place not yet laid out or marked to be laid out for any other Person or use, and if the Same should happen upon any Navigable river or river capable to be made Navigable you are to allow onely the fifth part of the depth thereof by the waterside and A certificate fully specifying the Situation and bounds thereof you are to returne to us wth all Convenient speed Dated this Second day of November 1678

To Captain Maurice Matthews
Surveyr: Generall.

Joseph West
Rich Conant: Jno Godfrey:
Andr Piercevall:

Carolina

You are forthwith to admeasure and Lay out for George Barratt Marrener one of the free persons of this Province one hundred acres of Land in some place not yet Laid out or marked to be Laid out for ay other person or use and if the same happen upon ay navigable River or River capable of being maid navigable you are only to allow the fifth part of the debth by the water side a sertificate fully specifiing the situation and bounds thereof you are to returne to us with all convenient speede dated this second day of Novembr. 1678/

To Capt: Maurice Mathews
Servayer Generall

Joseph West
Richard Connant John Godfrey
Andrew Percefull

Carolina:

You are furthwth to Admeasure and lay out for John Stock one of the ffree ꝑsons of this Province one hundred acres of Land in some place not yet Layd out or mrked to be Layd out for any other ꝑson or use And if the same happen upon any navigable River or River capable to be made navigable you are to allow only the fifth part of ye depth by the water Side & a certificate fully specifieing the situacon & bounds thereof you are to retourne to us wth all Convenient speede Dated this second Day of november 1678/

To Capt maur Mathewes Surv: Genll— Jo: West John Godfrey Rich Conant And: Percivall

Carolina ss:

You are furthwth to Admeasure and lay out for Wm Brockhurst and w^{m} Davies one hundred and fortie acres of Land in som place not yet laid out or marked to be laid out for any other ℘son or use and if ye same happen upon any Navigable river or river capable to be made Navigable you are to allowe only ye 5^{h} part of ye Depth thereof by ye waterside and a Certificat fully specfyeing ye bounds and scituacon thereof you are to returne to us with all Convenjent speede Dated ye 2^{d} Day of November 1678:

To Capt Maurice Mathews Survey^{r} generall Jo: West Rich: Conant J: Godfrey And^{r}: Piercevall:

Carolina S^{s}

You: are forth with to Cause to bee admeasured and laid unto John Godfreÿ Gent: in ye right of Henrÿ Jones deceased one hundred accres of Land in some place not yett laid out or marked to bee laid out for aney other ℘son or use and if ye same happen uppon aney navigable River or river Capable to bee made navigable yo^{u}: are to allow onelÿ ye fifth ℘te of ye depth thearof bÿ ye watter side & a Certif'cate fullÿ specifieing ye scituacon and bounds thereof, yo^{u}: are to returne to us with all Convenient speed, and for yor: soe doeing, this shall bee yor. sufficient warr^{t}: Given under our hands at Charles Towne this 2^{d} day of November: 1678

To Capt: Maurice Mathews Surveyo^{r}: Generall Richard Conant Joseph West Will: Owen

Carrolina

You are forth with to admeasure and lay out unto Sarah Yarpe one Towne lott in y^{e} oyster=point observing y^{e} Rules and method alreadie established for y^{e} building a Towne thear and not InJureing y^{e} lines of aneÿ other ℘son or ℘sones and a certificate fullÿ specie-

fieing metes bounds and scituacon thereof, you: returne to us with all Convenie^t: speed dated y^e 2^d: daÿ of November ano 1678
To Capt: Maurice Mathews Surveyo^r: Genll: Joseph West Andr: Percivall W: Owen: John Godfreÿ

Carrolina Yoü are forth with to admeasure and laÿ out unto Jno Norton plantor one Towne Lott in y^e oyster=point observinge y^e Rules and method alreadÿ established for y^e buildeing a Towne theare and not InJureing y^e lines of aneÿ other ℘son or ℘sons and a Certificate fullÿ speciefieing y^e metes boundes and scituacon thereof you: returne to us with all Convenient speed dated y^e 2°: day of November 1678/
To Capt. Maurice Mathews Surveyo^r Generll: Andrew Percivall Joseph West John Godfreÿ

Carrollina You are forthwith to admeasure and lay out unto Will: Owen one Towne lott in ye oyster pointe observeinge ye Rules and method alreadie established for ye building a Towne theare and not Injureing ye lines of aneÿ other ℘son or ℘sons and a Certiefiecate fully specifyinge ye metes bounds and scituacon: thearof, you: returne to us with all Convenient speed Dated ye 2°: daÿ of November 1678/
To Capt: Maurice Mathews Suryo^r: Genll: Richard Conant Andr. Percivall Joseph West John Godfreÿ

Carrolina
You are forthwith to admeasure and laÿ out for ffrancis Ladson one of ye free ℘sons of this Province one hundred accres of land in some place not yett laid out or marked to bee laid out for aneÿ other ℘son or use and if ye same happen upon aneÿ navigable River Capable of being made navigable you are onelÿ to allow ye fifth parte of ye depth bÿ ye watter side, and a Certifiecate fullÿ speciefieinge ye scituation and bounds thearof you: are to returne to us with all Convenient speede Dated this second day of November 1678
To Capt: Maurice Mathews Surveyr: Genll: Richard Conant Andr: Percivall Joseph West John Godfreÿ

Carrolina
You are forth with to admeasure and laÿ out for Maurice Mathews Gen^t. three hundred accres of land in some place not yett laid out or

marked to bee laid out for aneÿ other ꝑson or use and if ye same happen upon aneÿ navigable River or River Capable of being made navigable you: are to allow onelÿ ye fifth ꝑte of depth bÿ ye watter side and a Certiefiecate Specifieing the Scituation and bounds theareof you: are to retierne to us with all Convenient speed dated this second daÿ of November 1678/

To Capt: Maurice Mathews
Sirauyer: Genell

Richard Conant Joseph West
Andr: Percivall John Godfreÿ

Carrolina

You are forth with to admeasure and laÿ out for Abraham Smith in ye right of his wiffe two hundred and seventie accres of lands, in some place not yett laid out or marked to bee laid out for aneÿ other ꝑson or use and if ye same happen upon aneÿ navigable River or Rivers Capable of being made navigable you: are to allow onelÿ ye fifth ꝑte of ye depth bÿ ye watter=side and a Certificate fullÿ speciefieing ye Situation and bounds, thereof, you: are to returne to us with all Convenient speed dated this second day of November 1678/

To Capt: Maurice Mathews
Suryer: Generall

Joseph West
Richard Conant
Andw: Percevall John Godfrey

Carrolina You are forth with to admeasure and laÿ out for Richard Gilliard one of ye free ꝑsons of this Province one hundred accres of land in some place not yett laid out or marked to bee laid out for aneÿ other ꝑson or use, and if ye same happen uppon aneÿ Navigable River or River Capable of being made Navigable you: are to allow onlÿ ye fifth ꝑte of depthe bÿ ye watter-side and a Certificate fullÿ speciefieing ye sittuation and bounds thereof you: are to returne to us with all Convenient Speede dated this second daÿ of November 1678—

To Capt Maurice Mathews
Sureyr: Generall

Richard Conant Joseph West
Andw: Percevall John Godfrey

Carrolina

You are forth with to admeasure and lay out for Katharin Harding one of ye free persons of this Province one hundred accres of land in some place not yett laid out or marked to bee laid out for anÿ other ꝑson or use, and if ye same happen upon anÿ navigable River or Rivers Capable of being made navigable you: are to allow onelÿ ye fifth ℘te of ye depth thereof bÿ ye watter side and a Certificate fullÿ speciefieing ye sittuation and bounds thereof you: are to returne to us with all Convenient Speede dated this second day of November 1678—

To Capt: Maurice Mathews Suryor: Jenerall — Richard Conant, Joseph West, Andw: Percevall, John Godfrey

Carrolina

You are forth with to admeasure and laÿ out for John Godfreÿ Gentleman and a free ℘son of this Province one hundred accres of land in some place not yett laid out or marked to bee laid out for aneÿ other ℘son or use or if ye same happen uppon any navigable River or Rivers Capable of being made navigable you. are onlÿ to allow the fifth ℘te of ye depth bÿ ye watter side and a situation fullÿ Speciefÿing the sittuation and bounds theareof you: are to returne to use with all Convenient Speede dated this second daÿ of November 1678/

To Capt: Maurice Mathews Surveyor: Jenerall — Richard Conant, Joseph West, Andr Percivall, John Godfreÿ

Carrolina

You are forth with to admeasure and laÿ out for Will: Hatton one of ye.. free ℘sons of this Province one hundred seventie accres of land in some place not yett laid out or marked to bee laid out for aneÿ other ℘son or use and if ye same should happen upon any navigable River or Rivers Capable of being made navigable you are onelÿ to allow ye fifth ℘te of ye depth bÿ ye watter side and a Certificate fullÿ speciefieing the sittuation and bounds thereof you: to returne to us with all Convenient speede Dated this second daÿ of November 1678/

To Capt: Maurice Mathews Surveyr Jener: — Richard Conant, Joseph West, Andw: Percivall, John Godfrey

Carrolina Ss

You are forth with to cause to bee admeasured and laid out unto Robert Allerree seventÿ accres of land in some place not yett laid out or marked to bee laid out for anÿ other ℘son or use and if ye same happen upon aneÿ navigable River or Rivers Capable to bee made Navigable you: are to allow onlÿ ye fifth ℘te of ye depth theareof by ye watter side, and a Certificate fullÿ speciefieing ye sittuation & bounds theareof you: are to returne to us with all Convenient speede and for yor: soe doeing this shall bee yor: sufficient warrt:

Given under our hands at Charles towne this second day of november 1678

To Capt: Maurice Mathews Surveyr: Generall | Joseph West Richard Conant John Godfrey Andw: Percevall

Carrolina You are to lay out and admeasure unto Maurice Mathews Gent: three hundred and fortÿ eight accres of land being y remainder of seaven hundred and fiftie accres, in some place not yett laid out or marked to bee laid out for aneÿ other ꝑson or use and if it bee uppon aneÿ navigable River or River Capable to bee made navigable you are to allow onelÿ ye fifth ꝑte of ye depth theareof bÿ ye watter side and a Certificate fullÿ specifieing ye bounds and situation thearof you: are to returne to us with all Convenient speede. Given under our hands at Charles Towne this 2°: day of 9ber: 1678/

To Capt: Maurice Mathews Surveyr: Generall | Richard Conant Joseph West Andr: Percevall John Godfrey

Carrolina Ss./ You are to lay out and admeasure unto Richard ffowell Gent: seaventeene hundred therty accres of land in some place not yett laid out or marked to bee laid out for aneÿ other ꝑson or use and if ye same happen upon aneÿ navigable River or River Capable to bee made navigable you: are to allow onelÿ ye fifth ꝑte of ye depth thearof bÿ ye watter side & a Certificate fullÿ speciefieing ye bounds and situation theareof you: are to returne to us with all Convenient speede Given under our at Charles Towne ye 2°— day of November 1678/

To Capt: Maurice Mathews Surveyr: Generall | Richard Conant Joseph West Andw Percivall John Godfrey

Carrolina/ You are forth with to admeasure and lay out for Daniell ffreezell one of ye free men of this Province one hundred accres of land in some place not layd out or marked to bee laid out for aneÿ other ꝑson or use and if ye same happen upon aneÿ navigable River or River Capable of being made navigable you are to allow onelÿ ye fifth ꝑte of ye depth bÿ ye watter side and a Certificate fullÿ speciefieing ye situation and bounds theareof you: are to returne to us with all Convenient speede Given under our hands at Charles Towne ye 2°: day of 9ber: 1678

To Capt Maurice Mathews Suryer: Generall | Richard Conant Joseph West Andw: Percevall John Godfreÿ

Carrolina You are forth with to admeasure and laÿ out unto mr John Maverick one Towne lott in ye oyster Point observing ye Rules and Method already established for ye building a Towne theare and not InJuring ye lines of aneÿ other ꝑson or ꝑsons and a Certificat fullÿ specifieing metes bounds and situation theareof you: returne to us with all Convenient speede dated ye Second day of November 1678/

To Capt: Maurice Mathews Richard Conant Joseph West
Suryer: Generll Andw: Percevall John Godfreÿ

Carolina/

You are to admeasure and lay out for mr John Coming one of the ffreemen of this Province seaven hundred and fforty acres of Land in some place not yet layd out or mrked to be Laid out for any other ꝑson and if the same happen upon any navigable River or River capable to be made navigable you are to allow onely the fifth part of the depth thereof by the waterside and a Certificate fully specifieing the bounds and Scituacon thereof you are to retourne to us wth all Convenient speede dated this 30th day of Novemb 1678/

To Capt Maur Mathewes Richard Conant Joseph West
Surveyor Genll— Wm Owen—

Carolina/ You are to admeasure & lay out unto Charles Harliston ffreeman one hundred acres of Land in some place not yet layd out or marked to be layd out for any other ꝑson or use and if the same happen upon any navigable River or River capable to be made navigable you are to allow onely the fifth part of the depth thereof by the waterside and a certificate fully specifieing the bounds and scituacon thereof you are to retourne to us wth all Convenient Speede Dated this 30th day of novembr 1678./

To Capt. maur: Mathewes Rich Conant Joseph West
Survey: Genll— Wm Owen And: Piercevall:

Carolina:

You are furthwth to admeasure and lay out unto Jno Meader one Towne lott in ye Oyster point observeing ye rules and method alreadie established for ye building of a towne there and not Injureing ye lines of any other person or ꝑsons and a Certificat fully specifyeing ye bounds and Scituacon thereof you returne to us with all Convenient speed. Dated ye 2° day of November i678:

To Capt Maurice Mathews J. West
Surveyr genrall: R: Conant Jno Godfrey
And: Piercevalle

Carolina/
You are forthwith to admeasure & lay out unto Capt fflorence OSullivan one Towne Lott in the Oyster Point observing the Rules & method already established for the building a Towne there & not injureing the Lines of any other ꝑson or ꝑsons & a Certificate fully specifieing the metes bounds & scituacon thereof you retourne to us wth all Convenient speede dated the 30th day of Novembr 1678.

Josep: West
Rich Conant
And Percivall
Wm Owen—

To Capt Maur: Mathewes
Surveyor—

Carolina/
You are by virtue hereof to admeasure & lay out unto Edward Mayo one of the ffreemen of this Province seaven hundred & ffifty acres of Land which was formerly the Land laid out for Nich Cartwright & a Certificate fully specifieing the bounds & scituacon thereof you are to retourne to us wth all Convenient Speede Dated the 30th day of novembr 1678

To Capt Maur: Mathewes
Surveyor. Genll—

Rich Conant Jos: West
Wm Owen/

Carolina/
You are forthwth to admeasure & lay out for Mary Brotherhood one of the ffree ꝑsons of this Province Seaventy acres of Land in some convenient place not yet layd out or mrked to be layd out for any other ꝑson or use & if the same happen upon Navigable River or River capable to be made Navigable you are to allow onely the fifth part of the depth thereof by the water side & a Certificate fully specifieing the scituacon & bounds thereof you are to retourne to us wth all Convenient speede dated the 30th day of novembr 1678/

Joseph West
Rich Conant
Wm Owen

To Capt Maur: Mathewes
Surveyor Genll—

Carolina/
You are forthwith to admeasure & lay out for ffrancis Boult Gent one of the ffreemen of this province six hundred acres of Land for himselfe wife slaves & servants in some place not yet layd out or mrked to be layd out for any other ꝑson or use & if the same happen upon any navigable River or River capable to be made navigable

you are to allow onely the fifth part of the depth thereof by the waterside & a Certificate fully specifieing the scituacon & bounds thereof you are to retourne to us wth all Convenient speede dated the 30th day of novemb 1678

Joseph West
To Capt maur: Mathewes Rich Conant
Survey: Genll/. Wm Owen

Carolina.
You. are forthwth to admeasure and lay out for George Conway one of the ffreemen of this province three hundred acres of land in some place not yett laid out or marked to be laid out for any other person or use and if the same happen upon any navigable River or River capable to be made navigable you are to allow only the fifth part of the depth thereof by the water side And a Certificate fully specifying the scittuation and bounds thereof you are to returne to us wth. all convenient speed Dated this 30th. Novembr. 1678.
To Maurice Mathews Joseph West
Surveyor. Generall Richard Conant./ Will: Owen

Carolina: You are furthwth to admeasure and lay out for Thomas Greatebeach one hundred acres of Land in som place not yet laid out or marked to be laid out for any other ꝑson or use and if ye same happen upon any Navigable river or river capable to be made Navigable you are to allowe onlie ye 5th part of ye Depth by ye water side and a Certificat fully specifyeing ye bounds and scituacon thereof you are to returne to us with all Convenient speed Dated ye 30th Day of November i678

Jo: West
To Capt M: Maurice Mathews Rich: Connant:
Surveyr: genrall./ Will: Owen:

In pursuance of an order of the Grand Councill bearing date Aprill 23th. 1678 you are to admeasure and lay out for Jonathan Fitz one of the freemen of the Collony all that tract of land upon Ashley River formerly called Mr Bryans land and now in the possession of the sd. Mr. Fitz and a Certificate fully specifying the bounds scittuacon and quantity of acres therein you. are to returne to us wth. all convenient speed Dated this 30th: November 1678.—
To Capt. Maurice Mathews Joseph West
Surveyor Generall./ Will: Owen
Richard Conant

You are to Admeasure and lay out unto Neale m^{c}Donald one of ye freemen of this province one hundred acres of land in Som place not yet laid out or marked to be laid out for any other ꝑson or use and if ye same happen upon any Navigable river or river capable to be made Navigable you are to allowe onlie ye 5^{h} part of ye Depth thereof by ye waterside and a Certificat fully specifyeing ye bounds and Scituacon thereof you are to retorne to us with all Convenjent speede Dated this 30th Day of 9ber i678:

To Capt M: Mathews Surveyr generall:

R: Conant Joseph West
Will: Owen

Carolina:

You are furthwth to admeasure and lay out for Job Bishop one of ye freemen of this province twoe hundred acres of land in some place not yet laid out or marked to be laid out for any other ꝑson or use and if ye same happen upon any Navigable river or river capable to be made navigable you are to allowe onlie ye fifth part of ye Depth by ye water side and a Certificat fully specifyeing ye bounds and scituacon thereof you are to retorne to us with all Convenient speed Dated ye 30th Day of November i678:/

To Capt M: Mathews Survey^{r} generall — — — — —

Joseph West
Andr^{r}: Piercevall:
Will: Owen

You are to admeasure and lay out unto David Maybanck sen^{r} and David Maybanck Ju^{r}. twoe Towne Lotts in ye Oyster point observeing ye Rules and Method allready established for ye building of a towne there and not Injureing ye Lines of any other person or ꝑsons and a Certificat fully specifyeing ye metes bounds and scituacon thereof you are to retorne to us wth all Convenjent speede Dated ye 30th day of Nov^{br}: i678:

To Capt M: Mathews Surveyr gen^{r}all— —

Joseph West
Rich: Conant:
Will: Owen:

Carolina/

You are to admeasure & lay out unto Thomas Eakin one hundred acres of Land in some Convenient place not yet layd out or m^{r}ked to be layd out for any other ꝑson or use & if the same happen upon any navigable River or Any River Capable to be made navigable you are to allow onely the fifth part of the depth thereof by the water side & a Certificate fully specifieing the scituacon & bounds thereof you are to Retourne to us wth all Convenient speede & for yor soe doeing this shall be yor sufficient warn[t] Given under our hands at Charles Towne this 28[th] Day decem 1678./

To Capt Maur: Mathewes
Surveyor Generall

Joseph West
Andrew Percivall
W[m]. owen/

Carolina/

You are to admeasure & lay out unto Richard Searle Gent three hundred & Seaventy acres of Land in some place not yet Layd out or m[r]ked to be layd out for any other ꝑson or use & if the same happen upon any Navigable River or any River Capable to be made Navigable you are to allow onely the fifth part of the depth thereof by the water Side & a Certificate fully specifieing ye bounds & Scituacon thereof you are to Retourne to us wth all Conv[t] speede Given under our hands at Charles Towne the 9[th] day of decem 1678/

Joseph West
And Percivall
W[m] Owen

To Capt Maur: Mathewes:
Surveyo[r] Genll—

Carolina/

You are to admeasure & lay out for Abenezer Kyrtland one of the freemen of this Province one hundred of acres of Land in some Convenient place not yet layd out or m[r]ked to be Layd out for any other ꝑson or use & if the same happen upon any Navigable River or River Capable to be made navigable you are to allow onely the fifth part of the depth thereof by the water side & a Certificate fully specifieing the Scituacon & bounds thereof you are to Retourne to us wth all Convenient speede dated this 30th day of Novemb[r] 1678/

Joseph West
And: Percivall
W[m] owen

To Capt Maur: Mathewes
Surveyor Genll

Carolina/

You are to admeasure & lay out for m[r] Richard Quintin one of the freemen of this Province one hundred acres acres of Land in some place not yet layd out or marked to be layd out for any other ꝑson or use & if the same happen upon any Navigable River or River Capable to be made Navigable you are to allow onely the fifth part of the depth thereof by the water side & a Certificate fully specifieing the bounds & scituacon you are to Retourne to us wth all Convent speede Dated this 30th day of novemb 1678./

Joseph West

To Capt Maur: mathewes Surveyor Genll— } Richa Conant Wm Owen

Carolina/

You are to admeasure & lay out unto John Bristoll and Company one hundred & Seaventy acres of Land in some place not yett layd out or marked to be layd out for any other ꝑson or use & if the same happen upon any Navigable River or any River Capable to be made Navigable you are to allow onely the fifth part of the depth thereof by the water side and a Certificate fully specifieing the bounds & scituacon thereof you are to Retourne to us wth all Convenient speede Given under our hands at Charles Towne the 30 day of Novemb 1678./

Joseph West

To Capt maur mathewes Sur Genll— } Richa Conant Wm Owen—

Carolina/

You are to admeasure & lay out for John Miller gent one of the ffreemen of this Province ffive hundred & eighty acres of Land in some place not yet layd out or mrked to be layd out for any other ꝑson or use & if the same happen upon any Navigable River or River Capable to be made Navigable you are to allow onely the fifth part of the depth thereof by by the water side & a Certificate of the scituacon & bounds thereof you are to Retourne to us wth all Convent speede dated this 30th day of Novemb 1678/

Joseph West

To Capt maur: mathewes Sur Genll— } Richa Conant Wm—owen

Carolina/

You are forthwith to admeasure & lay out for George Miller Jane Miller and Martha Miller & John Miller Junior the free ꝑsons of this Province ffowre hundred acres of Land in some place not yet Layd out or mrked to be layd out for any other ꝑson or use & if the same happen upon any Navigable River or River Capable to be made navigable you are to allow onely the fifth part of the depth thereof by the water side & a Certificate fully specifieing the bounds

& scituacon thereof you are to Retourne to us wth all Convenint speede Dated this 30th day of novemb 1678.

To Capt maur mathewes Surveyor Gen[ll]

Rich[a] Conant Jos. West
W[m] Owen

Carolina

You are forthwith to admeasure & lay out unto M[r]s Sarah ffowell one of the free persons of this Province sixteen hundred and thirty acres of land in some convenient place not yet layd out or marked to be layd out for any oth[r] p[r]son & if it happen upon any navigable Riv[r], or Riv[r] capable to be made navigable you are onely to allow the fifth part of the depth thereof by the wat[r]. side, and a Certificate fully specifying the bounds & scituation thereof to returne to us with all convenient speed. Dated at Charlestown this 25° day of Jan[r]. 1678.

To Cap[t]. Maurice Mathews
Survey[r] Generall

Hen[r]. Woodward Joseph West
Will. Owen. And[r]. Percivall.

Yo[u] are forthwith to admeasure and lay out unto John Shepherd, one of y[e] free ꝑsons of this ꝑvince one hundred acres of Land in some convenient place not yett layd out or marked to be layd out for any other ꝑson, and if itt happen upon any Navigable River, or River capable to be made Navigable, yo[u] are onely to allow the fifth part of the Depth, thereof by the River side. and a Certificate fully Specifieing y[e] bounds & situation thereof yo[u]. returne to us wth all convenient speed. Dated att Charles Towne this 30th day of Jan[r] 1678/

To Cap[t]. Maurice Mathews. Surveyo[r]. Generall

Joseph: West
Richard Conant

Yo[u] are forthw[th]. to admeasure and lay out for Hugh Wiglesworth, one of y[e] ffree men of this Province. One hundred acres of Land in some place not yett layd out or marked to be layd out for any other ꝑson or use, and if the same happen upon any Navigable River or any River capable to bee made navigable, yo[u] are to allow onely the fifth part of y[e] debth thereof by the water side and a Certificate fully specifiinge the scituacon and bounds thereof yo[u] are to returne to us wth all convenient speed and for yo[r]. soe Doeinge this shall bee yo[r]. sufficient war[t]. Given und[r]. our hands this 30 ffebruary 1678/9

To Cap[t] Maurice Mathews
Surveyo[r]. Generall

Joseph West
Rich Conant

Yo^{u} are forthwth to admeasure and lay out for Jo^{n} Bullein one of ye free ꝑsons of this Province, one hundred acres of Land in some convenient place not yett layd out or marked to be laid out for any other ꝑson, and if itt happen upon any Navigable River or River Navigable to be made navigable, yo^{u} are onely to allow the fifth part of ye Depth thereof by the water side. and a Certificate fully specifieing the bounds & scituacon thereof yo^{u} returne to us with all convenient speed Dated att Charles Towne ye 24th day of Jan^{ry}. 1678/

To Capt Maurice Mathews Surveo^{r}. Generall/ — Henry Woodward Joseph: West Andrew Percevall/ Rich: Conant

You are furthwith to lay out and Admeasure unto Nathaniel Wigmor and Ann his wife free persons of this provinc^{e} one hundred and fortie acres of Land in som place not yet laid out or marked to be laid out for any other person or use and if ye Same happen upon any Navigable river or river capable to be made navigable you are to allowe only ye 5^{h} part of ye Depth thereof by ye water side and a Certificat fully specifyeing ye bounds and scituacon thereof you retorne to us with all Convenjent speed. Dated ye 25° Jan: 1678:

To Capt M: Mathews Surv^{r}: genall: — Hen: Woodward: Joseph West: Will: Owen:

You are forth with to Admeasure, & Lay out unto John Bird one of the free ꝑsons of this ꝑvince. 679 Acres of Land in some Convenient place not yett Layd out for any other ꝑson or marked to be Laid out, and if it happen upon any Navigable River or Rivers, the fifth ꝑte of the Depth thereof by y^{e}— water side, & a Certificate thereof fully specifying the Bounds & Scittuation there of you Returne to us wth— all Convenient Speed, dated at Charles Towne the 22°. day of March 1678/

To Capt. Mauris Mathews Surveyor Gener^{ll}./ — Jno. Godfrey Joseph West— W^{m}. Owen Andrew Percivall

Carolina:

You are furthwth to cause to be admeasured and laid out unto Joseph Hatchman one hundred acres of Land in som place not yet laid out or marked to be laid out for any other person or use and if ye Same happen upon any Navigable river or river capable to be made Navigable you are to allowe onlie ye 5^{h} part of ye Depth thereof by ye waterside and a Certificat fully specifyeing ye bounds and scituacons thereof you are to returne to us with all Convenjent speed and for yor soe Doeing this shalbe yor sufficient Warr^t Given und^r o^r hands att Charlestowne this 22th day of ffebr i678/9:

To Capt Maur: Mathews
Surveyr gen^rll:/

Jos: West:
Andr: Piercevall
Rich: Conant
John Godfrey:

You are furthw^th to Lay out for Jno Chambers one of ye freemen of this province thirtie five acres of Land in som place not not yet laid out or marked to be laid out for any other ꝑson or ꝑsons or use and if ye Same happen upon any navigable river or river capable to be made Navigable you are to allowe onlje ye 5^h part of the Depth thereof by ye water side and a Certificat fully specifyeing ye bounds and Scituacon thereof you are to retorne to us with all Convenjent speede Dated ye 3° of Aprill i679:

To Capt Maurice Mathews
Surveyr generall

Joseph West:
Rich Conant
Andr Piercevall
Will: Owen

Carolina

You are furthw^th to Admeasure and lay out unto Benjamin Andrews one of the freemen of this Province two hundred and forty acres of land in some convenient place not yett laid out or marked to be laid out for any other person or use and if it happen upon any navigable River or River capable to be made navigable yo^u: are to allow only the 5^h: part of the depth thereof by the water side and a Certificate fully specifying the bounds & scittuacon thereof yo^u. are to returne to us with all convenient speed, Dated the 19° Aprill 1679.

To Capt: M. Mathews
Surveyo^r. Generall./

Joseph West
Richard Conant
Will: Owen
Andr: Percivall./

Carolina You^u. are forthw^th. to lay out & admeasure unto Johna Lynch one hundred acres of Land marked & builded on by the said Lynch allready & if y^e. same happen upon any Navigable River or Rivers capable to be made Navigable you are to allow onely y^e. fifth parte of y^e. depth thereof by y^e. water syde, and a Certificat fully specifyeing y^e. bounds & Scituacon thereof you returne to us wth. all convenient speede, Given under our hands this 14th. day of May 1679

To Capt: Maurice Mathews Surveyor. Genall./

Joseph West
Jno: Godfrey
Richard Conant
Wm. Owen

Carolina:

You are furthwth to admeasure and lay out unto Jno Chaplin and Ann his wife free persons of this province one hundred and fortie acres of land in som convenient place not yet laid out or marked to be laid out for any other person or use and if it happen upon any Navigable or river capable to be made Navigable you are onlie to allow the 5th part of ye depth thereof by the waterside and a Certificat fullie specifyeing the bounds and its scituacon you retorne to us with all Convenient speed Dated ye 25th day of Janry i678:/

And: Piercevall J: West
Rich: Conant
Jno Godfrey——

To Capt M: Mathews Surveyr generall:/

You are furthwth to admeasure and lay out unto Jno Cottingham one towne lot at ye Oyster pointe observeing ye rules and method alreadie establisht for ye building a towne there and not injureing ye lines of any other person or persons and a Certificat fullie specifyeing ye scituacon and bounds thereof you retorne to us with all Convenjent speede Dated ye 19° Aprill i679

Joseph West
R: Conant:
Will: Owen And: Piercevall

To Capt M: Mathews Surveyr generall:

You are furthwth to cause to be Admeasured and laid out unto Jno Michell one towne lot att ye Oyster pointe observeing ye rules and method allreadie established for ye building a towne there and not Injureing ye lines of any other person or persons and a Certificat fully specifyeing ye bounds and scituacon thereof you are to retorne to us withall Convenjent speede Dated this 19° Aprill i679:

To Capt M Mathews Surveyr genall:

J West
R: Conant
Will: Owen:
Jno Godfrey:

You are forthwith to Cause to be admeasured & Laid out Unto William Murrill one Towne Lott at the Oysterpointe, observing the Rules and Method Already Established for the Building the said Towne, and not ꝑ^{r}judiceing the Lynes of any ꝑson or ꝑsons and a certificate fully Specifying the Scittuation & bounds Thereof you are to Returne to us wth- all convenient Speed dated 19th. Aprill 1679

Rich^{d}— Conant W^{m}— Owen Joseph West
Jno. Godfrey

To Capt— Maurice Mathews
Surveyo^{r}. Gener^{ll}—

You are furthwth to lay out and admeasure unto Charles Bulkley one of ye free persons of this province one hundred acres of Land in som convenjent place not yet laid out or marked to be laid out for any other person or use and if ye same happen upon any Navigable river or river capable to be made navigable you are to allowe onlje ye 5th part of of ye Depth thereof by ye water side and a Certificat fullie specifyeing ye bounds and Scituacon thereof you retorne to us with all Convenjent speede Dated att Charles towne this i9° Day of Aprill, i679

To Capt maurice Mathews Survey^{r} generall :/

Rich : Conant Joseph West
Will : Owen : And^{r} Piercevall

You are furthwth to admeasure and lay out unto Joseph Calfe one of the freemen of this province, Two hundred Acres of Land in some place not yett Layd out or marked to be Laid out for any other ꝑson or use, and if the same happen, upon any Navigable River or Rivers Capable to be made navigable, you are to Allow only a fifth ꝑte. of the Debth there of by the water side, and a Certificate fully specifieing the Scittuacon & bounds thereof, you are to Returne, unto us, wth— all convenient speede, dated the 3^{d} of Aprill, 1679./

To Capt. Maur. Mathews
Surveyo^{r}. Gener^{ll} :/

Rich^{d}. Conant Jos : West
W^{m}. Owen And^{r}. Percivall

You are forthwth. to Admeasure & Lay out Unto John Ellis for himselfe, & his wife John & James Theire Children, free ꝑsons of this ꝑvince, fower hundred Acres of Land, in some Convenient place not yett Laid out or marked to be laid out for any other ꝑson and if it happen upon any Navigable River, or Rivers capable to be made Navigable you are to Allow, only a fifth ꝑte of the Depth thereof by the water side, and a Certificate fully specifying y^{e}— bounds. Scittuation thereof you Returne to us wth— all convenient Speed, dated the 14th— of June 1679./

To Capt. Maure Mathews
Surveyo^{r} Gener^{ll}./

Rich^{d}. Conant Jos : West
Jno. Godfrey

Carolina. Ss./
You are forthwith to Admeasure, & Lay out Unto John Meader one of the ffree ꝑsons of this Province, Two hundred Acres of Land in Som convenient place, not yett Layd out, or marked, to be Laid out for any other ꝑson, and if it happen upon any Navigable River or Rivers capable to be made Navigable, you are only to Allow the fifth ꝑte thereof by the waterside, and a Certificate fully Specifieing the bounds & Scittuacon thereof you Returne to us wth. all Convenient Speed, dated at Charles Towne the 14th— day of June 1679.

To Capt. Maur: Mathews
Surveyo^{r}. Gener^{ll}./

Rich^{d}. Conant Jos: West
Jno. Godfrey—

You are to Admeasure and lay out unto James Mullrayne and Marie his wife free persons of this province one hundred and seaventie acres of land in som convenient place not yet laid out or marked to be laid out for any person or ꝑsons and if it happen upon any Navigable river or river capable to be made Navigable you are onlie to ollowe ye 5th part of the depth thereof by ye waterside and a Certificat fullie specifyeing ye bounds & scituacon thereof you retorne to us with all convenjent speed Dated ye 19° Mar: i679 att charles towne

Capt M: Mathews Survey^{r}/
generall/

Joseph West
R: Conant And^{r} Piercevall
Will: Owen:

You are forthwith to admeasure & Lay out unto Johna Lynch one of the free ꝑsons of this ꝑvince one hundred Acres of Land in some convenient place not yett Laid out or marked to be Laid out for any other ꝑson, and if it happen, upon any Navigable River, or River capable to be made Navigable, you are only to Allow the fifth ꝑte of the Depth thereof by the water side, and a Certificate fully Specifying the bounds Scittuation thereof, you, Returne to us, wth. all convenient speed, dated at Charles Towne, this 19th. of Ap^{r}ll 1679—

To Capt— Maur— Mathews
Survey^{r}— Gener^{ll}./

Jno. Godfrey Jos: West
Rich^{d}: Conant

Carolina. Ss./
You are forth^{wth}— to Admeasure and Layout unto John Thrusk one of the free ꝑsons of this Province, Seaventy acres of Land in some convenient place, not yett Laydout, or marked to be Laid out for any other ꝑson, and, and if it happen upon any Navigable River,

or Rivers capable to be made Navigable you are only to Allow the fifth Ꝑte of the Depth thereof by the water side and a Certificate fully specifying the bounds Scittuacon thereof you Returne to us wth— all convenient Speed, dated at Charles Towne, This 14th— day of June 1679

To Capt— Maur. Mathews
Surveyor Gener^{ll}./

Jos: West
Andrew Percivall
W^{m}— Owen

You are forthwith to Admeasure & Layout unto ffrancis Peele one of the free Ꝑsons of this Ꝑvince, one hundrd. Acres of Land, in some convenient place not yett Layd out or marked to be Laid out for any other Ꝑson, and if it happen upon any Navigable River, or River capable to be made Navigable you are only to allow the fifth Ꝑte of the Depth thereof by the waterside, and a Certificate fully Specifyeing the bounds, Scittuacon thereof, you returne to us wth. all convenient Speed, Dated at Charles Towne this 14th— day of June 1679

Jos: West

To Capt— Maur. Mathews
Survey^{r}— Gener^{ll}./

Rich^{d}. Conant
W^{m}= Owen

You are forthwith to Admeasure & Lay out unto Leah King, Thomas King, & Leah King ffree Ꝑsons of this Ꝑvince, Three hundred acres of Land, in some Convenient place not yett Laid out or marked to be Laid out for any Other Ꝑson, and if it happen upon any Navigable River, or River capable to be made Navigable you are only to allow the fifth Ꝑte of the Depth thereof by the water side and a Certificate fully Specifying the bounds & Scittuation thereof you Returne to us wth— all convenient Speed Dated at Charles Towne, this 23th— day of Jan^{r}y 1678—

To Capt. Maur. Mathews
Surv^{r}— Gen^{rll}—/

Hen. Woodward
Andr^{r}— Percivall
Jno. Godfrey

Jos: West
Rich^{d}. Conant

Carolina. Ss./

You are forthwith to admeasure & Lay out unto John Shepherd one of the free Ꝑsons of this Ꝑvince one hundrd— Acres of Land in Some convenient place not yett laid out or marked to be Laid out for any other Ꝑson, and if it happen Upon any Navigable River, or River capable to be made Navigable, you are only to Allow the fifth ꝑte of the Depth thereof by the waterside and a Certificate fully Specifying the Bounds the Bounds and Scittuation thereof you Returne to us w^th^— all convenient Speede, Dated at Charles Towne, this 3°— day of Jan^ry^. 1678./

To Capt. Maur. Mathews Surveyo^r^. Gener^ll^—/

Hen: Woodward Jos. West
W^m^= Owen, Rich^d^— Conant
Jno— Godfrey

You are forthw^th^. to Admeasure and Lay out unto Edward Wilson and Marieris his wife, one hund^rd^. acres of Land in Some place not yett Laid out, nor marked to be Laid out for any Other ꝑson or use and if the same happen upon any Navigable River, or River capable to be made Navigable, you are to Allow only the 5th— ꝑte of the Depth thereof by the water side, and a Certificate fully Specifying the Bounds & Scittuacon thereof you doe Returne to us w^th^— all convenient speed, dated the 22°. day of ffeb^y^.. 1678.

To Capt. Maur. Mathews Survey^r^— Gener^ll^,/

And^r^. Percivall Jos: West
Rich^d^. Conant, Jno. Godfrey

You are forthw^th^— to admeasure & Lay out unto Barn^d^.. Schenckingh one of the free ꝑsons of this Province Eleven hund^rd^— & fifty acres of Land in some Convenient place not yett Layd out, or marked to be Laid out for any other ꝑson and if it happen upon any Navigable River, or River Capable to be made Navigable, you are only to Allow the fifth ꝑte of the Depth there of by the waterside, and a Certificate fully Specifying the Bounds Scittuacon thereof, you Returne to us wth. all Convenient speed dated at Charles Towne this 22 day of March, 1678/

To Capt— Maur. Mathews Surveyo^r^— Gener^ll^— —

Jno. Godfrey Jos: West
W^m^— Owen And^r^. Percivall

Carolina. Ss./
You are forthwith to cause to be admeasured and Laid out unto Joseph Harrison one Towne Lott at the Oyster point observing the Rules and Method already Established for the Building a Towne There, and not Injuring the Lines of any other ꝑson, or ꝑsons, and, a Certificate fully Specifying the Scittuacon & bounds thereof you Returne to us w^th^— all Convenient Speed, dated the 19th— of Aprill 1679—

Jos: West
Richard Conant
W^m^= Owen

To Capt —Maur. Mathews Surveyo^r^. Gener^ll^—/

You are forthw[th]. to Admeasure and Lay out unto Deoniz Brodie one of the free ℘sons of this ℘vince, Seaventy acres of Land, in some convenient place, not yet Laid out or marked to be Laid out for any other ℘son, and if it happen upon any Navigable River, or River capable to be made Navigable, you are only to allow the fifth ℘te of the Depth thereof by the waterside, and a Certificate fully Specifying the bounds Scittuacon thereof you Returne to us w[th]— all convenient speed, dated at Charles Towne this day of

To Cap[t]— Maur. Mathews Rich[d]. Conant Jos: West
Surveyo[r]. Gener[ll]—/ W[m]= Owen And[r]—Percivall

You are forthwith to Cause to be Admeasured & Laid out unto James Colliton Landgrave, of this ℘vince a Barrony Cont[a]— Twelve Thousand Acres of Land, as by the Lords ℘prieto[rs]. of this ℘vince is directed, and a Certificate fully Specifying the Scittuation, & bounds thereof, you are to Returne to us w[th]— all convenient Speed Given Under our hands at Charles Towne, the Second day of Aprill in the yeare of our Lord, one Thousand Six hundred Seaventy & nine

To Cap[t]— Maur— Mathews
Surveyo[r]. Gener[ll]./

Joseph West.
Rich[d], Conant
W[m] Owen
And[r]. Percivall—

Carolina. Ss./
You are forthw[th]— to Admeasure & Lay out, Unto Edward Howard one of the free ℘sons of this ℘vince Seaventy Acres of Land in Some convenient place, not yet Laid out, or Marked to be Laid out for any Other ℘son, and if it happen upon any Navigable River, or River capable to be made Navigable you are only to Allow the fifth ℘te of the Depth thereof by the Waterside, and a Certificate fully specifying the Bounds & Scittuation thereof you Returne to us w[th]— all convenient Speed, Dated at Charles Towne, This day of

To Cap[t]. Maur: Mathews Rich[d]. Conant Joseph West—
Surv[r]— Gener[ll]./ W[m]= Owen And[r]. Percivall

You are forthw[th]. to Admeasure & Layout for Thomas Colliton Esq[r]. & Comp[a]., fower Thousand Acres of Land, in some place not yet Laid out, or marked to be Laid out for any other ℘son or Use, And, if the same happen upon any Navigable River—or River capable to be made Navigable, you are only to allow the fifth ꝑte of the Depth thereof by the waterside and a Certificate fully specifying the Scittuation & bounds thereof, You Returne to us, w^th^— all convenient speed Dated. 7°— die 7^ber^— 1678./

To Capt. Maur: Mathews
Surveyo^r^. Gener^ll^./

Joseph West
Wm Owen.
Rich^d^. Conant
And^r^. Percevall

You are forthw^th^. to Admeasure & Lay out, unto, William Cantey one of the free ꝑsons of this ꝑvince, one hund^rd^. Acres of Land in Some Convenient place, not yet Laid out, or marked to be Laid out for any other ꝑson, and if it happen upon any Navigable River, or River capable to be made Navigable, you are only to Allow the fifth ꝑte of the Depth thereof by the waterside and a Certificate fully Specifying the Bounds, and Scittuation thereof you Returne to us w^th^— all convenient Speed, dated at Charles Towne, June the 14th— 1679—

To Capt. Maur. Mathews
Surv^r^. Gener^ll^./

Jno. Godfrey Joseph West
Rich^d^— Conant./

Carrolina

You are forthwith to Admeasure unto Willi Paige one ye free persons &^c^: seaventy acres of Land in sum Convenient place not yet Laid Out: Nor Marked to be Laid out for any Oather ꝑson or use. and if the Same happen upon any Navigable River or River Capable to be made Navigable you are onely to Allow only the fift ꝑ^te^ of ye Depth thereof by the Waterside, and a Certifycate fuly spesifying the Bounds & Scittuation thereof you returne to us with all Convenient speed Given und^r^. our hands this 9 Day of Aug^t^: 1679/

To Capt Mor^s^: Mathews
Sury^r^. Gen^r^:

Joseph^h^: West
And^r^: Percivall
John: Godfrey

Carrolina

You are forthwith to admeasure and Lay out unto Willi Page two Hundred acres of Land in sum Convenient place not yet Layd Out for any Oather ꝑson or Use. and if the same Happen upon any Navigable River: or River Capable to be made Navigable, you are to Allow only the fift ꝑte of ye Depth thereof by the waterside, and a Certificate fully Specifying y^e^. bounds & Scittuation thereof: you

Returne to us with all Convenient speede: Given und^{r} our Hands this 9th: Day of Augs^{t}: 1679

To Capt. M: Mathews
Surveyr gen^{r}all:

J: West:
And^{r} piercevall
Jno Godfrey

Carolina./

You are forthwith to Admeasure and Lay out unto Moses Rivers one of the free ℘sons of this Province Seaventy Acres of Land in some Convenient place not yett Laid out nor marked to be Laid out for any other ℘son or use and if y^{e}. Same happen upon any navigable River or River capable to be made Navigable, you are to Allow only the fifth ℘te of the depth thereof by the waterside, and a Certificate fully specifying the bounds & scittuacon thereof you returne to us wth. all Convenient Speed given und^{r}. our hands this 9th— day of August 1679

To Capt. Maur. Mathews
Surveyr Gener^{ll}—

Jno. Godfrey Joseph West
W^{m}— Owen
Ste: Bull—

Carolina. Ss./

You are forthwith to Admeasure and Lay out unto Patrick Ohohj one of the free ℘sons of this ℘vince Seaventy Acres of Land, in Some Convenient place not yet Laid out or marked to be Laid out for any other ℘son or Use, and if it happen upon any Navigable River, or River capable to be made Navigable; you are only to Allow the fifth ℘te of the Depth thereof by the water side, and a Certificat fully specifying the bounds & scittuacon thereof you Returne to us wth— all convenient Speed, Given Und^{r}— our hands this 9th— day of August 1679./

To Capt— Maur— Mathews
Surv^{r}— Gener^{ll}—/

John Godfrey Joseph West
Ste: Bull—

Carolina Ss./

You are forthwith to Admeasure and Lay out unto John Cowen one of the free ℘sons of this Province, Seaventy Acres of Land in Some Convenient Place not yet Layd out nor marked to be Layd out for any other ℘son or Use, and if the same happen upon any Navigable River, or River Capable to be Made Navigable, you are to Allow only the fifth ℘te of the Depth thereof by the waterside, and a Certificate fully Specifying the Bounds & Scittuacon thereof you Returne to us wth— all convenient speed, given und^{r}— our hands this 9th— day of August 1679./

To Capt— Maur— Mathews
Surveyo^{r}— Gener^{ll}./

Joseph West
John Godfrey
Ste: Bull

Carolina Ss./

You are by virtue hereof to Admeasure and Lay out for m^{r}. Barnard Schenckingh, one Towne Lott in the Oyster pointe, Observing the Rules Established in Refference to the building of a Towne there, and a Certificate fully Specifying the Meates & bounds and Scittuacon thereof you Returne to us Given und^{r}— our hands this 12th— day of July, 1679./

To Capt— Maur— Mathews
Surveyo^{r}. Generall./

Joseph West
And^{r}. Persivall
Rich^{d}— Conant
W^{m}— Owen

Carolina Ss./

You are forthwth— to admeasure and Lay out unto Lawrance Saunders nine hundred & twentie acres of Land, in Some Convenient place not yet Laid out nor marked to be Laid out for any other ꝑson or Use, and if the same happen upon any Navigable River or River capable to be made Navigable, you are to Allow only the fifth ꝑte of the depth thereof by the waterside, and a Certificate fully Specifying the Bounds & Scittuacon thereof you are to Returne to us wth— all Convenient speed. Given und^{r}— our hands. this 12th— day of June 1679/

To Capt. Maur— Mathews
Surveyo^{r}. Gener^{ll}./

Joseph West
And^{r}. Percivall
Rich^{d}. Conant
W^{m}= Owen

Carolina Ss./

You are forthwith to Admeasure and Lay out unto W^{m}. Perriman, nine hundred & twentie acres of Land in convenient place not yet Laid out nor marked to be Laid out for any other ꝑson or use, and if the Same happen upon any Navigable River, or River Capable to be made Navigable, you are to Allow only the fifth ꝑte of the depth thereof by the waterside, and a Certificate fully specifying the bounds, & Scittuacon thereof you returne to us wth— all convenient Speed, Given und^{r}. our hands this 12th— July 1679./

To Capt. Maur. Mathews. Surveyo^{r}. Gener^{ll}./

Rich^{d}. Conant Joseph West
And^{r}. Persivall,
W^{m}. Owen

Carolina Ss./

You are forthwth— to Admeasure & Lay out unto m^{r}— Thomas Midwinter, Two Roodes and Three Perches of Land upon the Seamans Point, Nere Charles Towne, and you are to take care, you prejudice not the Rights of any other ℘son or ℘sons there, and a Certificate of the bounds & Scittuacon thereof you Returne to us wth— all Convenient Speed— dated the 8th— day of August 1679/

To Capt. Maur. Mathews Surveyo^{r}. Gener^{ll}/

Joseph West
And^{r}— Persivall
W^{m}— Owen
Jno. Godfrey

Carolina Ss./

You are forthwth— to Admeasure & Layout unto M^{r}— Alexand^{r}— Sympson, one hundred acres of Land, in Some Convenient Place, not yet Laid out nor marked to be Laid out for any Other ℘son or use, and if the same happen upon any Navigable River or River Capable to be made Navigable, you are to Allow only the fifth ℘te of the Depth thereof by the water side, and a Certificate fully Specifying the bounds & Scittuacon thereof you returne to us wth— all Convenient Speed Given und^{r}— our hands this ninth day of August 1679/

To Capt. Maur. Mathews Surveyo^{r}— Gener^{ll}— —

Joseph West
And^{r}— Persivall
Jno. Godfrey—

Carolina. Ss./

You are by vertue hereof to Admeasure & Lay out for M^{r}— Alexan^{dr} Symonds, one Towne Lott at the Oyster pointe Observing the Rules Established, in Refference to the building of a Towne there, and a Certificate fully specifying the Metes Bounds & Scittuacon thereof to returne to us given und^{r}. our hands this 8th— day of August 1679./

To Capt— Maur —Mathews Surveyo^{r}— Gener^{ll}./

Joseph West
And^{r}— Persivall Jno. Godfrey
W^{m}— Owen

Carolina. Ss./
You are By virtue hereof, to Admeasure and Lay out Unto mr. William Owen, one Towne Lott at the Oyster pointe, Observing the Rules Established in Refference to the building of a Towne There, and a Certificate fully specifying the Metes, Bounds and Scittuacon thereof to Returne to us Given undr— our hands this 30th— day of August 1679./

To Capt— Maur. Mathews
Surveyor— Generll— — —

Jos— West
Andr— Persivall Ste. Bull
Wm— Owen

Carolina. Ss./
You are by Virtue hereof to Admeasure and Lay out unto Thomas Rose one Towne Lott at the Oysterpoint, observing the Rules Established in Refference to the Building of a Towne there and a Certificate fully Specifying the metes Bounds & Scittuacon thereof to Returne to us— Given undr— our hands this 30th— day of August 1679—

To Capt— Maur— Mathews
Surveyor— Generll—

Joseph West
Andr. Persivall Ste: Bull—
Wm— Owen—

Carolina Ss/
You: are forthwth: to cause to be admeasured and laid out for James Donoho in the right of Priscilla his Wife seaventy acres of land in some place not yett laid out or marked to be laid out for any other person or use and if the same happen upon any navigable River or any River capable of being made navigable you are to allow only the fifth part of the depth thereof by the waterside and a Certificate fully specifying the scittuacon and bounds thereof you are to returne to us with all convenient speed, Dated at Charles Towne this 6°: day of 7ber: 1679

To Capt: Maurice Mathews
Surveyor— generall

Joseph West
Richard Conant
Maurice Mathews
Wm: Owen

You are furthwth to admeasure and lay out for Robert Donne and Jane his wife foure hundred and tenn acres of land in som place not yet laid out nor marked to be laid out for any other ꝑson or persons or use and if ye same happen upon any Navigable river or any river capable to be made Navigable you are to allowe onlje ye 5th part of ye depth thereof by ye waterside and a Certificat fullie specifyeing ye bounds and scituacon thereof you retorne to us with all convenjent speede Given undr or hands att Charles towne this 6h Day of 7ber i679

To Capt M: Mathews Srveyr. generall:

Joseph West
R: Conant
Will: Owen: M: Mathews

Carolina/

You. are forthwth. to admeasure and lay out for sr: Peter Colleton Barronett one of the Lords and absolute Proprietors of this province fower thousand fower hundred twenty three acres of land adjoyning to the South side of and of equall depth wth twelve thousand acres of land formerly laid out for the said Sr: Peter Colleton in the Westward branch of the Tee in Cooper River allowing the breadth of the said land proportionable to the said depth and a Certificate fully specifying the Scittuation & bounds thereof you. are to returne to us with all convenient speed and for yor: soe doeing this shall be yor: Warrt: Given under our hands this 20th: day of ffebruary 1678/9.

To Maurice Mathews Surveyor— Generall

Joseph West
Will: Owen

You are furthwth to Lay out and furthwth unto mr Thomas Hurt one hundred acres of Land in som place not yet laid out nor marked to be laid out for any other person or use and if ye same happen upon any Navigable river or river capable to be made Navigable you are to allowe onlje ye fifth parte of ye depth thereof by ye waterside and a certificate fullie specifyeing ye bounds and scituacon thereof you are to retorne to us with all convenient speede Given undr or hands att Charles towne ye 6h Day of 7ber i679

To Capt M: Mathews Surveyr generall/

Jo. West
Rich: Conant
Maurice: Mathews
Will: Owen:

Carolina Ss./

You are forthwith to Cause to be Admeasured and Layd out for Thomas Downing and Ellizabeth his wife and Thomas his Sonn, Three hundred Acres of Land in some place not yett Layd out or Marked to be Laid out for any Other ℘son or Use, & if the same happen upon any Navigable River, or River Capable of being made Navigable, you are to Allow only the fifth ℘te of the depth thereof by the water side, and a Certificate fully Specifying the Scittuacon and bounds thereof you Returne to us wth— all Convenient Speed. Given und^{r}— our hands at Charles Towne the 6th— day of 7^{ber}— 1679

To Capt. Maur. Mathews
Surveyo^{r}— Gener^{ll}.

W^{m}— Owen Jos: West
Rich^{d}. Conant
Maur: Mathews

Carolina. Ss./

You are forthwith to Cause to be Admeasured & Layd out unto m^{r}. Thomas Clowter one of the free ℘sons of this Province, Two hundred Acres of Land in Some Convenient place not yett Layd out or marked to be Laid out for any other ℘son or use, and if the same happen upon any Navigable River or River Capable to be made navigable, you are only to Allow the fifth ℘te of the Breadth thereof by the water side and a Certificate fully specifying the Scittuacon & bounds thereof, you Returne to us wth— all Convenient speed Given und^{r}— our hands at Charles Towne the 4th— day of 8^{ber} 1679./

To Capt— Maur: Mathews
Surveyo^{r}— Gener^{ll}./

Jos= West
Rich^{d}. Conant
And^{r} Persivall
W^{m}— Owen

Carolina Ss./

You are forthwith to Admeasure & Lay out unto m^{r}. Richard Quintyne, one of the free ℘sons of this province, six hundred & Seaventy acres of Land, in Some Convenient place, not yett Layd out or marked to be Laid out for any other ℘son or use, and if the same happen upon any Navigable River, or River Capable to be made navigable you are to Allow only the, fifth ℘te of the breadth thereof by the water side, and a Certificate fully specifyeing the bounds & scittuation thereof you returne to us wth— all Convenient Speed Given und^{r} our hands at Charles Towne, the 11th— day of October 1679,/

To Capt. Maur. Mathews
Surveyo^{r}— Gener^{ll}— —

Hen. Woodward Joseph West
W^{m}—ffuller. W^{m}— Owen—

Carolina/

You are forthwith to cause to bee admeasured and layd out for Bernard Schenckingh Gen[t]: one of the freemen of this province all that Eight hundred Ackers of Land that was formerly Run: out for m[r] Jonah Lynch acordinge to warr[tt]: and ꝑmission of y[e] Govern[r]. and councell; six hundred Ackers of y[e] S[d] Eight hundred by an Ord[r]: of Councell of the thirtith of Aprell 1677, as also two hundred Ackers by consent & further ꝑmission of the Govern[r] & Councell Exept one hundred Ackrs, part of the Sd: Eight hundred Since runn out for the Sd: m[r] Jonah Lynch by warr[t] bering date the 19[th] of Aprell 1678 and a certificate fully specifying the Situacon and Bounds, therof you are to returne to us with all convenient speed: Given under oure hands: This 5[th] of October 1679

To Cap[t] Maurice Mathews
Survey[r] Genn[r]all

Joseph West
M: Mathews Hen: Woodward
Will:ffuller: Will: Owen

Carolina ss:

You are forthwith to Admeasure & Lay out unto Thomas Hunt, & Elliner his Wife Two of the free ꝑsons of this ꝑvince, Seaventy Acres of Land in Some Convenient place, not yett Laid out or marked to be Laid out for any Other ꝑson, or Use, And if the Same Happen upon any Navigable River, or River Capable to be made Navigable, you are to Allow only the fifth ꝑte of the Breadth thereof by the water side, and a Certificate fully Specifying the bounds & Scittuacon thereof you Returne to us, w[th]— all Convenient Speed, Given und[r] our hands at Charles Towne, the 11th— day of October 1679./

To Cap[t]. Maur. Mathews
Surveyo[r]. Generall—

Henry Woodward Joseph West
W[m]—ffuller. W[m]. Owen

Carrolina ss:

Yo[u]: are forthw[th]: to Admeasure & Lay out Unto Richard Rowsar fower hundred and Twenty Acres of Land In Some Convenient Place nott yett Laid outt or Marked to be Laid outt for any other Parson or Parsons and If the Same happen upon Any navigable River or River Capable to be made navigable, yo[u] are to allow onely y[e]: fifth Parte of y[e]: deapth Thereof by y[e]: water Side, & A Certificate specifying y[e]: bounds & scituacon Thereof yo[u]: retourne to us wth: Convenient Speede dated at Charles Towne the 30th: of nor: 1679//

To Capt: Mau: Mathewes Surveyor: Generall// Wm: Owen: Richard Connant Joseph West Wm: ffullar

Carrolina ss:

You: are forthwth: to Admeasure & Lay out Unto John Birde one Towne Lott In ye: Oystar Poynt observinge the rules and Methods already Established for the Building A Towne There & nott Injureinge the Lines of Any other Pr:son or Pr:sons and A Certificate fully Specifieinge the Meates Bounds and Scituacon Thereof You: Tourne wth: all Convenient Speede dated the 30th: of nobr: 1679//

To: Capt: Mau: Mathewes Survayr: Genorall//// Richard Conant: Wm: Owen: Joseph West Wm: ffullar

Carrolina ss

You are forthwith to Admeasure and Lay out unto Mr. Will Bird one of the free persons of this province one hundred Acres of Land in some convenient place not yet Layd out, or marked to be Layd out for any other person or use, and if the same happen upon any navigable River or River capable to be made navigable you are onely to allow, one fifth part of the breadth by the water side, and a certifficate fully specifying the Bounds and scituacon thereof you returne to us wth all convenient speede Given under or: hands this 11th of Decembr: 1679/

To Capt Maur: Mathews Surveyr: Generll: Joseph West Rich: Connant Will Owen: Will ffuller}

Carrolina Ss

You are forthwith to Admeasure and Lay out unto Elizabeth Baker one of the free persons of this province one hundred Acres of Land in some convenient place not yet Layd out or marked to be Layd out for any other person or use, and if the same happen upon any Navigable River or River capable to be made navigable you are to allow onely one fifth part of the breadth thereof by the water side and a certifficate thereof fully specifying the bounds and scituation thereof you returne to us wth. all convenient speede Given undr: or: hands at Charles Towne ye 11th of Decemr: 1679/

To Capt: Mau: Mathews Surveyr Generll: Richard Conant Will owen Joseph West Will ffuller

Carolina: SS:/
You are furthw^th^ to Admeasure and lay out unto Jno Becknall shipp-wright one hundred acres of Land in som Convenjent place not yet laid out or marked to be laid out for any other ꝑson or use and if ye same happen upon any Navigable river or river capable to made Navigable you are onlje to allow ye fifth ꝑte of ye Depth thereof by ye water side and a Certificat fully specifyeing ye bounds and Scituacon thereof you retorne to us with all Convenient speede: Dated att Charles towne ye 11th of Dec i679

To Capt M: Mathews: Surveyr genrall:

W: Owen Jos: West
R: Connant W: ffuller

Carolina
You are furthw^th^ to cause to Admeasure and Laid out unto Edwd Johnson and Marie his wife one hundred and fortie acres of Land in som place not yet laid out or marked to be laid out for any other ꝑson or use and if ye same happen upon any Navigable river or river capable to be Navigable you are to allowe onlje ye fifth part of ye Depth thereof by ye water Side and a Certificate fully specifyeing ye bounds and Scituacon thereof you are to returne to us wth all Convenjent speede and for yor soe Doeing this shalbe yor. Warr^t^ Given und^r^ o^r^ hands att Charles towne y^e^ 13° day of October i679:

Capt M: Mathews Surveyr genrall:

J: West
R: Conant: W: ffuller:
W: Owen:

INDEX